The Empowering God

McMaster Divinity College Press
McMaster Theological Studies Series, Volume 8

Defining Issues in Pentecostalism (2008)

Pentecostalism and Globalization (2009)

You Mean I Don't Have to Tithe? (2009)

Baptism (2011)

Resurrection, Scripture, and Reformed Apologetics (2012)

The Globalization of Christianity (2014)

Salvation in the Flesh (2018)

The Empowering God
Redeeming the Prosperity Movement and Overcoming Victim Trauma in the Poor

by
Edward Y. Suh

foreword by
Veli-Matti Kärkkäinen

☙PICKWICK *Publications* · Eugene, Oregon

THE EMPOWERING GOD
Redeeming the Prosperity Movement and Overcoming Victim Trauma in the Poor

McMaster Theological Studies Series, Volume 8
McMaster Divinity College Press

Copyright © 2018 Edward Y. Suh. All rights reserved. Except for brief quotations in critical publications or reviews, no part of this book may be reproduced in any manner without prior written permission from the publisher. Write: Permissions, Wipf and Stock Publishers, 199 W. 8th Ave., Suite 3, Eugene, OR 97401.

Pickwick Publications
An Imprint of Wipf and Stock Publishers
199 W. 8th Ave., Suite 3
Eugene, OR 97401

McMaster Divinity College Press
1280 Main Street West
Hamilton, Ontario, Canada
L8S 4K1

www.wipfandstock.com

PAPERBACK ISBN: 978-1-7252-7703-8
HARDCOVER ISBN: 978-1-7252-7704-5
EBOOK ISBN: 978-1-7252-7705-2

Cataloguing-in-Publication data:

Names: Suh, Edward Y., author.

Title: The empowering god : redeeming the prosperity movement and overcoming victim trauma in the poor / Edward Y. Suh.

Description: Eugene, OR: Pickwick Publications, 2018. | McMaster Theological Studies Series 7. | Includes bibliographical references and index.

Identifiers: ISBN 978-1-7252-7703-8 (paperback). | ISBN 978-1-7252-7704-5 (hardcover). | ISBN 978-1-7252-7705-2 (ebook).

Subjects: LCSH: Pentecostalism. | Theology.

Classification: BR1643.5 S84 2021 (print) | BR1643.5 (ebook).

05/14/21

Cover art, "Arise and Walk" by Mike Moyers, used with permission. MikeMoyersFineArt.com

To Eunice
Jeremiah
Isaiah
Levi
and Aria

Contents

Foreword | ix

Acknowledgments | xi

Abbreviations | xii

1   Introduction and Statement of the Problem | 1

2   Towards a Broadly Credible Expression of Prosperity Theology | 11

3   An Orientation to the Contemporary Study of Human Flourishing | 30

4   The Liberative Elements of Prosperity Theologies | 71

5   Challenges to Flourishing Conceived of as Health and Prosperity | 105

6   The Good, Hospitable, and Liberating God: A *Kenotic* Model of God | 133

7   Conclusion: Towards a Theology of Empowerment and Abundance | 169

Bibliography | 181
Author Index | 193
Subject Index | 195

Foreword

COMPLAINTS AND CHARGES AGAINST the Prosperity gospel abound. Criticisms include the movement's overly (many say 'naïvely') positive stance toward life's struggles, such as poverty, sickness, and depression; that it unrealistically raises expectations about health and wealth; that it focuses on physical and material well-being at the expense of spiritual and inner peace; and that it replaces the cross for glory before the coming of the Kingdom.

These and related objections to the Prosperity gospel are largely valid and accurate. It is indeed incumbent upon the advocates of the movement to do serious soul-searching and engage in critical self-reflection. That said—and here we come to the genius of Edward Suh's innovative work *The Empowering God: Redeeming the Prosperity Movement and Overcoming Victim Trauma in the Poor*—there is also a need to raise an important theological "metaquestion": What is there behind the Prosperity gospel that is so appealing to folks across the globe? And even more: Notwithstanding the justified critique, might there be a constructive and healthy impulse buried in the midst of the fairly shallow and overly simplified "name and claim" preaching?

This is where Dr. Suh's work distinguishes itself among a growing number of fine studies and books on the ills of the Prosperity Movement. While it unambiguously affirms the critique of the movement, its focus is on this all-important question: *What might be the positive impulses behind the Prosperity gospel phenomenon so common among various types of Charismatic movements around the globe?* He wonders if the life-affirming, grounded, and liberative message about a loving and good God who facilitates human flourishing amidst life's hurdles can be distinguished from the mess of prosperity-hopes-gone-awry. Briefly put: this study is an attempt to

Foreword

redeem the biblical message of hope for life abundant, a message of liberation and flourishing, under the auspices of *The Empowering God*.

Tapping into contemporary systematic and liberation theologies as well as interdisciplinary resources (including those rooted in the behavioral sciences), the book argues that underlying the Prosperity gospel appeal rightly understood is a desire for personal and communal human flourishing. The result is a fascinating constructive recommendation not only for Pentecostal-Charismatics but for all Christians to envision ordinary human life—life in the quotidian, including sickness and suffering—as a life of abundance and liberation.

This book makes a fine contribution both to rapidly growing Pentecostal-Charismatic studies and to the wider international and ecumenical scholarship and literature. The hope for flourishing, empowerment, and liberation is not a commodity of one particular Christian tradition. It is an invitation to all Christians.

Veli-Matti Kärkkäinen
Professor of Systematic Theology, Fuller Theological Seminary
Docent of Ecumenics, Faculty of Theology, University of Helsinki

Acknowledgments

MANY THANKS TO DR. Veli-Matti Kärkkäinen, whose tremendous capacity to listen to and appreciate unique perspectives was demonstrated in his ability to see the potential in this thesis when few others could.

Many thanks also to Dr. Amos Yong, who consistently provided valuable feedback and recommendations for resources at every turn to the enrichment of both myself and this monograph.

Abbreviations

CCTPW   Kärkkäinen, Veli-Matti. *A Constructive Christian Theology for the Pluralistic World*. 5 vols. Grand Rapids: Eerdmans, 2013–2017.

EE   Kelsey, David H. *Eccentric Existence*. 2 vols. Louisville: Westminster John Knox, 2009.

IDC   Yong, Amos. *In the Days of Caesar: Pentecostalism and Political Theology*. Grand Rapids: Eerdmans, 2010.

LGFL   Moltmann, Jürgen. *The Living God and the Fullness of Life*. Translated by Margaret Kohl. Louisville: Westminster John Knox, 2015.

OTT   Goldingay, John. *Old Testament Theology*. 3 vols. Downers Grove, IL: IVP Academic, 2003–2009.

1

Introduction and Statement of the Problem

> In 1968 a conference of Latin American bishops meeting in Medellin, Colombia, proclaimed a "preferential option for the poor," which since then has become an important ingredient of Catholic social teaching and has influenced mainline Protestantism. Liberation theologians interpreted the "preferential option" as an option for socialism. But it is helpful to pay attention to the syntax. The option is *for* the poor. That is, it is an option to be taken by those who are not poor. The proposition is well-intentioned. But it is not surprising that many of the poor are opting for a less patronizing message. They do not think of themselves as dependent on the compassion of the rich.[1]

THE ABOVE QUOTATION FROM distinguished sociologist Peter Berger in *The Wall Street Journal* is a call for theologians and others who have voiced near universal criticism of the religious phenomenon known as the "Prosperity gospel" to listen more carefully to what this movement might actually be accomplishing in the lives of its adherents. In his surprising article, Berger acknowledges the validity of the many scholarly dismissals of this movement and does not even make a cursory attempt to challenge these critiques. However, as a sociologist, Berger notes that the effect of this theological movement on the social mobility of the poor in third world countries is not something to be dismissed out of hand. In Berger's estimation, the poor are the ones who know what is best for them, and all around the world they are opting for the Prosperity gospel in droves. There, they are finding a simple but profound message that does not glamorize poverty or the ascetic life.

1. Berger, "Pennies From Heaven."

They are hearing a message that empowers them to see themselves as responsible agents of change rather than as victims of over-arching systems of oppression. And from this message they are gaining a restored sense of self-worth that is critical to breaking the cycles of poverty that have shackled their families and communities for generations. Sociologically speaking, the Prosperity gospel is making a marked difference for good in the lives of the world's poor. So, why is it that so few in academia have been able to appreciate this?

Recently, there have been some Pentecostal scholars who have been more accepting of Berger's premise of the sociological benefits of the Prosperity gospel among the poor. Research compiled by Amos Yong and Katherine Attanasi points to this "upward mobility" as a positive contribution of this movement to the resourcing of the world's poor.[2] Their volume documents a diverse range of "thick" local contexts where the Pentecostal message of Prosperity has contributed to various forms of social uplift. Whether in the poor neighborhoods of Nigeria, the booming urban centers of modern China, or among professionals in the entertainment industry in Hollywood, various forms of the Prosperity message have demonstrated a socio-economic benefit to the lives of believers in these communities. This serves as a nice "elaboration" of the claims of sociological enrichment made by Berger and helps us to see how these communities intentionally seek to build self-reliance and a restored sense of personal agency in the lives of their congregants to position them to break out of the poverty narratives in their lives. If Berger's insights serve to show us how to hear the liberative voice of the Prosperity movement, Yong and Attanasi help us to see the diverse ways this liberative potential is being realized around the world.

Recognizing how and why the Prosperity movement can help contribute to the social uplift of the poor is certainly a theme worthy of deeper reflection which will be explored in this study from various perspectives. But, for the many critics of the Prosperity movement the extravagant lifestyles of the Prosperity preachers themselves are too much to overlook and are a clear indication of the exploitative tendencies that they fear are at the heart of this movement. Many of these concerns are no doubt justified, but a sociological perspective once again provides reason for a closer examination. In an in-depth exploration of the popular ministry of Prosperity preacher T. D. Jakes, Shayne Lee notes the role that the black preacher plays in the larger context of the African American community in America. There is a

---

2. Yong and Attanasi, *Pentecostalism and Prosperity*, 7.

Introduction and Statement of the Problem

"tribal" dimension at play where the pastor plays the role of tribal chieftain. Thus, the extreme wealth and luxurious lifestyles of some African American Prosperity preachers is sociologically acceptable for that community in ways that can transcend a critique from those outside of that community.[3] In a way, seeing a member of their own racial community achieve transcendent success is empowering to the whole community in some profound manner. From western perspectives such excesses appear immoral or even exploitative, but it is worth noting that sociologically these phenomena are not always so easy to critique. So, while we must critique the genuinely exploitative elements that may exist in pockets of this movement, we would be well-advised to do so mindful of the sociological dynamics at play. Moreover, a constructive approach may be best to preserve the positive effects this movement is having in promoting the flourishing of individuals and communities while minimizing its potential for excesses.

The sociological analyses of the Prosperity movement are important because they help us to see the good that it is doing amongst the poor in spite of the many concerns that have been raised about its purported role in exploiting the poor or of its theological inadequacies. The jarring disconnect between the theological guild's analysis of the Prosperity gospel and its broad appeal and utility amongst the poor suggests that some blind spots might be present in the way theologians have approached this movement in the past. And while the sociological insights give us reason to pause and pay closer attention to these movements, they also fall short of offering a sustained theological reflection on these positive dynamics in the Prosperity movement. A more nuanced theological perspective of this movement is needed. That is what this study aims to achieve.

A recent study by Lewis Brogdon exploring the potentials and pitfalls of the Prosperity movement as it contributes to the shape of future Pentecostalism revisits the various main criticisms that have been raised against the Prosperity movement over the years. According to these criticisms, the Prosperity movement has (1) a deficient view of God and of the Christian life; (2) an inadequate exegetical approach to Scripture; (3) an exploitative understanding of giving; and (4) an insensitivity to systemic issues identified by liberation theologians.[4] These issues leave Brogdon with little to say

---

3. Lee, *T. D. Jakes*, 1–7.

4. Brogdon (*An Introduction to the Prosperity Movement*, 64–70) suggests that these critiques encompass the ideas of legal right, binding faith, name it and claim it, dominionism, and license for greed.

in defense of the Prosperity movement's handling of the biblical texts and its own theological distinctives. However, his own experience and instincts regarding the good that this movement is doing in his local community leads him to suggest that perhaps what is needed is a new theology of Prosperity that can do justice to the biblical texts while still capturing the vibrant dynamics of the Prosperity movement's catalyzing effect on the poor.[5] This study will explore this idea of a new theology of Prosperity by looking at the Prosperity movement from the perspective of its radical affirmation of materiality and the various theological implications that undergird that affirmation.

In a nutshell, I believe that the liberative elements identified by sociological studies of the Prosperity movement are rooted in its inherent message of empowerment that calls people out of narratives of victimization and into narratives of self-determination. This derives from the Prosperity movement's radical affirmation of the concrete "this-worldly" dimensions of salvation and offers a critique of the ways that "other-worldly" views of salvation and ascetic values may have unintentionally played a role in trapping the poor in generational cycles of poverty. Consider the family who is told to learn to be content with their lot in life and to keep their attention on the heavenly rewards to come at the eschaton. What impetus might they have to put forth the herculean effort required to overcome their circumstances? In affirming the potential of the Kingdom of God to be made more fully manifest now, the Prosperity movement offers an inherent call to that family towards self-determination in order to bring forth that potential upon the earth.

Even more profoundly, this sense of self-determination requires the abandonment of internalized narratives of victimization. In affirming their role and responsibility for initiating transformative change, the Prosperity movement offers people who may have been immobilized by long-held internal narratives of victimization the empowerment they need to shed that victim-mentality and to instead cultivate a renewed sense of personal agency. Thus, rather than blame the system or misfortunes that may have befallen their lives such as being born into poverty or suffering calamity at the hands of others, the Prosperity movement focuses the attention of its adherents on the future they wish to build and in so doing it addresses the innate powerlessness of victimhood in a decisive way. Thus, it is not the promise of financial blessings that is transforming lives in the Prosperity

---

5. Brogdon, *An Introduction to the Prosperity Movement*, 70.

movement. Rather, it is the invitation to freedom from being defined and limited by the narratives of our past that is the true transformative factor in Prosperity theologies that then manifests in flourishing life.

To understand this "liberation of the victim" in Prosperity theologies helps to give perspective on the common misconception that the Prosperity movement is uninterested in issues of social justice. It is not that greed and self-interest blinds Prosperity proponents from engaging social justice causes. Rather, it is that they are focused on a different aspect of the problem. Namely, helping people who have seen themselves as victims of injustice find a way to rediscover their sense of personal agency. True to form, many Prosperity churches are deeply involved in issues of social justice—perhaps not by contributing to stoking public indignation in order to enact political and systemic changes, but rather by offering creative alternative solutions to societal problems. Think of churches offering micro-loans to the community to encourage entrepreneurship or relieving debt burdens by paying off a community's hospital bills. Prosperity churches are often committed not only to the welfare of their congregants, but also to the flourishing of their cities and communities. So, while both systemic approaches to social justice and community-oriented approaches to social justice have merit, it is understandable why the latter approach is more commonly found in the Prosperity movement.

Recognizing empowerment as central to the ethos of Prosperity theology helps us to appreciate the potential of this movement for broadly promoting human flourishing and shalom. As we try to discern what the Spirit might be doing through this movement it seems appropriate to move beyond simplistic critique of its theological naïveté and instead take a more constructive approach by formulating alternative theological perspectives that can support these newly articulated liberative values and perhaps even further advance them. The hope is that this can lead to an Evangelically sound theological expression of Prosperity theology that preserves and develops its liberative effectiveness while minimizing its exploitative excesses. I believe this can provide a valuable contribution to the theological dialogue on human flourishing taking place in academia today.

To develop this work following this introductory chapter, chapter 2 will seek to define what I mean by Prosperity theologies and where they stand in relation to the Pentecostal streams from which they arose. There is some contention about whether Prosperity theologies should be considered as an authentic offshoot of Pentecostalism or as a deviant and unwelcome branch. This project will seek to establish that Prosperity theologies are an authentic expression of Pentecostal themes and distinctives in order to help bridge the divide between "classical" Pentecostals and Prosperity theologies.

Appealing to the five-fold "full gospel" theological distinctives of Pentecostalism along with a composite sketch of Pentecostal spirituality drawn from contemporary Pentecostal scholars, I summarize the main contours of a contemporary understanding of Pentecostal identity. Then, in conversation with Kate Bowler and Lewis Brogdon in their historical analyses of the Prosperity movement's foundations, I distill the four distinctives of "Prosperity theologies" that fund its radical affirmation of materiality. From these four Prosperity distinctives, I demonstrate that they either align with Pentecostal identity or represent a natural "maturing" of the themes that make up that Pentecostal identity.

Having identified points for constructive rapprochement between classical Pentecostalism and Prosperity theology, I turn to attempt the same between Prosperity theologies and the wider Christian community. To overcome the many biblical critiques of Prosperity theology, I propose alternative theological foundations for it that can still maintain its affirmation of materiality. This also suggests moderated expressions of its distinctive practices that still retain its liberative power for the poor. This moderate Prosperity theology then positions us to take the study deeper into how Prosperity theologies affirm ordinary human flourishing and the effective liberation of the poor.

To frame the coming discussions in the rest of this study, chapter 3 provides an orientation to the contemporary study of human flourishing from biblical, theological, and behavioral science perspectives. I begin by laying out the case for why a theological affirmation of ordinary human flourishing is needed in light of the immanent frame of modern society as described by Charles Taylor in *A Secular Age*.[6] Then I connect this affirmation of ordinary human flourishing to biblical resources in the Old and New Testaments by appealing to the notion of *shalom* and the dynamics of the Kingdom of God. Turning to theological approaches to human flourishing, it is clear that Christian expressions of flourishing are fundamentally theocentric in orientation. So, the challenge becomes articulating a way that a

---

6. The immanent frame refers to modern society caught between a disenchanted view of the world on the one hand, and the recognition of the difficulty of finding meaning in that world on the other. It is the contemporary worldview grounded in materiality we must address to have a credible voice in modern society.

Introduction and Statement of the Problem

theo-centric view of flourishing can possibly align with a fully immanent "this-worldly" view of ordinary human flourishing, given that these have historically been seen to be at odds.

Looking at the proposals offered by Jürgen Moltmann, Richard Bauckham, and Miroslav Volf, I appropriate some of their respective insights while noting points where their proposals miss subtle dynamics that are important for a full embrace of ordinary human flourishing in its wide dimensions. For instance, Moltmann misses the lordship dynamics of a theo-centric view of God; Bauckham misses some of the subtleties of how the victimization caused by sin informs God's liberative action towards us; and Volf misses some of the dynamics of personal empowerment in his calls to mindfulness in the Christian life. I conclude this section with some reflections on a behavioral science contribution to the idea of human flourishing to give a basic target of the types of affirmations that need to be made for a theological view of human flourishing to align with contemporary views of ordinary human flourishing grounded in the sciences.

In chapter 4, I develop the relationship between human flourishing and theologies of liberation to make the case that Prosperity theologies function in liberative fashion to help people overcome the phenomenon of victimization. To address the missing sensitivity to some aspects of victimization in Bauckham's proposal, I offer a brief review of the key movements of contemporary liberation theologies from Gustavo Gutierrez, James Cone, and Elizabeth Johnson to show how they each contribute to expanding our understanding of the material dimensions of salvation. Then I propose that the broadest expression of liberation theology is the theology of the sinned-against, which explores victimization from the perspective of people who have experienced trauma or deep brokenness in their lives. Every other liberation theology merely addresses a specific form of this trauma of victimization.

This then leads me to my own reading and understanding of Prosperity theologies and what it is that makes them so appealing to the poor. I show that the liberative elements of Prosperity theologies at their deepest level are really about addressing the narratives of victimization that cause people to relinquish their sense of personal agency in life. As such, Prosperity theologies represent a very practical form of trauma recovery in the way that they empower believers to exercise the "good power" of personal agency in their lives in increasing measure. This fundamental value of "empowerment" at the heart of Prosperity theologies aligns with the research from the behavioral sciences about one of the most important factors that contributes to people feeling that their lives are flourishing: the sense of self-directedness.

As exhilarating as the message of empowerment in Prosperity theologies can be, it comes with inherent blind spots that must be addressed, which I work through in chapter 5. By encouraging the overcoming of all narratives of victimization, Prosperity theologies can seem insensitive to legitimate victimizations—especially of the systemic kind. This accounts for why Prosperity theologies have often been seen as being less than enthusiastic about the various agendas of liberation theologies to reform the societal factors contributing to systemic sin. Where this shows up most tragically is in the lack of any real messaging for people whose ability to flourish in traditional categories has been curtailed in some way—for example, people with disabilities or the chronically ill. David Kelsey also helps us to see the ways that theology has often lacked a proper value for the quotidian—the everyday processes of living life and the natural progression of life through stages towards eventual death. What does flourishing life look like in these contexts?

To address this lacuna in Prosperity theologies, I propose that we need to affirm a healthy tension between a hunger for breakthroughs and a contentment in our limitations. Merely hungering for breakthroughs can leave disillusionment and a discontented life. Merely being content in limitations can miss out on potential breakthroughs of the Kingdom of God in one's life. In this sense, Miroslav Volf's call to mindfulness has the potential to affirm this tension, though I think Prosperity theologies have the potential to affirm it more dynamically.

Finally, having painted a picture of the value and potential of Prosperity theologies for a vibrant affirmation of ordinary human flourishing, I attempt to bring out this full potential by deducing the implicit model of God that lies behind Prosperity theologies in chapter 6. I propose that a *kenotic* model of the Good God who is oriented towards enabling the flourishing of others is capable of funding all of the liberative elements of Prosperity theologies and their value for personal empowerment.[7] But I note here that an even more comprehensive model would incorporate the insights of the Hospitable God movement and Liberation theologies as well. So, I set out to show that a *kenotic* model of God's mode of relationality can support the

---

7. *Kenotic* is being used here to refer to a mode of relationality, not to make some claim about ontology.

Introduction and Statement of the Problem

personal empowerment of Prosperity theologies, the interpersonal mutuality of the hospitable God movement, and the societal justice-making of Liberation theologies. That is why I propose a model for the Empowering, Hospitable, and Liberating God to address every level of the overcoming of victimizations in a believer's life.

In contrast to Moltmann, who rejects any notion of the lordship of God, a biblically based theo-centric view of human flourishing must acknowledge that a Christian view of flourishing places humanity under the lordship of God. That said, a *kenotic* model of God's relationality qualifies how we understand the way that God exercises His lordship. God's lordship is meant to lead us into flourishing and *shalom*. And as we established earlier in chapter 3, *shalom* corresponds well with ordinary human flourishing. Thus, submitting to the lordship of God is akin to entering a process of rehabilitation with the aim being our ordinary human flourishing in relationship with God. And that relationship with God is critical for human flourishing for two reasons: (1) to lead us into dealing with issues of pride and fear that we would have difficulty facing voluntarily on our own, and (2) to be a source of limitless generosity into our lives enabling us to live from abundance and be a source of generosity to the lives of others. That is the heart of a theology of abundance based on the *kenotic* generosity of God. And this is how a theo-centric view of human flourishing can correspond comprehensively with ordinary human flourishing and *shalom*.

In the concluding chapter, I then present three dimensions of a theology of empowerment and abundance. First, such a theology reflects a robust affirmation of empowerment in the form of healthy self-care that precedes living for others. Second, such a theology emphasizes the ways that we were created to live *from* the abundance and overflow of God's generosity towards us. And third, such a theology encourages us to live *for* enabling the abundant life and flourishing of others. Three areas where this theology of empowerment and abundance can be naturally extended are: (1) in deepening the connections between research in the behavioral and medical sciences with the theology of empowerment and abundance to further define our understanding of healthy self-expression and behavioral science/medical perspectives on flourishing life; (2) to explore the differences between scarcity-based thinking and abundance-based thinking to position the church at the forefront of creative justice-making promoting the *shalom* of all; and (3) to consider how a theology of empowerment and abundance in a *kenotic* model of God's relationality can provide a fresh paradigm for Christian political engagement with the world.

This is a broad-ranging project, to be sure, but one I believe whose time has come. I hope this study allows others to appreciate the work of the Spirit in the midst of the still maturing Prosperity movement and how it contributes to our understanding of human flourishing in theo-centric perspective.

2

Towards a Broadly Credible Expression of Prosperity Theology

INTRODUCTION

As WE BEGIN OUR study of the liberative elements of Prosperity theologies and how they contribute to an affirmation of ordinary human flourishing, it is interesting to note that even within the Pentecostal tradition itself Prosperity theologies have often failed to gain legitimacy. So, one of the first tasks of this project is to ask the question "why?" and to see if there might be ways to demonstrate that Prosperity theologies represent an authentic extension of Pentecostal values, or a natural maturing of Pentecostal initiatives. To that end, this chapter (1) explores ways to think about Pentecostal identity, (2) asks what we mean by Prosperity theologies, (3) seeks to bridge the divide between classical Pentecostals and Prosperity theologies, and (4) seeks to articulate a mature form of Prosperity theology that has more points of connection with a broader theological audience. The goal of this exploration is to set the stage for a recovery of the liberative elements of Prosperity theologies towards the development of a constructive theology of empowerment and abundance in the chapters to come.

THE ROOTS OF PENTECOSTAL IDENTITY

We begin with a summary of contemporary Pentecostal identity rooted in two primary sources: (1) the five-fold full gospel of early Pentecostalism, and (2) the shape of Pentecostal spirituality. Both of these methods have been championed as proven ways to demarcate the borders of what can be considered Pentecostal and what might lie beyond that designation.

The Five-Fold Full Gospel of Early Pentecostalism

When it comes to the question of Pentecostal identity, contemporary theologians diverge between those who find the roots of that identity in the narratives of Azusa Street and those who believe that there are many complementary movements that contributed to the evolution of contemporary Pentecostal identity. Amos Yong advocates for the latter perspective, arguing that a historiographical view radiating outward from Azusa Street "[u]ltimately cannot be sustained since historical movements develop much more dynamically in multiple rather than unilateral directions."[8] And while I agree that many of these movements have unique insights to offer, this project builds on the former suggestion that there are "roots" to Pentecostal identity that can be traced to Azusa street and that contemporary Pentecostal movements are best understood to be evolutions of these roots in fundamental ways. Otherwise, why continue to call them Pentecostal?

Work on Pentecostal identity from Donald Dayton in the 1980s focused on the Wesleyan roots of the movement centered around the five themes of Christ as (1) our Savior, (2) our Sanctifier, (3) our Baptizer in the Spirit, (4) our Healer, and (5) our Soon and Coming King.[9] This "full gospel" reflected commitments held in common by nearly all of the early Pentecostal groups.[10] "Christ our Savior" referred to the revivalistic and

---

8. Yong, *IDC*, 96. McClymond ("Charismatic Renewal," 44) says, "[i]t is time to abandon what one might call the Big Bang theory of global Pentecostalism, namely, the notion that all the major elements of later Pentecostal-charismatic theory and practice were already present in early twentieth century American Pentecostalism. Instead of a Big Bang—where everything emanates from a single center—we should think of the twentieth century as a String-of-Firecrackers. Each bang was separated from the others in time and space and represented a diffusive center for new Pentecostal-charismatic ideas or practices."

9. Dayton (*Theological Roots of Pentecostalism*, 21) explains that the five-fold formulation was prevalent in Wesleyan Pentecostals while a four-fold one merging Savior and Sanctifier was more common in non-Wesleyan Pentecostalism.

10. Kärkkäinen ("Pentecostal Mission and Encounter with Religions," 299) agrees: "At the heart of Pentecostal spirituality lies the idea of the 'Full Gospel,' the template of Jesus Christ in his fivefold role as Savior, Sanctifier, Baptizer with the Spirit, Healer, and Soon-Coming King."

Towards a Broadly Credible Expression of Prosperity Theology

conversionist values of Pentecostalism and its embrace of the doctrine of justification by faith. Speaking of Christ as Sanctifier was a nod to the Wesleyan focus on subsequent works of grace in the life of the believer that could lead to the experience of "entire sanctification" (Christian perfection) by faith where the entire life of the believer was brought in line with the will of God. The baptism in the Spirit referred to the empowerment of believers for witness and service—later to be associated with the initial evidence of speaking in tongues. The focus on "Christ our Healer" was an outworking of the Wesleyan understanding of instantaneous sanctification of the soul from sin. In line with this present deliverance from the effects of sin in the believer's life, Dayton explains the Pentecostal belief that "[t]he Atonement has provided for the body all that it has provided for the soul . . . [thus] he who finds in Jesus the perfect cleansing of the soul and the keeping power against all sin, can be equally consistent in placing his body beneath the same wonderful salvation."[11] Finally, the doctrine of the Soon and Coming King represented a key element of the Pentecostal self-understanding captured in the idea of the "latter rain." The latter rain was a teaching based on the book of Joel that prophesied that in the "latter days" the Spirit would be poured out upon all humanity.[12] The recovery of spiritual gifts during the time of the birth of the Pentecostal movement suggested to believers that the time of this "latter rain" had come, signifying the victorious maturing of the church and the imminent return of Christ. This "full gospel" offered a coherent way to think about Pentecostal distinctiveness in the language of theology and doctrine.

The Shape of Pentecostal Spirituality

While this "full gospel" message was broadly accepted as an accurate reflection of the key doctrinal commitments of a Pentecostal identity, other theologians argued that Pentecostal distinctiveness could not be captured in a set of doctrines alone. Instead, they proposed that Pentecostal identity had more to do with a distinctive Pentecostal spirituality or worldview that was essential to an authentic Pentecostal experience and understanding. Thus, for Henry L. Lederle and Matthew S. Clark, Pentecostals had in common an experience of God's power that inaugurated a life of power in the

---

11. Dayton (*Theological Roots of Pentecostalism*, 130) is quoting from Carter, *The Atonement for Sin and Sickness*, 17, 38.

12. Dayton, *Theological Roots of Pentecostalism*, 27.

believer.[13] Steven J. Land expanded this to say that beyond Pentecostal-like experiences of God's power, there was a distinctive Pentecostal spirituality that was "[a]pocalyptic, corporate, missional, and essentially affective."[14] If a Pentecostal spirituality was to be the focus, this suggested that worship and prayerful responsiveness to the Holy Spirit were central to a Pentecostal "theology as spirituality."[15] Here, the Holy Spirit was seen as the agent of the Kingdom of God working to recover the ascetic and power-filled Apostolic life of the first-century church for contemporary believers.[16]

Walter J. Hollenweger furthered the case for a distinctive Pentecostal spirituality by arguing that Pentecostal theology was an oral theology rather than primarily a literary one.[17] He traced the origins of this oral theology to African-American spirituality and its traditions of oral liturgy, narrative theology and witness, reconciliatory and participatory community, the inclusion of visions and dreams in worship, and an understanding of the relationship between body and mind revealed in healing by prayer and liturgical dance. Likewise, Keith Warrington emphasized that Pentecostal theology was a theology of encounter, so any doctrine that did not help to lead believers into dynamic experiences of God in praxis was suspect.[18] Daniel E. Albrecht and Evan B. Howard agreed, saying "Pentecostalism is a renewal movement that emphasizes the experience of God. Certainly, Pentecostals reflect on theology. Certainly, Pentecostals maintain structures of ecclesiastical life. However, what is most distinctive about Pentecostals is not their theology or their ecclesiastical structure, but rather their sense of the experience of God."[19]

More recently, Kenneth J. Archer has proposed that it is helpful to think of a distinctive Pentecostal narrative identity to help give contour to the notion of a Pentecostal spirituality. That narrative identity was based on the doctrine of the Latter Rain where Pentecostals saw themselves as called

---

13. According to Clark and Lederle (*What is Distinctive*, 44, 46), this was in contrast to the contemplative life of pietism.

14. Land, *Pentecostal Spirituality*, 31.

15. For Land (*Pentecostal Spirituality*, 35), that spirituality is an integration of belief, affection, and action—otherwise we fall into intellectualism, sentimentalism, or activism.

16. Land, *Pentecostal Spirituality*, 53.

17. Hollenweger, *Pentecostalism*, 18–19, 269–72.

18. Warrington (*Pentecostal Theology*, 188) says, "Pentecostals believe that the main purpose of the Bible is to help them develop their experience of and relationship with God..."

19. Albrecht and Howard, "Pentecostal Spirituality," 235.

Towards a Broadly Credible Expression of Prosperity Theology

to bring the Church to perfection through an empowered supernatural witness to the world that would usher in the return of Christ.[20] Archer says of the impact of this narrative identity: "They read Scripture as the marginalized people of the 'Latter Rain.' At the center of the story stood Jesus. Their Jesus was the God-human messiah. Jesus was a mighty miracle worker because he was a holy man empowered by the Holy Spirit, not necessarily because he was God. The five-fold gospel, then, was the experientially and relationally understood extension of one's participatory salvific relationship with the Living God."[21]

For James K. A. Smith, Pentecostal spirituality implied a particular worshipping culture, and that worshipping culture in turn implied a particular worldview.[22] Thus, he sets out to give expression to some of the key elements of this implicit Pentecostal worldview, suggesting that it consists of (1) a radical openness to God acting in new and surprising ways in the world, (2) an "enchanted" view of a world full of spiritual forces and influences, (3) a radical affirmation of materiality expressed in healing and perhaps in Prosperity gospels, and (4) an eschatological orientation to mission and justice based on the "latter rain" desire to embody and model the coming Kingdom of God in this present world.[23]

Each of these "developments" can be understood to be complementary to one another—like exploring Pentecostal spirituality from a variety of angles where each snapshot contributes to a clearer view of the whole. And while most tend to use either the five-fold gospel or the appeal to a distinctive Pentecostal spirituality to define Pentecostalism, I find value in both approaches and do not consider them to be mutually exclusive. Rather, I find they both contribute to a fuller picture of what Pentecostalism entails.[24]

---

20. Archer, *Pentecostal Hermeneutics*, 109.

21. Archer, *Pentecostal Hermeneutics*, 118.

22. Smith (*Thinking in Tongues*, xvii–xviii) says "[I] will *not* define 'Pentecostal' *theologically*, that is, I do not locate the center or defining traits of Pentecostalism in a set of doctrines. Instead, I will unpack the elements that make up what I'll describe as a pentecostal 'worldview' or, following Charles Taylor, a Pentecostal 'social imaginary' I do so to honor the lived nature of Pentecostalism as a *spirituality*, an embodied set of practices and disciplines that implicitly 'carry' a worldview or social imaginary."

23. Smith, *Thinking in Tongues*, 12.

24. If pressed, I would say that I prefer the five-fold gospel approach to defining Pentecostalism both for its historical rootedness and for its theological commitments. A Pentecostal spirituality alone seems a bit too broad to be the sole factor for defining Pentecostalism. However, I do feel that taken together they present the strongest expression of what can be considered genuinely Pentecostal.

Thus, taking the five-fold gospel together with the composite Pentecostal spirituality sketched here gives us a contemporary understanding of what constitutes Pentecostal identity both regarding the early expressions of the movement and for evaluating any new expressions that might arise.

Prosperity Theologies and the Evolution of Pentecostal Themes

Having reviewed the major elements of contemporary Pentecostal identity, we turn to consider what we mean by Prosperity theologies and whether or not they align with that Pentecostal identity. Specifically, are Prosperity theologies a forgetting of the roots of Pentecostalism? Or are they rather a natural maturing of its key themes?

What is Prosperity Theology?

In discussing the Prosperity movement that has now spread all over the world, one of the challenges one finds is how to speak responsibly about this movement in the face of the myriad expressions of it that have come to light. Even limiting oneself to American expressions of Prosperity themes leads to at least eight different varieties of it to be catalogued merely among its most recognized practitioners.[25] Each of these has its own idiosyncratic reading of favorite Scriptures and its own customs and culture as the case may be. As my aim in this project is to speak broadly of this movement, I will attempt to generalize the types of distinctives that many of these Prosperity expressions have in common as a way of talking about "Prosperity theologies" typologically.

Taking this broad approach, I propose that the key theological values of Prosperity theologies are: (1) some affirmation of health and prosperity as blessings in this life that can be accessed by faith, (2) some recognition of the power of spoken words to facilitate breakthroughs, (3) some transition away from ascetic values towards an engagement with the world and the things in the world, and (4) some positive view of a vibrant church in the eschaton rather than a vision of world-flight.[26] There are some more

25. Brogdon, *New Pentecostal Message*, 11.

26. This composite sketch is derived from the analysis of various Prosperity movements by Brogdon (*New Pentecostal Message*, 1–24) and alternatively by Bowler (*Blessed*, 11–41).

Towards a Broadly Credible Expression of Prosperity Theology

controversial expressions of these values (see the near-universal rejection of "name it and claim it" variants) and some more broadly acceptable expressions as well. But these values taken together represent the set of convictions that seems to enable the radical embrace of materiality that we find in all Prosperity theologies. And that embrace of materiality is what makes Prosperity theologies so promising for a theological affirmation of ordinary human flourishing.

Forgetting the Roots of Pentecostal Identity? Or a Maturing of Pentecostal Themes?

It is no secret that the Prosperity movement is not embraced by all those in the larger Pentecostal movement. In particular, "classical" Pentecostal denominations have distanced themselves from it and have even written formal statements against some of its teachings.[27] Many Pentecostal scholars from the "classical" Pentecostal denominations have bemoaned the loss of the Holiness ethic of early Pentecostalism and have issued calls for Pentecostalism to return to these roots in order to fund its revitalization.[28] However, there is an open question as to whether Prosperity theologies do diverge from the historical roots of Pentecostalism or if instead they represent a maturing of some of its most basic themes.

If we consider Dayton's five-fold theological distinctives of Pentecostalism, we can see how the values of Prosperity theologies can be understood as a maturing of some of these basic doctrines in ways that are consistent with the narrative of a Pentecostal identity. For instance, the affirmation of health and prosperity as blessings in this life that can be accessed by faith is nothing more than a logical extension of the Pentecostal conviction that divine healing is a provision in the atonement.[29] If the forgiveness of sins can be accessed by faith in the atonement, and divine healing can too, then why not prosperity to overcome the ills of poverty as well?[30] While we may

---

27. For example, the largest Pentecostal denomination, the Assemblies of God, has a position paper denouncing the Prosperity movement entitled "The Believer and Positive Confession."

28. Land (*Pentecostal Spirituality*, 180–200) has issued just such a call in his landmark work on Pentecostal Spirituality.

29. Brogdon (*New Pentecostal Message*, 56) says, "[P]rosperity teachers believe that sin, sickness, poverty, and death were once and for all overcome by Jesus on the cross. That is their understanding or application of the atonement."

30. Kärkkäinen ("Pentecostal Mission and Encounter with Religions," 300) states that

question this application of atonement theology in general, it is clear at least that the Prosperity theology use of this doctrine aligns with the spirit of the classical Pentecostal use of it.

Where this value has been criticized most strenuously is when the blessings held in the atonement are thought to be some sort of a believer's "legal right" to be accessed by faith. Or that a positive confession "binds" God to act in accordance with spiritual laws of faith that govern the universe.[31] Obviously, these extremes are problematic on a great many fronts—not the least of which is to ensnare God to the whims of human will. But these extremes are not "essential" to Prosperity theologies and there are more moderate ways to uphold these values that we will explore in the third section of this chapter.

At heart, the challenge for believers to access the provisions laid up in the atonement is a call to exercise active faith. If justification of sins is within the reach of faith and healing has been shown to be within the reach of faith, then what other heavenly resources might believers tap into by faith? It is in this context that the Prosperity theology recognition of the power of spoken words to facilitate breakthroughs should be seen.[32] Encouraging believers to use their vocalized words to help focus their faith can be a very helpful way to stimulate active faith in the life of the believer. Moreover, this emphasis on the active expression of faith to pursue greater breakthroughs in Christian life is not so far off from the emphasis in Pentecostal Spirituality for believers to pursue encounters and experiences of God by this same type of probing faith. The difference is that in Prosperity theologies this theology of encounter becomes a theology of breakthrough. Still, this emphasis on active faith is the lifeblood of Pentecostal Spirituality, so Prosperity theologies affirming the power of spoken words to activate faith clearly reflect this Pentecostal distinctive as well.

Perhaps the area where Prosperity theologies have come under the most critique by the "classical" branches of Pentecostalism is in their transition away from ascetic values towards an engagement with the world and

---

"No doubt, in their yearning and search for a holistic account of the Full Gospel, Pentecostals came to embrace the notion of 'holistic salvation' long before the term gained fame in some mainline theologies."

31. Brogdon, *New Pentecostal Message*, 53.

32. Bowler (*Blessed*, 11) believes the roots of Prosperity theology are in New Thought metaphysics through the influence of E. W. Kenyon. Brogdon (*New Pentecostal Message*, 4) disagrees and tries to locate the roots of Prosperity theology firmly within Pentecostalism's own traditions.

the things in the world. We have already mentioned how many "classical" Pentecostal theologians have called for a return to the ascetic values of the early Pentecostal movement to revitalize the vibrancy of the movement. So, how can this divide be overcome? I think the common ground here is actually in the joint passion for revival that both "classical" Pentecostals and Prosperity theologies hold and that is a fundamental part of Pentecostal identity.

When confronted with the question of what revival looks like, "classical" Pentecostals might paint a narrative of godly men and women fasting and praying for years for a breakthrough of God's Spirit in revival fervor throughout the community. We might hear about how New York City came to a standstill at noon each day so that believers could pray—such was the widespread impact of the great revivals in that region in the mid-nineteenth century. But as great and powerful as these religious awakenings were, the one thing they all had in common was that they eventually came to an end. Prosperity theologies thus ask the question, "What would revival look like that was sustainable for a lifetime?"[33] How would it manifest in our families? In our workplaces? In our neighborhoods? What would allow it to avoid the burnout that inevitably followed history's great revivals? Prosperity theologies answer these questions by claiming that sustained revival is only possible if the presence of God begins to consecrate every area of life and every human endeavor. In short, sustained revival looks like the presence and blessings of *shalom*.[34]

Theologically, one of the main issues here lies between a view of holiness as asceticism and a view of holiness as consecration.[35] An ascetic view of holiness sees material things as potential contaminants or distractions from a life of holiness and emphasizes the importance of a believer's separation from the material things of the world. In contrast, a consecrationist

---

33. Pastor Bill Johnson of Bethel Church in Redding often poses this question to new students at the Bethel School of Supernatural Ministry.

34. Sustainable revival will look like lives becoming whole, communities flourishing, and justice for the marginalized being realized. It will be defined less by what it stands against than by what it stands for. It will be more feasting, rather than more fasting. More celebration of life than somber fear of sin and death.

35. Yong (*IDC*, 172) speaks of this distinction as a tension within Pentecostalism generally between an appropriate cleansing *from* the world and a missional consecration *for* the world. While this is a legitimate point to make when discussing Pentecostal political theology, I am using the terms to speak to a larger metanarrative that governs Pentecostal thought and behavior—an overall ascetic orientation vs. an overall consecrationist orientation.

view of holiness sees the potential of every material thing to be utilized in ways that can promote the work of the Spirit and thus not inherently corrupt or contaminated. For "classical" Pentecostals, a return to the ascetic lifestyle of the apostles in the early church is the model for a return to the Pentecostal power of the early church. As such, they continue to emphasize separation from the world and from material things in a disciplined life of self-sacrifice that stands against worldliness in its many varieties—among them, the dangers of the love of money.[36] But for Prosperity theologies which had made the shift to valuing financial breakthroughs out of poverty as a provision of the atonement, the good that could be brought into a life through money began to be recognized as well. And if even money could be consecrated to be used for the holy purposes of God, then why not other aspects of material life and society as well? Indeed, if revival looks like *shalom*, that would require that every dimension of material life becomes consecrated to the holy purposes of God.

Pastor Bill Johnson of Bethel Church in Redding, California is fond of saying that in the Old Testament, if you touch a leper *you* become unclean; in the New Testament, if you touch a leper, *they* become clean. The point being that believers can consecrate relationships and material things in the world to align with the purposes of God rather than be afraid that they will be contaminated by those interactions. Under this consecrationist model of holiness, material blessings are not an evil to be shunned or a temptation to be avoided but are simply tools that can be used for good purposes or bad. Charlie Self would seem to agree with this consecrationist model when he affirms the value of ordinary work saying that Pentecostals used to value Spiritual, missional things more than normal vocations. This, he felt, was a failure of discipleship. Spirit-empowered discipleship was meant to encompass the whole of life. Indeed, legitimate work done well glorifies God, flourishes communities, and dignifies the individual.[37] Thus, while we can see that in Prosperity theologies the Pentecostal doctrine of sanctification is preserved, it is preserved in the vein of a new orientation of holiness as consecration to the material world rather than preservation from it.

Of course, where critics rightly take offense is when this recognition of the potential consecrated use of money and material things becomes a

---

36. Cartledge ("Pentecostal Theology," 254–72) suggests that Steven Land has articulated a distinctly Wesleyan Pentecostal theology of spirituality with this ascetic view of holiness.

37. Self, *Flourishing Churches and Communities*, xxi–xxxvii.

license for greed or an uncritical embrace of consumerism.[38] Where exactly does one draw a healthy line to say enough is enough? Is this just a baptism of American capitalism? While these challenges are important, there are certainly ways to encourage healthy financial practices in the context of community *shalom*. And we should be sensitive to the social uplift that can result when people who have been trapped in generational cycles of poverty hear that pursuing financial breakthrough for their families is not a manifestation of unspiritual greed. I will fully explore these liberative elements of Prosperity theologies in later chapters, but for now, it is enough to point out that there are broader sociological dynamics at play here than simple overtures to greed. Accordingly, perhaps Prosperity theologies stand in need of refinement and development more than outright dismissal.

The fourth value of Prosperity theologies that we identified above was a positive view of a vibrant church in the eschaton rather than a vision of world-flight. This is interesting because the Prosperity theology view actually reflects the early Pentecostal doctrine of the "Latter Rain" perfectly as well as the Pentecostal narrative identity as the "people of the Latter Rain" that Kenneth Archer detailed.[39] In fact, the entire reason that this can be thought of as a retrieval is because early Pentecostalism, under the influence of Fundamentalism, moved away from this "Latter Rain" eschatology towards a pre-millenial expectation of the annihilation of the world and apostasy of the church. That often left believers primarily concerned with self-preservation instead of imagining a victorious church that was full of the presence and power of the Spirit and demonstrated the wisdom of God to the world in every sphere of life. Peter Althouse has written an exploration of the original "Latter Rain" roots of early Pentecostalism looking at David Wesley Myland's *The Latter Rain Covenant* and putting it in conversation with the contemporary eschatological perspectives of Jürgen Moltmann and others. He recommends a return to this "Latter Rain" eschatological orientation rather than the premillennial dispensationalism that has been prevalent in Pentecostalism ever since its partnership with early Fundamentalism.[40] To that, I say that Prosperity theologies heeded this call long ago, and on this point, it is perhaps "classical" Pentecostalism that has moved away from this Pentecostal distinctive and narrative identity.

---

38. For a critique that Prosperity theology is just an accommodation to the worldly values of America, see McConnell (*The Promise of Health and Wealth*, 183).

39. Archer, *Pentecostal Hermeneutics*, 109–10.

40. Althouse, *Spirit of Last Days*, 16–20.

The Empowering God

While the recovery of a "Latter Rain" orientation in eschatology is an important factor in the vibrant embrace of materiality in Prosperity theologies, there are some practices here that can again raise concerns. In light of the historical abuses of World War II, due perhaps in part to over-realized eschatological delusions, it is clear that one group's idea of the Kingdom of God manifested on earth can be another group's worst nightmare. With that in mind, a word of caution about Dominion theologies and Kingdom Now expressions is in order. In the 1980s and early 1990s "[s]ome influential North American Pentecostal leaders ditched their theology of an imminent rapture and embraced a version of post-millennialism sometimes referred to as kingdom theology (or Kingdom Now), emphasizing engagement with and capture of the social and political realms to help establish the Kingdom of God on earth (and in the process hasten the Second Coming)."[41] Certain expressions of Dominion theology seem to have made a significant impact for good in their communities—such as the Redeemed Christian Church of God in Nigeria where they have established an alternative polis providing social services to the community well beyond what the government has been able to provide.[42] But beyond the concerns of an over-realized eschatology, history is rife with examples of the dangers and myopia that often come with visions of the church ruling over the affairs of state. While better models of this dynamic between church and state can be proposed, it is perhaps most important to remember just how easily this dynamic can become oppressive as an initial way to hold chiliastic zeal accountable. Despite this call to sobriety, the enhanced engagement with the world that a "Latter Rain" orientation inspires is another welcome shift that Prosperity theologies have made—in this case, to recover an important Pentecostal distinctive that had been lost.

From this analysis it seems clear that Prosperity theologies can be authentic expressions of Pentecostalism given their alignment with the theological distinctives of Pentecostalism and their expression of a Pentecostal Spirituality that values active faith, revival, and experiences of the power of the Spirit. Indeed, with their extension of the provision for divine healing to include a more holistic view of health and their adoption of a consecrationist view of holiness rather than an ascetic one, the case can certainly be made that Prosperity theologies represent a healthy "maturing" of Pentecostal themes beyond their initial roots. It is hoped that this

---

41. Smith, "Politics and Economics," 184.
42. Ukah, *A New Paradigm of Pentecostal Power*, 171–218.

analysis can clarify points for dialogue between Prosperity theologies and the many branches of the Pentecostal movement that remain wary of its message—especially as it regards the competing visions of holiness. There is much richness to be mined here and a cooperative effort to refine the insights offered by Prosperity theologies would be welcome indeed.

A Broadening of Theological Resources for Prosperity Theology Values

A large part of the reason Prosperity theologies have such a bad reputation among scholars and observers both inside the church and outside of it is because of questionable practices in lifestyle and ministry among its leaders that bring forth legitimate questions about the exploitation of the poor or the use of manipulative practices to induce giving that mainly benefit the leaders of these ministries.[43] The concerns people have over these sorts of practices are certainly not to be casually dismissed. But I wonder if the spectacle of many Prosperity ministries is getting in the way of our ability to recognize themes and insights in these movements that might have a broader application for all Christians. I will lay my cards on the table—personally, I also find many of the televised appeals for money to be shameless and exploitative. I dislike the whipping up of the crowd and the promise of hundredfold returns in exchange for hundred-dollar bills. And I most certainly get uncomfortable with the "name it and claim it" varieties that seem to feed into the unhealthy obsession with consumption in much of the Western world. But if we were to take away all of these "hard to stomach" elements, could we find an expression of these practices that is actually healthy?

To this end, I want to explore ways to fund the four values of Prosperity theologies we identified earlier with alternative theological constructions that could provide it with more biblically sound and broadly appealing foundations. In other words, I want to retain the values of Prosperity theologies that seem to have had such a liberative effect on the lives of the poor while giving them different theological support that will appeal to traditions beyond Pentecostalism. My goal is to make a contribution to the refinement of Prosperity theologies towards a mature expression that

---

43. David Williams ("The Heresy of Prosperity Teaching," 33) talks about these manipulative practices when he refers to "[t]he casualties of the faith message." See also Brogdon, *New Pentecostal Message*, 57.

affirms ordinary human flourishing and communal *shalom* that the wider body of Christ can embrace.

Alternative Theological Support for Prosperity Theology Values and Practices

The first alternative theological support I would like to propose is to replace the theology of healing and prosperity as legal rights of the believer in the atonement with George E. Ladd's theology of the "already–not yet" dynamics of the Kingdom of God. According to Ladd, many Christians erroneously believe that the eschatological Kingdom of God will only come when this present world has passed away. While that is not necessarily wrong, there are other biblical passages that suggest that the Kingdom of God came decisively in the life and ministry of Christ and that this Kingdom can be accessed even now by believers. Thus, Ladd says, "The Kingdom is a present reality (Matt. 12:28), and yet it is a future blessing (1 Cor. 15:50) . . . The Kingdom is a realm into which men enter now (Matt. 21:31), and yet it is a realm into which they will enter tomorrow (Matt. 8:11)."[44] Many theologians from a wide variety of denominations have come to embrace this tension between the "already" and the "not yet"—perhaps none more vigorously than Pentecostal groups as it provides a useful way to understand how some manifestations of the Kingdom can be experienced now (such as healings and miracles), while the world at large remains largely unchanged awaiting its full redemption at the eschaton.

To say that the kingdom can be accessed now actually is more all-encompassing than the Prosperity theology belief that sin, sickness, poverty, and death were paid for in the atonement. After all, that would mean that every blessing of the eschaton was now within the reach of faith. In this construction, that is precisely what Prosperity theologies believe. And Prosperity theologies differ from other theologies in their extreme optimism about exactly how much of heaven they believe can be manifested here on earth (hint: a whole lot).[45] This language of "optimism" for the Kingdom is

---

44. Ladd, *The Gospel of the Kingdom*, 18.

45. Even among those who believe in the theology of the Kingdom of God, some hold a "pessimistic" orientation expecting very little of the eschaton to manifest in the present. Most Pentecostals hold an "optimistic" view but limit their expectations to the charismata and such. Prosperity theologies express the greatest optimism that every aspect of kingdom *shalom* can be accessed for today. And while that can border on something close to an over-realized eschatology, the language of "optimism" and "mystery"

Towards a Broadly Credible Expression of Prosperity Theology

better than language of a "legal right" because it manages to retain some role for mystery in how the dynamics of faith and the Kingdom of God work, which avoids impinging on the freedom of God. Removing the language of "legal right" also helps to put the value for the power of spoken words into a more moderate framework. So, instead of positive confessions "binding" God to act, these confessions become ways to help activate faith that welcomes the Kingdom of God to manifest on earth according to its ultimately mysterious ways.[46]

The second alternative theological support I propose is to move from a "Latter Rain" eschatological orientation to an eschatology of hope à la Jürgen Moltmann.[47] While both of these eschatological views can be considered "victorious" eschatologies where the church is expected to flourish as it progresses towards the end-times, the main difference between them lies in where they draw their respective visions for the flourishing church. For the "Latter Rain" narrative, the ideal is the apostolic power of the first-century church of the past—but that is an awkward fit with Prosperity theologies given the early church values of asceticism and self-sacrifice. In the eschatological vision of Jürgen Moltmann on the other hand, the ideal is the vision of *shalom* in the future Kingdom of God. That is clearly a better fit for Prosperity theologies.

This eschatological vision of the future Kingdom of God is not just a wishful dream. Rather, it is meant to activate believers to work to transform present social structures and relational dynamics to align with those future heavenly realities. Thus, if there is no discrimination between male and female in the future Kingdom, then there should be no such discrimination now. If there is no poverty or sickness in the future Kingdom, then we should endeavor to also eliminate them now. Hence, the obvious link to the potential liberative dynamics of Prosperity theologies. In fact, adding the Moltmannian eschatology of hope to Prosperity theologies might naturally instill values for liberation and *shalom* for all in them that can provide a

---

helps to mitigate those accusations.

46. In appealing to mystery, Prosperity theologies do not think faith is just a crapshoot. They would still believe that certain best practices get the best results from faith even if it no longer can be thought of formulaically.

47. For Moltmann's famous eschatological proposal, see *Theology of Hope*. Many prominent theologians and biblical scholars from various streams of faith either directly owe their eschatological views to Moltmann or align closely with his views. A small sampling of such scholars would include: N. T. Wright, Richard Bauckham, Walter Brueggemann, and Miroslav Volf.

check to any tendencies towards unfettered greed or consumerism. A nice side-bonus.

Contrary to the ascetic values inherent in the "Latter Rain" eschatologies, the eschatology of hope is consecrationist through and through. After all, the end vision is the *shalom* of all things where everything is in proper relationship with God again. That means everything becomes consecrated to holiness over time as it is brought to align more and more with the values of the eschaton.[48]

So, by making these two slight shifts in the theological supports for Prosperity theologies, we have been able to retain all of the four core values that are the root of their radical affirmation of materiality while allaying many of the theological and biblical objections raised against them. Ladd's Kingdom of God theology managed (1) some affirmation of health and prosperity as blessings in this life that can be accessed by faith, and (2) some recognition of the power of spoken words to facilitate breakthroughs. Moltmann's eschatology of hope contributed (3) some transition away from ascetic values towards an engagement with the world and the things in the world, and (4) some positive view of a vibrant church in the eschaton rather than a vision of world-flight. Now, I want to consider some common Prosperity theology practices to see if we can also frame them in a way that is more broadly compelling.

Towards More Broadly Accessible Practices for Prosperity Theology Values

We have already covered some of the more well-documented examples of questionable practices in Prosperity theologies—legal right, name it and claim it, binding faith, license for greed, Dominionism, etc. So, what might responsible and healthy expressions of these practices look like? And if healthy practices can be identified, what benefits might they confer to the believer and the community of faith?

---

48. We could add many other things here such as a non-dualistic view of the human person or even a theology of creation that affirms the goodness of the world. But for the sake of simplicity, I will leave these for future exploration. Regarding the non-dualistic view of humanity, Joel Green (*Body, Soul, and Human Life*, 4–6) says that the human person doesn't consist of a body and a soul, but rather is a complete entity—an embodied life. That challenges every *gnostic*-type tendency to value "spiritual" life over "material" life.

Towards a Broadly Credible Expression of Prosperity Theology

For starters, we have already proposed how the notion of legal rights in the atonement can be superseded by the theology of the "already–not yet" dynamics of the Kingdom of God. So, a healthy expression of the idea of "legal rights" in this new context would simply be the manifestation of vibrant optimism regarding just how much of the Kingdom one believes it is possible to access in this life by faith. And while believers can certainly argue about just how much optimism is appropriate, this sort of debate is not likely to lead to a charge of heterodoxy. Indeed, for most believers exercising a little more optimism regarding the inbreaking of the Kingdom of God in their present realities would be a healthy challenge to embrace.

Removing the basis for the appeal to "legal rights" also undermines much of the logic behind the "name it and claim it" phenomenon in Prosperity theologies. But positive confessions still can play an important role in the spiritual formation of the believer. Take, for instance, the practice of making declarations that is practiced in some of the more moderate Prosperity theologies. The practice of making declarations is an expression of the process of daily renewing one's mind with the truth—in this case, the truth about God's desire to bring everyone into *shalom*.[49] The power of declarations in shaping mindsets can be vividly seen in the Civil Rights Movement's anthem declaration: "We shall overcome! We shall overcome! We shall overcome someday!" Seen in this light, it is clear how powerful of a galvanizing force declarations can be. Prosperity theologies tap into the formative power of this practice to imprint their most basic theological conviction—that God is good and is passionate about bringing all of His creation into flourishing and *shalom*.

Another of the more controversial practices in Prosperity theologies is the idea of seed faith as developed by Oral Roberts during the years of his television ministry in America.[50] In its worst forms, it amounts to manipulative appeals for donations with the promise of exorbitant returns that seem to fuel human greed. But at its root it is meant to be about the cultivation of practices of generosity and active faith. It is meant to help believers shift their attention away from the oftentimes heavy circumstances of their own lives and live generously towards others, even when they have little by way of finances to give. A recovery of this practice in a more broadly

---

49. Green (*Body, Soul, and Human Life*, 123) points out that repentance in Luke–Acts is "[a]imed at a transformation of day-to-day patterns of thinking, feeling, believing, and behaving." That is precisely what the practice of making declarations aims to do.

50. Roberts, *The Miracle of Seed Faith*, 5–94.

affirmative way might focus on giving to others in the hope that it will produce a hundred-fold return in *their* lives, not in our own. It might mean choosing to see the best in someone when they can't see it in themselves. It might mean making room at the table to befriend a stranger. Such practices of generosity and faith are the bedrock of thriving personal and community life.

Lastly, regarding the tendencies towards Dominion theology in some Prosperity theologies, the value for engaging a Christian presence in every sphere of society is not problematic in itself. Indeed, that is one of the strengths of Prosperity theology's radical embrace of the material. Rather, what is in question is the mode of that engagement. Prosperity theologies would benefit from a shift towards a posture of generosity here as well. In such a stance, rather than replace civic authorities and institutions with Christian ones, the church would come alongside civic authorities in the mode of servant-heartedness—thereby modeling the values of Christ without having to dominate over others to do so. All of these moderated Prosperity practices are already being modeled in churches and communities of faith.[51] I have just compiled and curated them here to demonstrate that more broadly accessible forms of Prosperity theology and practice do exist and to show the real value that a radical embrace of the material dimensions of salvation can bring.

Conclusion

Part of my goal in this chapter was to try to find an expression of Prosperity theology that could be credible theologically and in its practical expression in the church. That would serve both as an internal critique to extreme versions of Prosperity theologies and as an invitation to other Christian traditions to engage in constructive dialogue with Prosperity theologies regarding their robust vision for ordinary human flourishing. In the coming chapters, I will dive more deeply into an exploration of what it is about this radical embrace of materiality that has been so liberating for the poor. The answer surely goes deeper than a simple license for greed.

---

51. For instance, all of these moderated practices can be found at Bethel Church in Redding, California led by Pastor Bill Johnson. The attitude of active generosity and servant-heartedness is characteristic of what they call their "culture of honor," which they consider to be the bedrock of a sustainable revival culture. See Silk, *Culture of Honor*, 29–46.

Towards a Broadly Credible Expression of Prosperity Theology

I hope to discern the ways that the Spirit is using Prosperity theologies beyond the categories of health and wealth and towards a broader empowerment to wholeness in the life of the believer and in the community. By extending the scope of Prosperity theologies in this way, we can incorporate a sensitivity to circumstances in life where "idealized" standards of prosperity might be curtailed, such as for people with disabilities or those in the process of dying. Beyond that, we can think about the core theological claims being made about the nature and character of God. It is there that we will see most clearly if Prosperity theologies really have something to contribute to our understanding of the Triune God revealed in the life of Christ. I believe that they do and the remainder of this study is dedicated to teasing out the shape of that distinctive contribution.[52]

---

52. In many ways, I am taking up the challenge presented by Yong ("Instead of a Conclusion," 318) "[P]entecostal theologians need to take up this issue of prosperity as a central theme within their broader soteriological and theological considerations. What is the problem and how does the gospel provide a response? These are the issues underneath the debates about Prosperity theology. Answers to these questions will influence the next generation of Pentecostal churches as well as their impact on these wider social, political, and economic domains."

3

An Orientation to the Contemporary Study of Human Flourishing

Introduction

IN THE PREVIOUS CHAPTER, I tried to normalize Prosperity theologies in light of the fact that they have proven effective at actually helping the poor to experience social uplift in many areas of the world. One of the main reasons that they have been able to do this is because of their embrace of some of the potential "this-worldly" benefits of salvation—namely health and prosperity. As this study progresses, I want to see if it can be demonstrated that Prosperity theologies affirm ordinary human flourishing more broadly, which is something I suspect results from the deeper liberative elements in its message that have not yet been fully appreciated.

To properly frame this exploration of the deeper liberative elements of Prosperity theologies in the coming chapters, this chapter offers an orientation to the contemporary study of human flourishing from the perspective of biblical, theological, and behavioral science resources. The reason for this background is that it allows us to (1) recognize where theo-centric views of flourishing have historically diverged from ordinary views of human flourishing on the subject of the lordship of God, (2) identify ways that contemporary theological proposals have missed some important dimensions of ordinary human flourishing in understanding victimization, and (3) see if the liberative impulses to be explored in Prosperity theologies line up with contemporary views of human flourishing from the behavioral sciences. Ultimately, any theo-centric view of flourishing that wishes to also

An Orientation to the Contemporary Study of Human Flourishing

be seen as an affirmation of ordinary human flourishing has to show how submission to the lordship of God is vital to ordinary human flourishing—no easy challenge by any stretch of the imagination.

A Brief Orientation to the Study of Human Flourishing

This brief orientation first addresses the modern worldview and why the study of human flourishing must be done in a way that makes sense to both theistic and secular scholars. Afterwards, it offers a simple typology of theistic visions of the flourishing life that will be useful for this study.

The Modern Worldview and the Immanent Frame

One of the great themes that has occupied the minds of countless philosophers and theologians over the centuries is the question of what constitutes a flourishing human life—or in more common vernacular, what is the meaning of life? In *A Secular Age*, Charles Taylor notes that every society he has observed over the last two thousand years has had its own definition of what makes for a flourishing life.

> Every person, and every society, lives with or by some conceptions(s) of what human flourishing is: what constitutes a fulfilled life? What makes life really worth living? What would we most admire people for? We can't help asking these and related questions in our lives. And our struggles to answer them define the view or views that we try to live by, or between which we hover. At another level, these views are codified, sometimes in philosophical theories, sometimes in moral codes, sometimes in religious practices and devotion. These and the various ill-formulated practices which people around us engage in constitute the resources that our society offers each one of us as we try to lead our lives.[53]

Indeed, throughout history, many competing visions for the flourishing life have each had their moments of prominence in various cultures around the world. Ancient Greece was famous for the competing schools of the philosophers each making a claim to discerning the definitive answer to this riddle. The Epicureans promoted a hedonic view of flourishing—the

---

53. Taylor, *A Secular Age*, 16.

pleasure-seeking and experientially satisfying life. Contrast that with the Stoics—champions of the life of reason and self-mastery, a version of the life well-lived (the *eudaimonic* life). While these perspectives differed as to what the highest goal of the human life might be, they shared the assumption that whatever that highest good turned out to be, it was something objective that could be applied to every person in a similar way. It was not until the philosopher Immanuel Kant popularized the idea that beauty was in the eye of the beholder that popular opinions about flourishing life took on a greater degree of subjective relativity. Friedrich Nietzsche took this perhaps furthest in exhorting everyone to embrace the will to power—what he considered the fullest expression of the flourishing life. This will to power was the tendency of all beings "[n]ot just to survive, but to enlarge and expand—to flourish, so to speak, even at the expense of others."[54]

There are many other factors that gave rise to the shift from a communal understanding of identity and flourishing to the individualistic vision that seems to dominate Western thought today. Charles Taylor maps out many of these factors when he develops his theory of how the modern worldview arose out of the cultural shifts that took place during the Reformation. The Reformation era challenge to the "enchanted" view of the world and the empowerment of the laity through its rejection of the sacred orders of the church paved the way for developments like the disenchanting of the world, the initial creation of a buffered view of the self, the molding of that self into a disciplined and civilized self, the invention of privacy, and ultimately, the rise of individualism.[55] These changes, Taylor notes, are not likely to be rolled back to a semblance of the prior enchanted view of the world. As a result, we now live in a society where transcendent "otherworldly" views of flourishing have come under deep suspicion. Instead, modern society now focuses on the "this-worldly" dimensions of flourishing life.

The heightened emphasis on the "this-worldly" dimensions of flourishing has led to one of the most commonly cited problems of modernity, namely, the loss of depth and meaning in life. Thus, Taylor sees modern

---

54. Volf, *A Public Faith*, 67.

55. Taylor (*A Secular Age*, 473) describes the last half-decade as an "age of authenticity" where the individualistic trajectories of the reformation have shifted into an "expressive" individualism in modern Western society. Also, Taylor's "buffered self" contrasts with the "vulnerable self" that required the sacred orders of the church for protection from cosmic forces. A "buffered self" no longer needs that outside protection from others.

society caught between the forces of two rival cross pressures: the narratives of a closed immanence on the one hand and an awareness of the inadequacy of those narratives on the other.[56] This tension is what Taylor refers to as the "immanent frame" and together with the parallel rise of modern science, it constitutes the rough boundaries of the modern worldview.

Rather than join the chorus of those who critique and reject modernism outright for the flatness of its view of the world, Taylor believes modernity is here to stay and that it does have some redeeming qualities.[57] Thus, Taylor suggests that we need to engage this worldview with some challenges to its propensity to lean towards a flat view of the world and with an embrace of its program for "ordinary" human flourishing rather than pine for a return to the enchanted worldview of an era long since passed. But how do Christians embrace the modern worldview's program for "ordinary" human flourishing if indeed the religious viewpoint aims at God and thus beyond ordinary human flourishing (and sometimes starkly against ordinary human flourishing) as Taylor suspects?[58]

This challenge of articulating a Christian response to the immanent frame and the question of ordinary human flourishing has become a key task of theology. David Kelsey provides us with a clear picture of this task when he says,

> Christian theology has a large stake in making it clear that its affirmations about God and God's ways of relating to human beings underwrite human beings' flourishing. It has been especially important to emphasize this claim in the context of "late modernity," in which Friedrich Nietzsche is often cited as the most powerful spokesman for a widespread and deep suspicion that Christians magnify God and God's power and dominion by systematically minimizing human beings, making them small, weak, and servile—anything but flourishing.[59]

---

56. Taylor, *A Secular Age*, 555.

57. Taylor (*A Secular Age*, 548) claims that "What emerges from all this is that we can either see the transcendent as a threat, a dangerous temptation, a distraction, or an obstacle to our greatest good. Or we can read it as answering to our deepest craving, need, fulfillment of the good."

58. Taylor's (*A Secular Age*, 18) own view of the relationship between religious and humanistic flourishing remains fairly classical: "There remains a fundamental tension in Christianity. Flourishing is good, nevertheless seeking it is not our ultimate goal. But even where we renounce it, we re-affirm it, because we follow God's will in being a channel for it to others, and ultimately to all."

59. Kelsey, "On Human Flourishing," 1.

This suspicion that the Christian vision of human flourishing undermines ordinary flourishing is a common one and not quite so easy to overcome. What is clear is that a suitable response will have to go beyond dogma if it hopes to engage the modern worldview. Indeed, it will likely have to frame itself in a way that affirms ordinary flourishing for it to pass the authenticity test. I will explore a basic typology of theistic responses to this issue below before turning to a deeper exploration of the contributions of key contemporary theologians on this issue.

A Typology of Theistic Visions of the Flourishing Life

When we consider theistic visions for the flourishing life, we find they are grounded on convictions about the nature and character of God, the dynamics of the relationship between God and people, and the extension of these dynamics to relationships with other people, other religions, and the world. But through the different eras of the church and in the many divergent theological traditions that have persisted through the centuries, varying theistic visions have led to a variety of different understandings of human flourishing. For some, human flourishing entails escaping from the trappings of this world to perfect the soul. For others, following the sovereign God means a life of sacrificial service to the ends of the earth. What these views have in common is a sense that flourishing life is to be found in God and apart from the worldly concerns that non-believers might normally associate with the trappings of a flourishing life. Worldly things are either dangerous distractions from the more noble spiritual pursuits, or they are things that need to be sacrificed in the name of service to the higher purposes of God in the world. These types of theistic visions for flourishing life amount to what Taylor identifies as visions of flourishing that contradict "ordinary flourishing"—meaning that in these formulations, the goal of flourishing lies somewhere beyond the immanent frame of this world.[60] We will call such views *ascetic* views of human flourishing because they constitute a withdrawal from ordinary flourishing.

Alternatively, there have arisen some Christian visions of the flourishing life that seek to affirm ordinary human flourishing as precisely what it

---

60. These ascetic views have been a part of church tradition for centuries, perhaps dating back to the desert fathers and Anthony the Great. Monastic orders of the middle ages might also be represented in this category. For a biblical challenge to these ascetic views, see Bauckham, *God and the Crisis of Freedom*, 20.

An Orientation to the Contemporary Study of Human Flourishing

means to find true flourishing in God. We will call these views *humanistic* views of human flourishing. Among these views, perhaps none is more provocative than Ludwig Feuerbach's desire to conflate the two together into one. Feuerbach's project to recover a theology of life that fully embraces the this-worldliness of faith and refuses to dialectically separate this world from the world to come has caused much consternation for theologians over the centuries. He has said, "Life is God. The enjoyment of life is the enjoyment of God. A true love of life is the true religion."[61] But if theistic human flourishing is nothing more than humanistic human flourishing, why add God to the conversation at all? How can we be sure that our preconceived convictions about flourishing life do not inappropriately frame our theologies? Shouldn't authentic theology retain the ability to re-orient our values (discipleship) and provide some sense of perspectival critique to conceptions of human flourishing in light of the Christian revelation of the triune God? These are important questions for views that equate ordinary flourishing completely with Christian flourishing.

The quest to articulate an authentically Christian vision of human flourishing that is firmly engaged in this immanent frame is one of the more exciting trajectories of contemporary theology as evidenced by the number and quality of scholars who have engaged in this dialogue of late.[62] It is precisely here that much theological attention has been focused in attempts to either retain some measure of the divide between theistic and humanistic views of human flourishing or to bridge it in some way. Many theologians are willing to keep the language of human flourishing, but they have spoken of the need for a redefinition of the values that underlie humanistic views of flourishing in the light of Christ. What we understand by the terms freedom, love, and goodness (among others) are determined by values that arise from the dominant culture that often go un-critiqued. Is freedom simply the ability to do whatever we desire? Is love primarily something pleasurable for us to enjoy? Is goodness merely that which is good from our perspective? Theologians have often challenged the cultural preconceptions of these values and offered their own set of contrasting values from their varying biblical hermeneutics. The resulting critiques of modernity, consumerism, and individualism bring important categories to the

---

61. I am indebted to Moltmann (*LGFL*, 11) for this quote and translation from Feuerbach, *Gedanken über Tod und Unsterblichkeit*.

62. Besides Jürgen Moltmann and Miroslav Volf, David Kelsey, Veli-Matti Kärkkäinen, and N. T. Wright among many others have all contributed richly to this discussion.

fore in the contemporary conversation on human flourishing in the light of Christ. We might call these views *redefined* views of human flourishing.

Perhaps a definitive response that silences all other views is not really feasible here in light of the enduring mysteries surrounding human existence in the universe. There will always be a conflict of ideas arising from contrasting philosophies and value systems such that, at best, we can only present our theories to the marketplace of ideas to see where consensus might occur. Following that line of thinking, the best proposals will harmonize the widest diversity of truths from the religious metanarratives, the behavioral sciences, and the creative humanities. Consequently, the contention of this study is that Prosperity theologies thoughtfully developed provide a promising new way to harmonize the internal narratives of Christianity on human flourishing with the external narratives of the behavioral sciences and humanities. While that is a *redefined* view of human flourishing, it is a redefined view that tries to achieve consensus such that it can also be recognized as an authentically *humanistic* view as well. This mutually respectful bridging between the theistic and the humanistic is what makes Prosperity theologies so potentially fascinating for this study.

Biblical Perspectives on Human Flourishing

Having established the need to harmonize theories of human flourishing from both theistic and humanistic perspectives, we explore Biblical resources that can be used to help bridge that divide. In particular, this includes the idea of *shalom* from the Old Testament and of the Kingdom of God from the New Testament.

Old Testament Perspectives on Human Flourishing

Turning to the issue of Prosperity theology's internal coherence with the Christian narratives, it is helpful to begin with a look at what the Old Testament Scriptures have to say about flourishing life. Recently, I had the opportunity to engage in extended conversations with Rabbi Michael Cohen of the Arava Institute for Environmental Studies regarding Jewish ideas of flourishing life.[63] In our wide-ranging discussion, Rabbi Cohen talked about holiness as something embedded in the way we live our everyday

---

63. Cohen interview by author.

lives. This was no ascetic retreat from the world, but rather an attentiveness towards God in the midst of the simple goings on of life. Flourishing, then, had a lot to do with the idea of *shalom* and its holistic reach into every dimension of life. Indeed, the division between secular and sacred was nonsensical because everything belonged to God.

The concept of *shalom* at the heart of the Old Testament view of a flourishing life goes far beyond a simple peace that reflects the absence of a conflict. Rather, John Goldingay points out that "*Shalom* stands potentially for all forms of well-being. It covers peace, but it is another positive term that embraces fullness of life, prosperity, contentment, harmony and happiness."[64] In the context of relationships, Malinda Berry says that the Hebrew notion of *shalom* points to "[w]holeness, completeness, security, friendship, well-being, and even salvation of the people both individually and collectively."[65] Just from these two brief snapshots, we see that it is impossible to overstate how comprehensive this vision of flourishing captured in the Hebrew notion of *shalom* really is.

While the Hebrew notion of *shalom* is remarkable in the breadth with which it addresses every conceivable aspect of flourishing life, it is equally focused on the quality of that flourishing life.[66] So, *shalom* speaks not just to having enough to be satisfied, but even to having an abundance that allows for generosity and for sharing amongst the entire community. *Shalom* is so characteristic of the way things ought to be that Cornelius Plantinga Jr. literally defines sin as the absence of *shalom*. He says, "In the Bible, *shalom* means *universal flourishing, wholeness, and delight*—a rich state of affairs in which natural needs are satisfied and natural gifts fruitfully employed, a state of affairs that inspires joyful wonder as its Creator and Savior opens doors and welcomes the creatures in whom he delights. Shalom, in other words, is the way things ought to be."[67]

Perhaps the most provocative way that *shalom* has been applied is to describe the way that God rules His creation. John Goldingay says, "[t]his Everlasting Father is one who rules in such a way as to ensure *shalom*. Both the narrower and the broader connotations of *shalom* are significant here.

64. Goldingay, *OTT*, 2:79.

65. Berry, "Mission of God," 167–73.

66. Swinton (*From Bedlam to Shalom*, 58) says that shalom "[h]as in essence to do with the quality of a person's life and quality of their relationship with God, with one another, and with the rest of creation."

67. Plantinga (*Not the Way*, 10) is drawing from Wolterstorff, *Justice and Peace Embrace*, 69–72.

As a ruler who brings *shalom*, this mighty God takes king and people from oppression and conflict to release and peace. But in addition, this Father sees that his son's people enjoy blessing, fruitfulness, prosperity and well-being in their life together."[68] This image of God ruling with the intention of ensuring *shalom* for all contrasts sharply with the common perception of a God who demands obedience for His own inscrutable purposes. If God's purposes include the promotion of *shalom* in His creation, then in a very profound way ordinary human flourishing is an important part of the will of God.

This idea is given further credence when we acknowledge that in the Hebraic way of thinking, there is no stark duality between the material and the spiritual. Rather, the Hebraic understanding is that of an embodied life that represented a unity of body and soul. Brevard Childs says that the human is "[a] complete entity and not a composite of parts from body, soul and spirit."[69] Contemporary Christian philosophy might refer to this as a nonreductive physicalism where "we are our bodies—there is no additional metaphysical element such as mind or soul or spirit. But . . . this 'physicalist' position need not deny that we are intelligent, moral and spiritual . . . we are *Spirited* bodies."[70] Thus, when speaking of a flourishing of the soul, it is hard to separate that from a concurrent flourishing of the body as well.

If the purposes of God are to ensure the *shalom* of all and holiness is to be set apart for the purposes of God, then there is an overlap between holiness and *shalom*. As such, it would not be wrong to suggest that holiness can be thought of in the context of wholeness, provided that wholeness is also thought of in the context of *shalom*. This fits well with Rabbi Cohen's depiction of holiness as something embedded in the way we live our daily lives in mindful relationship with God.

New Testament Perspectives on Human Flourishing

When we consider the teachings of the New Testament on the shape of a flourishing life, we naturally gravitate towards the life and teachings of Christ. What we find there, however, is not always so easy to interpret. First, we see in the life that Christ lived a certain downward mobility and a

68. Goldingay, *OTT*, 2:480.

69. Childs, *Canonical Context*, 199. Cf. Green, *Body, Soul, and Human Life*, 9.

70. Murphy, *Bodies and Souls*, ix. For a nuanced discussion of nonreductive physicalism, emergence, and two-way supervenience, see Kärkkäinen, *CCTPW*, 3:306–49.

challenge for the rich to use their wealth to address the injustices being experienced by the poor.[71] Then we see Jesus directing Peter to put his nets on the opposite side of the boat to reveal an extraordinary abundance of fish, directing Peter to pull money from the mouth of a fish to pay temple taxes, and providing endless quantities of fish and bread to feed the multitudes listening to him. So, on one side we seem to have a call to downward mobility and regard for the poor while on the other side we have a revelation of the super-abundance available in the Kingdom of God to meet every need. Which of these is the true Kingdom economics?

I believe that the best way to navigate this strange state of affairs is to interpret Jesus' downward mobility and calls for justice-making among believers as an invitation to a lifestyle oriented towards generosity. But that lifestyle of generosity is limited if it is not paired with a great optimism regarding the degree to which we can see the super-abundance of the eschatological Kingdom of God manifest in our lives by faith. The primary message of Jesus during his earthly ministry was about the nearness of the Kingdom of God. We have already detailed George E. Ladd's theology of the "already–not yet" dynamics of the Kingdom of God where we recognize that while the fullness of the Kingdom of God will not be revealed until the eschaton, proleptic (anticipatory) experiences of that Kingdom can be accessed in this epoch through faith.[72] The question is: To what degree can we expect the Kingdom of God to manifest in this life? To what degree can we expect the *shalom* of heaven to become a reality on this side of the eschaton?

If our answer veers more to the side of "not yet," then we might be rightly challenged about why we require so little of our faith.[73] If instead we veer more towards affirming that the super-abundance of heaven can be accessed now or that heaven's *shalom* should be our model for earthly life and community now, we risk being challenged for having an over-realized eschatology. But while the dangers of an over-realized eschatology are clear in the history of the church's political engagement with the state, when it comes to accessing the super-abundance of heaven as a resource for today,

---

71. See the Jubilee economics of Jesus detailed in Yoder, *The Politics of Jesus*, 60–75.

72. Ladd, *The Gospel of the Kingdom*, 18. Regarding the proleptic experiences of the Kingdom of God, Yong (*IDC*, 310) says, "The result will not be *the* shalom of the coming kingdom, but will be intimations of the peace, justice, and righteousness that will be established on that day of the Lord."

73. Bill Johnson (*God is Good*, 55, 155) says that choosing to err on the side of "not yet" can be a form of settling for a life that requires little faith.

is more faith ever wrong? Is setting a vision of the super-abundance of *shalom* in the eschaton as our model for ideal community life here ever inappropriate? Amos Yong offers a moderated view here saying, "[a] pneumatological theology of shalom neither idealizes poverty nor uncritically embraces a theology of Prosperity. Neither poverty nor riches for their own sake are the will of God, although both poverty and riches are redeemable within the scope of God's redemptive work in the world . . . The Spirit's redemption of poverty is not necessarily the production of wealth, although the healing of the world will involve, finally, the provision of what is more than sufficient for all."[74]

So, while *shalom* can serve as the ultimate standard of the New Testament vision of flourishing life, the dynamics of the "already–not yet" Kingdom of God govern how much of that *shalom* can be experienced in this life. Still, it is helpful to recognize that beyond advocacy regarding the justice issues facing society, the New Testament joins the Old in affirming the comprehensive scope of God's commitment to ordinary human flourishing in its affirmation of *shalom*.[75] Justice-making is best seen in the context of *shalom*.

Some Reflections on the Biblical Resources and Prosperity Theologies

Remembering that *shalom* is the ultimate objective of both the Old and New Testaments puts a lot of things into perspective. If we pair that with the unmatched optimism of Prosperity theologies regarding how much of the Kingdom of God it is possible to access in this life, we begin to appreciate how Prosperity theology's embracing of ordinary human flourishing amounts to a recovery of the centrality of *shalom* in the Christian vision of flourishing life. This is especially true of the moderated version of Prosperity theology that I proposed in the previous chapter.

Still, many nuances of that *shalom* life remain to be explored. For instance, in both the Old and New Testaments, a key dimension of this life of *shalom* is to live in obedience and submission to the lordship of God.

---

74. Yong, *IDC*, 315.

75. This notwithstanding the fact that there is evidence that Greek dualistic thought separating the spiritual and the material marginally influenced some of the writers of the New Testament—though the extent of this influence has been challenged by Joel Green (*Body, Soul, and Human Life*, 51).

An Orientation to the Contemporary Study of Human Flourishing

This is perhaps where there has been the most distortion and confusion regarding the Christian vision of a flourishing life and its perceived incompatibility with ordinary human flourishing, particularly as seen from the perspective of the humanities. How can a life of submission be an expression of a liberated life? And how can that life of submission to God result in the comprehensive *shalom* that we have documented in the Scriptures? Furthermore, what kind of God is this with whom we are called to be in relationship? And what are the dynamics of that relationship? How is this relationship vital to human flourishing? We will explore some responses to these questions in the proposals of contemporary theologians in the next section of this chapter.

THEOLOGICAL PERSPECTIVES ON HUMAN FLOURISHING

Among theologians who have advocated for an optimistic vision of how much of the Kingdom of God we might be able to experience now on earth, Jürgen Moltmann stands as a towering figure for his recognition that eschatology was not meant to be used as a vision for escaping this corrupt world, but rather as a roadmap for the transformation of the present towards that vision of *shalom*. He offers us one of the most comprehensive "affirmations of life" that is available in modern theology, and thus, one of the most sturdy affirmations of ordinary human flourishing. Building on Moltmann's work, Richard Bauckham attempts to provide some biblical correctives to some of Moltmann's proposals to recover a sense of the lordship of God and the relational nature of Christian freedom. His is an important contribution as well. Finally, we will explore the developing work from Miroslav Volf with his affirmation of virtue and the Christian call to work for the common good.

Jürgen Moltmann and the Parameters of the Affirmation of Life

One step removed from Feuerbach's full embrace of the humanistic vision of life might be the musings of Jürgen Moltmann who insists that there must remain some transcendent elements that condition the this-worldly visions for the flourishing life. Moltmann says, "The modern world takes its bearings from humanistic and naturalistic concepts of life, and in so doing, what it experiences is a diminished life. Christian life takes its bearings from 'the living God,' and in doing so, it experiences the fullness of life."[76] This aligns with Moltmann's steady insistence since at least the writing of *The Crucified God* that he is, in fact, doing dialectical theology despite any appearances to the contrary.[77] That is important to remember when faced with the opening paragraphs of Moltmann's *Spirit of Life* where he seems to equate the work of the Spirit with the work of promoting life when he says, "'[s]pirit' is the love of life which delights us, and the energies of the spirit are the living energies which this love of life awakens in us."[78] Indeed, when *Spirit of Life* first came out, many commentators expressed the fear that he had completely conflated the work of the Spirit with the principle of life in creation.[79] Others pointed out that the category of "life" could be subject to any number of interpretive nuances. Moltmann sets out to put some of these concerns to rest in his most recent work, *The Living God and the Fullness of Life*. We will explore his maturing contribution to see if it helps to better define what is meant by the universal affirmation of life he has proposed.

Moltmann begins by discussing the many aspects of our understanding of the nature and character of God that we need to redefine in order to recognize the Living God who affirms life. So, ancient conceptions of the immutable God need to be understood not as statements of a God who cannot change ontologically, but rather as statements of a God whose *character* cannot change in regards to His faithfulness upon which we can rely.[80] Or consider the belief that the Almighty God is the all-determining reality who determines everything that happens in creation. Moltmann suggests that such a view results in the Almighty being effectually powerless and a prisoner of the universe.[81] Regarding ancient views of the impassibility of the divine, Moltmann repeats a key theme of his work in *The Crucified God* in saying that the passion of Christ is at the center of the Christian story and a God who cannot feel is not the God revealed in Christ.[82]

---

76. Moltmann, *LGFL*, 1.

77. Moltmann, *Crucified God*, 25–26.

78. Moltmann, *Spirit of Life*, x.

79. As an example, see Macchia's response ("A North American Response," 25–33), which he later clarified after a reply from Moltmann.

80. Moltmann, *LGFL*, 31.

81. Moltmann, *LGFL*, 44.

82. Moltmann (*Crucified God*, 222) states that "[a] God who cannot suffer is poorer than any man. For a God who is incapable of suffering is a being who cannot be involved."

Moltmann next turns his attention to the notion of God's self-limitation and suggests that "The limitation of God's unending power is an act of God's power over Godself. Only God can limit God."[83] This hearkens back to themes from *God in Creation* where Moltmann appeals to Jewish *zimsum* theology to describe how God makes space within himself for creation to flourish.[84] Next, regarding God's omnipresence, Moltmann suggests that God is not present in everything in the same way—something that hints at his appropriation of the notion of *Shekinah* in *The Coming of God* to describe the presence of God's eschatological Sabbath in moments and places today in anticipation of its full manifestation in the eschaton.[85] But even in godforsaken spaces and situations today and in the face of godless powers, God is present in the crucified Christ.[86]

Finally, Moltmann asks, "Is God omniscient?" Here he appeals to his theology of promise in *Theology of Hope* to say, "God's providence is directed not to future realities, but to future possibilities . . . It is the advance knowledge of the living God intended for a cooperation with those God has created, especially with human beings, God's image, for a shared future."[87] As foreign as this iteration of God's providence might sound to Western audiences, it is more in line with a Jewish perspective of providence, which is certainly not fatalistic, but instead is, as Moltmann says, an invitation to cooperate with God's spirit in bringing about more of the coming Kingdom into our present realities.

Having established the many re-orientations needed to conceive of the God who affirms life, Moltmann then turns his attention to some meditations on what he means by the phrase, "the fullness of life." First of all, Moltmann clarifies that eternal life is meant for life in this world—for the hope of a transformed earth. Any iteration of eternal life that expects the annihilation of the earthly world is, according to Moltmann, "a vision hostile to life and a destructive spirituality."[88] Instead, Christianity is called

---

83. Moltmann, *LGFL*, 45.

84. Moltmann, *God in Creation*, 86.

85. Moltmann (*God in Creation*, 333) states that "The Shekinah, the descent and dwelling of God among human beings, originally in the Ark of the Covenant and in the temple on Zion, can be imagined as a self-differentiation in God. God does not just restrict himself in order to concede human beings freedom; he differentiates himself from himself in order to be beside them in their wanderings."

86. Moltmann, *LGFL*, 49.

87. Moltmann, *LGFL*, 51. Cf. Moltmann, *Theology of Hope*, 42.

88. Moltmann, *LGFL*, 84

to transform pain into joy in *this* life in solidarity with the eschatological purposes of the Spirit.

In the context of these eschatological purposes, if we were to condense into one word the heart of Moltmann's understanding of the fullness of life, that word would likely be "liberation." Moltmann says, "God is 'the Lord' because God is the liberator. Israel's fundamental experience of God is this *experience of freedom*. To believe in God means nothing other than to trust in God's liberating power."[89] But it wouldn't be Moltmannian theology without some nuanced reframing of what these terms ought to mean. And so we must ask, if flourishing life is the liberated free life, then what does it mean to be free?

Modern conceptions of freedom tend to move towards ideas of self-determination among an infinitude of options available to us. We suppose that our dream is that we could do whatever we like whenever we wanted. But Moltmann points out that if this is the definition of freedom, then God himself is not free because God always acts for the right and the good. Instead, Moltmann leans on Hannah Arendt's definition of freedom to say that the real human freedom is the ability to begin something new. "Freedom means that we ourselves take the initiative and begin something new with our abilities and the potentialities we see before us."[90] I want to pause here to reflect a bit on this idea. Freedom for the addict would mean the ability to do something other than what one had felt compelled to do before. Freedom for the traumatized would mean the power to escape one's self-repeating internal narratives of victimization and begin a new chapter of one's life afresh. These themes will be important in our discussion of the potential of Prosperity theologies to contribute to a contemporary Christian view of human flourishing rooted in the immanent frame. But for now, let us continue exploring the shape of Moltmann's affirmation of life in more detail.

Moltmann continues his meditation on the shape of what it means to be free by turning to a sustained reflection on relationships and communal living. He bemoans the tendency of people to become more and more closed to others as mistrust, competition, and the disappointments of life take root. Rather, the free life is enriched by social interaction and demonstrates a willingness to be open to friendship again. If indifference to

---

89. Moltmann, *LGFL*, 106.

90. Moltmann, *LGFL*, 110. Moltmann is referencing Hannah Arendt's work in: Arendt, *Vita Activa*, 168.

An Orientation to the Contemporary Study of Human Flourishing

relationships is a sign that one is no longer alive, then interest in forming new connections with others and creating healthy communities with others are expressions of the life that is free.[91] It should come as no surprise to anyone that healthy relationships and the ability to embrace new relationships is a vital part of any vision of human flourishing given the fundamentally social nature of human life.

Finally, in contrast to the traditions that encourage the mortifying of the senses in order to progress in spirituality, Moltmann believes that the liberative work of the Spirit should cause the senses to come back to life. He says "Human beings are in harmony with God's love for those God has created when they love life, the life of their neighbor, the life they share, and the life of the earth."[92] Just as grief, apathy, and the routinization of life can dull the senses, love, hope, rest, mystery and attentiveness can bring the senses back to life.[93] A human life fully alive is marked by joyfulness and feasting where "a radiance of the divine life can emanate from the feast of the resurrection and fall on the human life . . . in the everyday world."[94] All of this, Moltmann suggests, flows from being in a relationship of mutual friendship with God which is modeled from the mutual relationships of the Trinity.[95]

Moltmann's contributions effectively work to bridge the divide between traditional theistic approaches to flourishing and the modern worldview's ordinary understanding of flourishing from both sides. His many theological re-framings regarding the character of God allow for a theological affirmation of ordinary flourishing while his qualifications of the modern concept of freedom redefine the parameters of what healthy freedom might entail. But while Moltmann's dialogical model provides a substantive contribution to these efforts, the common objections to Moltmann's main theological writings will likely apply to his vision for the flourishing human life as well—particularly critiques of his continued allergy to all things hierarchical and aversion to any dynamics of power, even if they might be used benevolently or as moments for human self-actualization.

---

91. Moltmann, *LGFL*, 150.
92. Moltmann, *LGFL*, 149.
93. Moltmann, *LGFL*, 165.
94. Moltmann, *LGFL*, 196.
95. Moltmann (*Trinity and the Kingdom*, 157) states that "The history of God's trinitarian relationships of fellowship corresponds to the eternal perichoresis of the Trinity . . . The history of salvation is the history of the eternally living, triune God who draws us into and includes us in his eternal triune life with all the fullness of its relationships."

Many question how such a radical commitment to mutuality can be reconciled with the lordship language used in Scripture to characterize the relationship between God and humanity. Furthermore, for some, Moltmann's view of freedom as self-determination and, more recently, as the ability to begin something new, seems to largely embrace the modern view of the autonomous self. Ellen Charry suggests that this freedom needs to be better framed in the context of the believer's dependence upon being in relationship with God.[96] We will explore some of these points and alternatives in the work by Richard Bauckham in *God and the Crisis of Freedom*.

Richard Bauckham on Christian Freedom and Divine Authority

For Richard Bauckham, modern understandings of freedom tend to revolve around a more basic value for the autonomous self. He feels that despite Moltmann's calls to mutuality in human relationships and responsible stewardship of the environment, Moltmann does not do enough to bring this modernistic value for autonomy under biblical critique. Likely, this is somewhat attributable to Moltmann's aversion to authority and the abuses of power that any form of authoritarianism could allow.[97] Moltmann, in his implicit commitment to liberation, is compelled to re-frame every traditional power-dynamic in the language of "friendship" and "mutuality." As a result, Bauckham believes it is difficult to avoid a built-in autonomous vision of the self within Moltmann's commitment to mutuality.

One of the issues that Bauckham finds with having an autonomous view of freedom is that he believes it results in seeing other people as a limitation on that freedom.[98] After all, the autonomous freedom of others can result in constrained options available to us. When this autonomy is expressed as an insistence on having unrestricted choice, other people might be seen as obstacles to the achievement or maintenance of that autonomy.

---

96. Charry ("The Crisis of Modernity," 88–112) suggests that Moltmann is affirming a modern view of the self with its value for individual autonomy.

97. Of Moltmann, Bauckham (*Crisis of Freedom*, 193) says, "He evidently treats individual self-determination as an absolute not to be compromised by any concession to a notion of community that might qualify it. In this sense Moltmann remains profoundly modern in his thinking about the self and community."

98. Bauckham (*Crisis of Freedom*, 45) states that "If my freedom consists in abolishing all limits to what I may do and have, then other people are bound to appear as limits to my freedom."

The reason this is problematic for Bauckham is that it conceives of freedom in the context of domination, which he defines as "a means of securing the freedom of some at the expense of the freedom of others."[99] Using the example of the global free market, Bauckham argues that the proliferation of free choices available to the wealthy often comes at the expense of the growing oppression of the poor.[100] Thus, the privileging of infinite choice results in an unhealthy "consumerism" that oppresses the freedoms of the many for the whims of the few.[101]

Perhaps partially in response to Bauckham's critiques of his view of freedom as self-determination, Moltmann shifts his view of freedom in later writings to Arendt's view of freedom as the ability to begin something new or to act unexpectedly. That would constitute a view of freedom that everyone has by virtue of being born and that no other person could ever fundamentally take away from someone else. The benefit of this approach is that it enables people, no matter their circumstances, to always find a source of freedom (and thus a source of power) within themselves. In both of these formulations, freedom is power. And the degree to which one has freedom is the degree to which one has power. In a consumerist society, the one with the most choice has the most power. And, by extension, the one with the least choice has the least power, or even no power at all. The beauty of Arendt's view is that everyone has equal access to the same freedom, and thus to the same power. No matter the oppression that someone might be experiencing, they always retain the ability to act in a new or unexpected way—for instance, by forgiving their oppressors. The power to grant or withhold forgiveness is a real power that every person has that can never be fully extinguished by another without one's consent. Building on

---

99. Bauckham, *Crisis of Freedom*, 190.

100. Bauckham (*Crisis of Freedom*, 189) states that "consumerism constitutes a deeply interconnected relationship between increasing individualism and the global free market and, highly significant for our subject, enables the oppression of the latter to be perceived as liberating."

101. Both Bauckham and Volf believe that modern society is characterized by this "consumerism" that values the multiplicity of choices as a reflection of postmodernism. Bauckham (*Crisis of Freedom*, 68) says, "The postmodern critique at this point consists in the appeal to diversity: there is an indefinite variety of life-goals one may choose, and to pronounce one better than others is to impose one's own choice on others. But this is, as so often turns out to be the case with postmodernism, the philosophy of consumerism, which exalts choice as the supreme value in itself, irrespective of the content of choice." Bauckham is drawing from the work of Storkey ("Post-Modernism Is Consumption," 100–17).

this inalienable source of freedom within oneself, Moltmann envisions that vibrant autonomous selves capable of mutually respecting relationships can arise.

However, Bauckham would still be critical of even Arendt's view of freedom because it continues to hold to a distinctly autonomous view of the self. Whether freedom is conceived of as the multiplicity of choices or as the ability to begin something new, the self at the center of that freedom is the autonomous individual self. Bauckham takes issue with these views because they fail to account for the fact that the Christian idea of freedom is framed in terms of a relationship of dependence upon God and not in autonomous mutuality. Likewise, the Lordship language used in Scripture calls believers to a life of obedience where some freedoms might be restricted. So how do we reconcile these dynamics with Bauckham's otherwise enthusiastic embrace of Moltmann's vision for a theology that in many ways affirms ordinary human flourishing?

There are three main trajectories that Bauckham follows to make his point. First, he says that while obedience is at the center of the believer's relationship with God, that obedience is not heavy-handed, but is rather a responsive obedience to the generosity and love of God towards us. Or better yet, that obedience is nothing more than the expression of love and gratitude of someone who values being in close relationship with the God who has poured out grace upon them. Thus, Bauckham is able to say, "Freedom is here not the rejection of all limits, but the free acceptance of those limits that enable loving relationships."[102] Here Bauckham is making the simple point that to be in a genuine relationship with anyone requires a limitation on one's choices to those that honor and respect that relationship. So, while that might appear as a limitation to freedom, it is a willing embrace of that limitation in order to make room for love. Put another way, if the greatest human happiness comes from deep relationships of love, then the pursuit of happiness ultimately longs for the restriction of freedoms to allow love and respect to arise. Far from undermining human flourishing by restricting choices, the life of obedience is a life of love and respect towards the God who desires for all His creation to experience *shalom*.

The second thing that Bauckham notes is that this life of obedience to God is meant to allow God to set us free from the things that already limit our ability to flourish whether we know it or not. He calls these things "compulsions to sin" and they can be both the inner compulsions of sin in

---

102. Bauckham, *Crisis of Freedom*, 68.

An Orientation to the Contemporary Study of Human Flourishing

human nature or the outward compulsions of sin that influence us through distorted cultural values such as consumerism.[103] He says, "Loving obedience to God is not, as so many see it today, an alienating loss of personal freedom but liberation from all the compulsions to which would-be independent selves so often find themselves subject."[104] So, people who imagine that they have a multitude of choices open to them don't often realize that those choices are already constrained by cultural norms and values. This gives the lie to the myth of free choices. Allowing God to re-shape our values through obedience to Him is how we are set free from any cultural values that might predispose us to act in ways inconsistent with our own flourishing.

Finally, Bauckham argues that a biblical understanding of freedom recognizes that it is not so much freedom *from* others as it is freedom *for* others and for their liberation.[105] Bauckham agrees with Moltmann that the basic message of the Old Testament and of the ministry of Jesus is that of liberation. He reads the Old Testament as a rejection of all forms of exploitative relationships and finds in Jesus someone who worked to liberate people from sin, guilt, sickness and even death itself.[106] But Bauckham again rejects a reading of biblical freedom that focuses on the development of an autonomous self, even if it is for a liberated self. For him, the freedom spoken of in Scripture is the freedom to live a life in service to others. Thus, the mark of a liberated life would not be in their liberty, but rather in their orientation to serve others. Indeed, he even says, "Outward liberation

---

103. Bauckham (*Crisis of Freedom*, 17) says, "If we wish to put it concretely in terms of some of the prime realities of our culture, we should think of the compulsions of sin, from whose grip we cannot get free by ourselves, as not just the inner compulsion to sin in fallen human nature, but also the forces outside individual persons, such as consumerism, which appeal to the base desires of human nature and exploit people by latching onto the human tendencies to greed, lust, envy and excess."

104. Bauckham (*Crisis of Freedom*, 17) states that "It becomes possible to resist the otherwise irresistible pressures because we have something above and beyond them that enables us to see through and to resist them."

105. Bauckham (*Crisis of Freedom*, 11) says, "The New Testament's understanding of freedom, as not so much *from* others as *for* others, is already implicit in the Old Testament sense of social responsibility."

106. Bauckham (*Crisis of Freedom*, 13) notes that "All relationships of subjection that permit the exploitation of one human being by another are contrary to the fundamental will of God as the Old Testament reveals it."

worthy of the name requires people who have been freed to live for others, and for all others, even for their oppressors."[107]

At the heart of Bauckham's proposal for the liberated life are the three dimensions of loving God, self, and others properly. The life of obedience to God is the expression of a life of loving relationship that results in liberation from the compulsions to sin in oneself and an orientation to serving the needs of others. Moltmann says that we are called to mutual relationships of friendship based on the model of Trinitarian mutuality. Bauckham says that we are in a Creater/created relationship with God which does call for obedience, but it is an obedience that leads to our flourishing. The benefit of Bauckham's contribution is that it more closely ties ideas about flourishing to traditional biblical categories while still re-framing them enough to affirm the liberative goals of a modern view of ordinary human flourishing.

While I appreciate Bauckham's recovery of the lordship dynamics in the believer's relationship with God, it does leave open the question of whether that lordship dynamic might ever become an unhealthy one. Particularly for people who have experienced horrific trauma, such as the holocaust, such language and imagery could trigger post-traumatic stress reactions that ultimately prevent healthy encounters with God. A more nuanced exploration of this lordship dynamic from the perspective of a liberation theology for the victims of sin might be helpful. Additionally, Bauckham's emphatic efforts to move away from an autonomous view of the self towards a relational view make me wonder if perhaps he overstates the case a bit. On the one hand, I think of Charles Taylor's arguments about the immanent frame and the unlikeliness that society could ever return to an enchanted view of the world and an unbuffered view of the self. On the other, I suspect that both an autonomous and a relational view of the self are parts of a healthy integrated view of a flourishing human life. I think, for example, of sociological studies that find that people who are able to be gracious and generous towards themselves tend to be more gracious and generous towards others as well.[108] But despite these qualifications, I think Bauckham makes an important contribution towards refining Moltmann's original project of liberation and moving us closer to a Christian view of flourishing that engages the modern worldview.

---

107. Bauckham (*Crisis of Freedom*, 25) states that "[f]reedom in this form, as the spirit of glad and loving service, creates not a collection of independent and competitive individuals, but a *real* community of mutual dependence."

108. Neff, "Self-compassion," 85–101.

An Orientation to the Contemporary Study of Human Flourishing

Miroslav Volf on the Life of Mindfulness

One of the broadest contemporary meditations on the Christian vision of human flourishing in the immanent frame comes from Miroslav Volf and the Yale Center for Faith and Culture that he directs in New Haven. Volf has turned his whole attention to exploring the many dimensions of what a Christian vision of human flourishing might entail using resources from philosophy, theology, and the world's religions. His own definitive statement about human flourishing has yet to be written, but the many dialogues that have been started through this center have brought a rich diversity of perspectives to this topic. An exploration of some of the key insights from his works and these discussions helps to enrich our discussion of what constitutes flourishing life.

For Volf, the question of how a Christian vision of flourishing engages the modern world is at the heart of the Christian life.[109] In Volf's estimation, contemporary society is characterized by an exclusive humanist view of the good life which holds that a flourishing life is an experientially satisfying one. In this view, "[w]hat justifies a given lifestyle or activity is the satisfaction it generates—the pleasure. And when [people] experience satisfaction, people feel that they flourish."[110] When this perspective infiltrates the Christian faith, it results in a malfunction of faith where "[f]aith will shed its power to orient people and will be reduced to a servant of experiential satisfaction."[111] People come to God solely to get their needs met or to have their wounds soothed. And while the soothing of wounds is certainly a part of the ministry of the Spirit, when that is all that faith provides it ceases to truly orient a life to the vision of the hopeful future that God intends.[112]

The vision of God in such an orientation is difficult to reconcile with the lordship language used in Scripture and forgets that God, as the Creator and Master of the universe, determines precisely who we are and how we should live. When discipleship ceases to be a core element of the Christian life Volf laments that "Take up your cross and follow me" morphs into "I'll

---

109. Volf (*A Public Faith*, 5) states that "[i]t is important for Christians to keep focused on God and on the proper understanding of human flourishing. For this, in the end, is what the Christian faith as a prophetic religion is all about—being an instrument of God for the sake of human flourishing, in this life and the next."

110. Volf, *A Public Faith*, 57.

111. Volf, *A Public Faith*, 68.

112. Volf (*A Public Faith*, 16) says, "[i]f faith *only* heals and energizes, then it is merely a crutch to use at will, not a way of life."

bring out the champion in you."¹¹³ Instead, Volf embraces a tri-partite vision of flourishing life that (1) goes well (circumstantial), (2) is lived well (agential), and (3) is pleasurable (affective).¹¹⁴ These three dimensions he defines as a life of joy because "[j]oy is the emotional dimension of life that goes well and that is led well."¹¹⁵

For life to go well is what Nicholas Wolterstorff believes is at the heart of the biblical notion of *shalom* and is marked either by some objective indicators of well-being or a subjective one where life is satisfying.[116] A simple example of this would be to measure whether or not one's basic needs for food, shelter, and community are being met. The life that is lived well is one which is lived according to our highest good—in the case of the Christian, that is in accordance with our true nature in Christ and in obedience to divine commands. And the life that is pleasurable is better defined as the life of joy, where joy itself is the feeling one has when life is going well and being lived well.

Of the three categories of flourishing life identified by Volf, perhaps the one that is most subject to diverging opinion is the question of what constitutes a life that is well-lived? Is it one spent in noble public service? Is it one of great personal achievement? While these dimensions can certainly be included in a well-lived life, Volf believes that the indispensable aspect of such a life is that it centers around loving God and our neighbor according to God's greatest commands. He says, "[i]f we believe that God is love and that we are created for love, we will reject the notion that flourishing consists in being experientially satisfied. Instead, we will believe that we will be experientially satisfied when we truly flourish. When is it that we truly flourish? When is it that we lead our lives well, and our lives are going well? We lead our lives well when we love God with our whole being and when we love our neighbors as we (properly) love ourselves."[117]

---

113. See Volf (*A Public Faith*, 12). I will note that these two ideas are not necessarily in conflict with one another, but the larger point Volf is making is still valid.

114. Volf ("Crown of the Good Life," 133) states that "[I]n my judgment, any plausible candidate for the good life has to incorporate all three: life is truly and fully good when (1) it goes well, (2) we lead it well, and (3) when it is pleasurable."

115. Volf, "Crown of the Good Life," 134.

116. Wolterstorff ("God's Power and Human Flourishing") notes that "Let me tip my hand. Shalom is flourishing. That is to say, shalom, as understood by the writers of the Old Testament, is not the life that is lived well, and is certainly not the life that is experientially satisfying; it is the life that goes well."

117. Volf, *A Public Faith*, 72.

An Orientation to the Contemporary Study of Human Flourishing

Accordingly, Volf believes that "malfunctions" of faith happen when people fail to love God or their neighbor as they should.[118] Ascent malfunctions happen when we fail to love God wholeheartedly or have a faulty vision of the character of God. Return malfunctions happen when we fail to love our neighbor or ourselves properly.[119] But if one is able to love God, others, and self rightly, then Volf believes that Christians can show the world how the life of faith can lead to a flourishing life in every sphere of society.[120]

So, what would Volf consider to be a proper vision of God given his concerns? Admittedly his thoughts at this point in his work are little more than a sketch, but they still provide provocative themes that enrich our discussion here. First, he speaks of the God of love and of how this God orients us to love others and ourselves rightly. But to give this more dimension, he then paints a picture of a loving Creator who intends for His creatures to genuinely enjoy His creation. He says,

> [i]f God created the material world inhabited by sentient beings (Gen. 1:1), if God became flesh in the person of Jesus of Nazareth (Jn. 1:14), if the bodies of those bound to God in faith and love are the temples of the Spirit (1 Cor. 6:19), all central claims Christians make, the opposition between attachment to God and the enjoyment of the ordinary things of life must be false. More: not only is there no necessary opposition between them, but the two can be aligned: *attachment to God amplifies and deepens enjoyment of the world.*[121]

How does attachment to God amplify and deepen our enjoyment of the world? Volf believes this derives from the fact that attachment to God infuses the world and the things in the world with meaning. He argues that the objects that we find in the world are more than simply 'things.' Rather, they are social relations in a sacramental way in that they are "[c]arriers of the presence of another."[122] Drawing on the work of Paul Bloom, he says,

---

118. Volf (*A Public Faith*, 73) "Most malfunctions of faith are rooted in a failure to love the God of love or a failure to love the neighbor."

119. Volf, *A Public Faith*, 73.

120. Volf (*A Public Faith*, 19) "Christians should show how faith, though prone to misuse, is a salutary way of life and inculcate its vision of lives well lived in all spheres."

121. Volf, *Flourishing*, 203.

122. Volf (*Flourishing*, 204) states that "To put it in theological language, we enjoy things the most when we experience them as sacraments—as carriers of the presence of another."

The Empowering God

"What matters most for pleasure isn't the object 'as it appears to our senses' but an experience of the object as a thing that is also a particular relationship to other persons."[123] A pen handed down from one's grandfather; a letter sent by a loved one—these objects are imbued with deeper meaning, significance, and perhaps pleasure because they are social relations with people we cherish. In similar fashion, the world is a gift given to us by the God of love. When we learn to see it in this way, then the ordinary things in the world become extraordinary. Volf concludes, "[t]he right kind of love for the right kind of God bathes our world in the light of transcendent glory and turns it into a theater of joy."[124]

Embedded in Volf's view of the good life is an affirmation of a classical view of freedom where one restricts one's freedom in some dimensions in order to achieve the freedom of excellence in another. Anyone who has learned to play a musical instrument understands the discipline (restriction of freedom) required to master the instrument well enough to attain a freedom of excellence that allows free expression through that instrument. Volf's vision for the good life echoes this process—it is the cultivation of mindfulness towards God in every dimension of life that ultimately allows us to truly enjoy all of the things we have been gifted with in life.

The tri-partite vision of flourishing that Volf articulates demonstrates how putting a priority on living a life mindful of God can result in a life that goes well and is pleasurable within that context. The important aspects for this study are in how it connects a life of meaning with a life that is pleasurable (two things that have historically been put in opposition to one another), and in how it shows that attachment to God can deepen our enjoyment of the world.[125] These recoveries are valuable in their own right, but taken at face value, they can appear to support an exhortation to finding contentment in the limited circumstances of our lives. And as we will see when we explore liberation theologies in the next chapter, sometimes the call to contentment results in an acceptance of the status quo—which can have the effect of entrapping the poor in their cycles of poverty. Volf's calls to public theology for the common good would seem to suggest that

---

123. Volf (*Flourishing*, 204) is drawing from Bloom (*How Pleasure Works*, 24).

124. Volf, *Flourishing*, 206.

125. Volf (*Flourishing*, 201) says, "In choosing between meaning and pleasure we *always* make the wrong choice. Pleasure without meaning is vapid; meaning without pleasure is crushing. In its own way, each is nihilistic without the other. But we don't need to choose between the two. The unity of meaning and pleasure, which we experience as joy, is given with the God who is Love."

his understanding of mindfulness of God includes an activist component, but even there, I would suspect that the focus on the common good would miss many of the daily victimizations that people experience in their personal lives. These and other questions raised by liberation theology deserve a careful reading.

Some Reflections on the Theologians and Prosperity Theologies

I find the contributions of each of these theologians to be wonderfully illuminating to our discussion in myriad ways. That said, I do believe that Prosperity theologies offer a way to critique and extend each of these viewpoints in important ways as well. For instance, Moltmann's turn to activist eschatology and his influence in originating liberation theologies has given us a deeper ability to recognize the systemic effects of sin and an appreciation for the materiality of salvation. But his rejection of every form of hierarchy, especially of the lordship dynamics between the believer and God, leave his proposal lacking in critical dimensions. I will propose a model of God that derives from Prosperity theologies that affirms the lordship of God while seeking to retain the liberative strengths of Moltmann's work. Furthermore, Richard Bauckham's retrieval of the lordship of God and his framing of the life of obedience as a derivation of the life of responsive love is very close to the view that I propose. However, his focus on obedience leading to a deliverance from the compulsions to sin, while important, is only half of the picture. I will demonstrate that Prosperity theologies add to this a sensitivity to the victimizations that result from sin and a prescription for how these victimizations can be overcome. Finally, Miroslav Volf's depiction of the life mindful of God is a wonderful way to frame the fulfilled Christian life. However, calls to mindfulness in present circumstances can often settle into calls to learning contentment in the midst of our limitations. That can have the unintended effect of disempowering people from seeking change. This is where Prosperity theologies offer the clearest counterpoint in their constant calls for people to hunger for breakthroughs in their lives. And rather than say one of these routes is better than the other, I propose that some combination of these values is important for a healthy stance toward life that celebrates God's current work while pressing in faith for more of the Kingdom of God to be manifest in our lives and communities. Each of these arguments will be presented in the chapters to follow.

Human Flourishing in the Behavioral Sciences

Before turning to develop these constructive dimensions of Prosperity theology, I want to offer a brief orientation to some recent research from the behavioral sciences regarding human flourishing. The reason for this is to be able to connect my future proposals about the liberative elements of Prosperity theologies with corroborating research from the behavioral sciences to further make the concrete connection between Prosperity theologies and the affirmation of ordinary human flourishing. As such, this section will explore relevant contributions from the behavioral sciences in the fields of Psychology, Sociology, Economics, Political science, and Anthropology.

Psychological Perspectives on Human Flourishing

The contemporary preoccupation with the topic of human flourishing extends beyond the theological discussion and can be found in many of the modern sciences as well. In the field of psychology, Martin Seligman is often recognized as one of the founding fathers of the positive psychology movement who recognized that while psychology had a wealth of detailed knowledge about abnormal behavior traits, it lacked a clear articulation of what a healthy psychology might entail.

> For the last half century psychology has been consumed with a single topic only—mental illness—and has done fairly well with it . . . But people want more than just to correct their weaknesses. They want lives imbued with meaning . . . The time has finally arrived for a science that seeks to understand positive emotion, build strength and virtue, and provide guideposts for finding what Aristotle called the "good life."[126]

To address this lacuna, Seligman and others began to formulate a vision for achieving "authentic happiness" in life through the cultivation of good habits, values, and character. The goal of such a program was to help guide people to experience positive emotions about their past, present and futures while using their strengths to do things that filled their lives with meaning and a sense of significance.[127] As such, he characterized the happy

---

126. Seligman, *Authentic Happiness*, ix.

127. See Seligman (*Authentic Happiness*, 261–63). Pope ("Christ and Human Flourishing," 10–11) says, "Martin Seligman and his collaborators maintain that people

life as one which sought positive emotion, engagement of one's signature strengths, and meaningfulness through serving a cause or community greater than oneself. It was a simple message and it was spectacularly well received by the public and the media spawning a number of best-selling books and personalities in the process.[128]

Years later, Seligman would revisit his theories to move away from the simple idea of "happiness" and towards a broader sense of "well-being" because: (1) the notion of "happiness" was too culturally saddled with ideas of cheerfulness; (2) how much life satisfaction people reported was highly correlated with how good their mood was at the moment they were asked the question; and (3) positive emotion, engagement and meaning did not exhaust the things that people chose for their own sake.[129] His new theory was meant to highlight the fact that positive emotion was simply one aspect of what made up well-being and that a broader understanding of well-being would include things such as positive relationships and a sense of accomplishment in addition to meaningfulness and a sense of deep engagement in life.[130] This is a helpful formulation in that it gives some measurable categories by which one might assess an individual's relative psychological well-being.

Robert Cloninger, a leading research psychiatrist, has similarly attempted to distill the hallmarks of a flourishing state of life using data collected from his Temperament and Character Index. Of the four temperament traits and three character traits measured by this index, Cloninger found that high marks in the three character traits correlated to states of biopsychosocial well-being in people.[131] Conversely, low marks in the three character traits correlated to instances of psychosis or other dysfunctions. The three character traits were self-directedness, cooperativeness, and

generally pursue happiness in one of three ways: they seek the 'pleasant life' (hedonic values like pleasure, enjoyment, and comfort), the 'good life' (which he defines in terms of living in ways that allow one to exercise one's 'signature strengths' to achieve one's goals), or the 'meaningful life' (found in serving a cause or community greater than oneself)."

128. The best-selling book *The Secret* came out of this movement. Alternatively, some such as Barbara Ehrenreich (*Bright-sided*, 177–206) did provide the important caution that positive psychology could be misused to perpetuate self-delusion or to prevent people from feeling a motivational level of anxiety about the future.

129. Seligman, *Flourish*, 13.

130. Seligman, *Flourish*, 24.

131. Cloninger was one of the early advocates for an integrated biopsychosocial view of people. His TPI incorporates elements of the biological (temperaments), psychological (character), and sociological (cooperativeness, self-transcendence).

self-transcendence.¹³² It is worthwhile to reprint his descriptions of these traits here:

> *Self-Directedness:*
>
> Highly self-directed persons are described as mature, strong, self-sufficient, responsible, reliable, goal-oriented, constructive, and well-integrated individuals when they have the opportunity for personal leadership. They have good self-esteem and self-reliance. The most distinctive characteristics of self-directed individuals is that they are effective, able to adapt their behavior in accord with individually chosen, voluntary goals. When a self-directed individual is required to follow the orders of others in authority, they may be viewed as a rebellious trouble maker because they challenge the goals and values of those in authority.
>
> In contrast, individuals who are low in Self-Directedness are described as immature, weak, fragile, blaming, destructive, ineffective, irresponsible, unreliable, and poorly integrated when they are not conforming to the direction of a mature leader. They are frequently described by clinicians as immature or having a personality disorder. They seem to be lacking an internal organizational principle, which renders them unable to define, set, and pursue meaningful goals. Instead, they experience numerous minor, short-term, frequently mutually exclusive motives, none of which can develop to the point of long lasting personal significance and realization.¹³³
>
> *Cooperativeness:*
>
> Highly cooperative people are described as empathetic, tolerant, compassionate, supportive, fair, and principled individuals who enjoy being of service to others and try to cooperate with others as much as possible. They understand and respect the preferences and needs of others as well as their own. This capacity is important

---

132. Cloninger et al., "Psychobiological Model," 975–90.

133. Cloninger et al. ("Psychobiological Model," 979) say that self-directedness is measured by evaluating (1) responsibility vs. blaming, (2) purposefulness vs. lack of goal direction, (3) resourcefulness vs. inertia, (4) self-acceptance vs. self-striving, and (5) congruent second nature vs. incongruent habits. Measuring responsibility and blaming tendencies has to do with whether one feels that the locus of control is within oneself or if it is outside. Lacking goal direction manifests as a simple life of satisfying immediate desires rather than focusing on long-term goals. Resourcefulness is really about whether one believes they are capable of attaining their goals. Self-acceptance is the mark of a person who recognizes their own strengths and limitations and accepts them. And having a congruent second nature means that one is acting in ways that demonstrate integrity with one's goals.

in teamwork and social groups for harmonious and balanced relationships to flourish, but is not needed by solitary individuals.

In contrast, low scorers on the Cooperativeness dimension are described as self absorbed, intolerant, critical, unhelpful, revengeful, and opportunistic. These individuals primarily look out for themselves. They tend to be inconsiderate of other's rights or feelings.[134]

Self-Transcendence

Self-transcendent individuals are described as unpretentious, satisfied, patient, creative, selfless, and spiritual . . . These individuals seem to tolerate ambiguity and uncertainty. They can fully enjoy most of their activities without having to know the outcome and without feeling the urge to control it. Self-transcendent individuals impress others as humble and modest persons who are content to accept the failure even of their best efforts and who are thankful for both their failures and their successes. High Self-Transcendence has adaptive advantages when a person is confronted with suffering and death, which is inevitable with advancing age.

In contrast, low scorers in Self-Transcendence tend to be proud, impatient, and unimaginative, unappreciative of art, self-aware, materialistic, and unfulfilled. They cannot tolerate ambiguity, uncertainty, and surprises. Instead, they strive for more control over almost everything. Low scorers on this dimension may impress others as pretentious persons who seem to be unable to be satisfied with what they have. Individuals low in Self-Transcendence are often admired in Western societies for their rational, scientific, and materialistic success. But, they may have difficulty accepting suffering and death, which leads to difficulties in adjustment with advancing age.[135]

Cloninger's index is useful because it points out character traits that are important for biopsychosocial well-being.[136] Elsewhere, Cloninger goes

---

134. Cloninger et al. ("Psychobiological Model," 980–81) suggest that cooperativeness is measured by evaluating (1) social acceptance vs. intolerance, (2) empathy vs. social disinterest, (3) helpfulness vs. unhelpfulness, (4) compassion vs. revengefulness, and (5) principles vs. self-advantage.

135. Cloninger et al. ("Psychobiological Model," 981–82) say self-transcendence is measured by evaluating (1) self-forgetful vs. self-conscious experience, (2) transpersonal identification vs. self-isolation, (3) spiritual acceptance vs. rational materialism, (4) enlightened vs. objective, and (5) idealistic vs. practical.

136. Cloninger et al. ("Psychobiological Model," 982) find that self-directedness and cooperativeness are the traits most correlated with well-being while self-transcendence can be thought of as a measure of relative well-being among those who are well.

on to connect these character traits with the biblical categories of faith (self-transcendence), hope (self-directedness), and love (cooperativeness).[137] He says that they demonstrate three different levels of advancing self-awareness that culminate in an understanding of biopsychosocial well-being that avoids common psychoses and indicate a "healthy" biopsychosocial specimen. The first level of self-awareness (average adult cognition) demonstrates good self-directedness, but low cooperativeness and low self-transcendence. Such individuals might be seen as purposeful and able to delay gratification, but also egocentric and unable to consider others or to cooperate effectively with them. The second level of self-awareness (metacognition) demonstrates good self-directedness and cooperativeness, but low self-transcendence. Such individuals are able to set and achieve goals while also being considerate of the needs of others around them. At this stage, Cloninger says, a person is able to "[o]bserve herself and others for understanding without judging or blaming."[138] At the third stage of self-awareness (contemplation), an individual demonstrates high self-directedness, cooperativeness, and self-transcendence. Such an individual becomes aware of the factors influencing their behaviors which allows "[t]he enlarging of consciousness by accessing previously unconscious material, thereby letting go of wishful thinking and allowing the impartial questioning of basic assumptions and core beliefs about life."[139] For Cloninger, the journey towards well-being is thus a journey towards growing self-awareness. His claim that the highest stage of self-awareness correlates with the highest degree of well-being is supported by research that shows that individuals who are above average in these three character traits "[h]ave the highest levels of positive emotions and the lowest levels of negative emotions of all possible character configurations."[140]

Cloninger's attempts to identify factors that correspond with biopsychosocial well-being provide an interesting new tool for theologians to use to consider different theistic visions of human flourishing. Would there be a correlation between these biopsychosocial portraits of well-being and common theistic portrayals of such? Might some theistic visions of human flourishing actually correspond with low levels of self-awareness—in particular low levels of self-directedness? If self-directedness can indeed be

---

137. Cloninger, "Science of Feeling Good," 740–43.
138. Cloninger, "Science of Feeling Good," 741–42.
139. Cloninger, "Science of Feeling Good," 742.
140. Cloninger, "Science of Feeling Good," 742.

An Orientation to the Contemporary Study of Human Flourishing

affirmed as an integral part of biopsychosocial well-being, what sorts of theological considerations might promote the growth of self-directedness in healthy ways? A key question for this study might be whether growing self-awareness is an important factor in growing other-regard. If so, that would seem to support other sociological research that found that people who love themselves in a healthy way tend to be the most generous towards the needs of others.

If we accept Cloninger's proposal that the three key character traits for self-awareness correspond to the biblical values of Faith, Hope, and Love, then perhaps we have the beginnings of a bridge here between a theistic vision of human flourishing and the immanent frame of modern scientific society. To further explore these convergences, I will next consider the contributions of sociological studies on human flourishing and wellness.

Sociological Perspectives on Human Flourishing

Between 1939 and 1944, researchers at Harvard University recruited 268 of the school's students for the longest longitudinal study of adult development of its kind.[141] A similar study was launched from 1940–1945 to study the development of 456 inner-city youths in the area. Every one or two years, researchers would send participants an extensive questionnaire about their mental and physical health, careers, and familial life dynamics with the purpose of identifying correlations with healthy aging. Over 75 years later, researchers published their findings with the somewhat surprising conclusion that the greatest predictor of flourishing life at the age of 80 was not cholesterol levels at 50 years of age, but rather the quality of people's relationships at that half-century mark. People with strong social connections were physically healthier and had less instances of dementia than people who did not. This was true even across both longitudinal studies of the Harvard-educated students and the inner-city youth. The conclusion? Healthy social connections lead to more happiness, healthiness, and longer life.

Brené Brown has been studying the factors that promote healthy social connections and defines connection as "[t]he energy that exists between people when they feel seen, heard, and valued; when they can give and

---

141. The original study findings were reported in Vaillant's *Adaptation to Life*. A follow-up was published in 2002 titled *Aging Well*. His further reflections were recorded in 2012 in *Triumphs of Experience*.

receive without judgment; and when they derive sustenance and strength from the relationship."[142] In her research, she has found that the major obstacle to healthy connection in relationships is shame, which she defines as the fear of disconnection.[143] Shame is the sense that there is something about oneself that makes one unworthy of connection.[144] She goes on to identify twelve categories where shame commonly occurs in contemporary society and where people often don't feel that they are good enough: appearance and body image, money and work, motherhood/fatherhood, family, parenting, mental and physical health, addiction, sex, aging, religion, surviving trauma, and being stereotyped or labeled.[145] These categories are helpful in giving us ways to measure the likely health of someone's social connections as gauged by the degrees of shame they experience in these metrics. That has clear implications for a modern view of human flourishing where coopertiveness (Cloninger) and connection (Brown) are key traits of people who are flourishing.

This type of sociological perspective is helpful because it allows us to penetrate a layer beneath the surface of how the dynamics of social health and unhealth work in a given social context and how those vectors intersect with physical, mental, and spiritual health. One example of this that I find particularly insightful is the sociological evaluation of the phenomenon of narcissism—according to many, a growing epidemic in modern society. Brené Brown suggests that rather than see narcissism as a manifestation of hyper-autonomy and the embrace of rampant consumerism, sociology sees narcissism as a symptom of the fear of being ordinary in a postmodern culture where ordinary is devalued. Brown says, "[w]hen I look at narcissism . . . I see the fear of never feeling extraordinary enough to be noticed, to be lovable, to belong, or to cultivate a sense of purpose."[146] Seen in this light, it is not simply a vice to be rebuked, but rather a trauma to be understood. And I believe it gives us helpful ways to examine theological stances as well. Does our view of kingdom life alleviate or exacerbate tendencies towards

---

142. Brown, *Gifts of Imperfection*, 19.

143. Brown (*Daring Greatly*, 71) says, "In a 2011 study funded by the National Institute of Mental Health and by the National Institute on Drug Abuse, researchers found that, as far as the brain is concerned, physical pain and intense experiences of social rejection hurt in the same way." Brown is referring to Kross et al., "Social rejection," 6270–75.

144. Brown, *Daring Greatly*, 68.

145. Brown, *Daring Greatly*, 69.

146. Brown, *Daring Greatly*, 22.

shame in believer's lives? What of our view of the character of God? Is our interaction with the Lordship of God free of the manipulations of unhealthy shame?

The sociological remedy for a shame-dominated social context is, fittingly enough, vulnerability. It is a bit counter-intuitive because shame is based in feelings of insecurity about our areas of vulnerability. For women, that shame tends to manifest in trying to do everything perfectly and look good while doing it. For men, it manifests in trying to never show any signs of weakness. But vulnerability is the courage to be imperfect and to have the compassion to treat oneself generously about it, which is a form of healthy self-love.[147] Likewise, far from being a sign of weakness, when we see vulnerability in others, it comes across to us as profoundly courageous. Think of the alcoholic who finally admits his problem and asks for help. Such vulnerability, says Brown, is what gives us access to vital emotions like love, belonging, joy, courage, empathy, and creativity.[148] And these vital emotions are key to any conceptions of the flourishing human life.

The embrace of shame-free vulnerability and the healthy self-love that it entails is significant for this study because it challenges views of Christian flourishing that emphasize total sacrifice of the self for the sake of love for others. Stephen Pope suggests just such a Christian vision for flourishing when he says, "[a]gape sacrifices the self for the sake of the neighbor."[149] And while this is both noble and true, we do well to ask if there is a way to reconcile this call to selflessness with the humanistic call for a balance between healthy self-love and healthy love for our neighbors.

Economic and Political Perspectives on Inequality, Justice and Human Flourishing

Another perspective to consider comes from the fields of economics and political science. It has long been thought that once basic needs were met, a continued rise in income did not correlate with a rise in subjective measures of well-being. Indeed, many have argued that more financial wealth led to more complications and stress in life and less overall well-being. In a 2012 article on absolute income levels and subjective well-being, Daniel

---

147. Brown, *Daring Greatly*, 34.

148. Brown (*Daring Greatly*, 33–34) notes that "Vulnerability is the birthplace of love, belonging, joy, courage, empathy, and creativity."

149. Pope, "Christ and Human Flourishing," 21.

Sacks et al. found that this was not quite accurate.[150] Rather, they found that well-being rose with levels of income whether that was comparing people within one country or across different countries. They found that economic growth in a country correlated with greater well-being for the people in that country. And, perhaps most surprisingly of all, they found that there was no plateau in levels of well-being but rather a logarithmic curve that indicated higher levels of absolute income correlated with higher degrees of well-being with seemingly no limit.[151]

While it is of course possible to read these trends cynically as evidence that people are never satisfied and always longing for more, there are reasons for a more optimistic reading that posits that there are real benefits to well-being as income levels rise. One possible such reading draws from the work of Yona Kifer et al., who found that putting people in positions of power correlated with increased subjective well-being.[152] The reason for this correlation was that being placed in a position of power allowed people to be free to act in ways that were more consistent with their true thoughts, beliefs, personality, or internal values. As a result, they felt more authentically themselves and that led to a higher sense of subjective well-being. Thus, the researchers concluded that "[g]iving people a sense of power may go a long way towards improving their well-being."[153]

What I want to extrapolate from these studies is the relationship between rising income (a form of enhanced power) and the ability to be authentic (free). At what level would such a metric be deemed to indicate health? At what point poverty? Is there such a thing as power poverty? What of good healthy power? And should Christians, who have historically been taught to eschew power, embrace sacrifice, and be content in every circumstance, ever seek such power?

The question of how to measure poverty has been helpfully addressed by Amartya Sen and his capabilities approach to human development.[154] Rather than focus on the fair distribution of resources or the utility of something for a person's well-being, Sen draws attention to capabilities and

---

150. Sacks et al., "Income and Subjective Well-Being," 1181–87.

151. Sacks et al., "Income and Subjective Well-Being," 1186.

152. Kifer et al., "The Good Life," 280–88.

153. Kifer et al., "The Good Life," 286.

154. Sen's work in *Commodities and Capabilities* has been instrumental in helping develop the UN Human Development Index and many other measures of practical development in countries around the world.

An Orientation to the Contemporary Study of Human Flourishing

functionings because of inadequacies he finds with these other approaches. In a resource-focused approach, attention is given to improving access to income and resources for the poor in the expectation that this would enable them to flourish. However, one bag of rice for a very large man vs. that same bag of rice for a smaller man does not allow for the same development for both. Thus, the resource approach does not adequately address differences among people in age, ability, or any number of other individual factors at play.[155] Furthermore, with the utility approach attention is given to what contributes to a person's happiness. But Sen argues that some people can become conditioned to adapt to oppressive circumstances and imagine that they are doing well when they are in fact being deprived of basic rights and freedoms. Others might value certain rights and freedoms even if they do not contribute to their well-being. For these reasons, Sen offers a capabilities approach to avoid the pitfalls of a focus on resource equality or utility development.

In contrast to the resource approach and the utility approach, Sen suggests that we focus on helping people gain the capabilities to achieve valuable (to them) functioning in society. Sen is intentionally vague about what capabilities and functionings are basic and has steadily maintained a refusal to codify any standardized list. This is because he firmly believes that the capabilities and functionings that are valuable to one person might not be the same ones that are valued by another. At the heart of Sen's capabilities model is an embrace of the diversity of every individual and a recognition that the resources needed to give them the capability to reach their own valued potential will be different for each person. Think of an athlete or an artist and of how different the resources needed to cultivate their capabilities would be. Sen says, "The capability approach sees human progress, ultimately, as 'the progress of human freedom and capability to lead the kind of lives that people have reason to value.'"[156]

If we harken back to the Yona Kifer et al. study on the correlation of power and authenticity, we can say that a growth in capabilities and valued functionings is like a growth in power and authenticity. People who become more capable of pursuing the functionings in society that they value experience that as a heightening of healthy power and deepened authenticity. Seen in this light, it becomes clear how such power might be perceived

---

155. Sen's critiques of the resource model and utility model can be found in his book, *Development as Freedom*.

156. Dréze and Sen, *An Uncertain Glory*, 43.

of as "good" power. When thinking about how a society might cultivate human development, it is helpful to put it in this context of healthy empowerment towards greater authenticity by developing capabilities for valued functioning.

Finally, while Amartya Sen hesitates to offer a list of basic capabilities for a just society to cultivate in its citizens, Martha Nussbaum suggests ten capabilities that she believes a just society should develop in order to respect basic human dignity and provide a bare minimum for a flourishing life. Those capabilities are the right to a complete life (not dying prematurely), bodily health, freedom to use the senses to imagine, think, and reason, control over one's body, being able to form attachments to people or things outside ourselves, being able to associate with whom we please, being able to make rational choices according to practical reason, being able to form one's own conception of a flourishing life, respecting nature and other species, and some sort of control over one's material and political environment.[157] Although not meant to be an exhaustive list, it provides a good starting point for discussions about basic human capabilities that pose interesting questions for traditional theological approaches to human flourishing.

Anthropological Perspectives on Human Flourishing

Anyone with cross-cultural experience would immediately recognize the Western flavor of the ten core capabilities affirmed by Nussbaum in the section above. As such, it is important to add the voice of alternative conceptions of human flourishing from cultures that are more collectivistic in values than the starkly individualistic values prevalent in the West. Adam Cohen and Kathryn Johnson help to point out the practical dimensions of this difference when they say that "[i]n industrialized nations, self-satisfaction, the collection of pleasurable experiences, frequently experiencing positive affect, and personal freedoms are highly correlated with happiness, life satisfaction, and subjective well-being. However, in collectivist societies (e.g., India, China, or the Middle East), acceptance of others and achieving goals to make others happy is paramount."[158]

---

157. Nussbaum, *Creating Capabilities*, 32–33.

158. Cohen and Johnson, "Religion and Well-Being," 11. Cohen and Johnson are referring to work by Diener et al. ("Subjective Well-Being," 403–25) on cultural considerations in subjective appraisals of well-being.

An Orientation to the Contemporary Study of Human Flourishing

This raises the question of whether the basic capabilities identified by Nussbaum are merely a reflection of her own values, culture, and religious views.[159] Eastern culture is typically recognized to be a more shame-based culture than Western culture, which is integrally related to its collectivistic values. That is part of the social fabric and is what safeguards the orderliness of society there. Would it be appropriate to say that this shame-based culture is in error? Would it be appropriate to say that the individualistic Western society is in error?

While definitive stances on these questions continue to elude us, Richard Shweder et al. provides us with a three-dimensional approach to ethics that offers a helpful way to frame this dilemma. Shweder and his colleagues suggest that flourishing life can be framed in the light of three different ethics: (1) the ethic of autonomy where moral reasoning is focused on individual concerns; (2) the ethic of community where the objective of ethical behavior is social cohesion and duty rather than self-interest; and (3) the ethic of divinity where obedience to the commands and purposes of deity are paramount and personal or group concerns are discounted.[160] Which of these dimensions of well-being should get priority?[161] Is there a way to reconcile these three separate ethics into a single comprehensive ethic? These are questions that I hope to address through the course of this study.

Some Reflections on the Behavioral Sciences and Prosperity Theologies

While these insights from behavioral sciences have been developed largely outside of a Christian context, I believe that they express important categories of what flourishing life looks like that can help to nuance our theological constructions of what flourishing life is meant to be. For instance, what do healthy self-love, healthy power that leads to authenticity, and a healthy sense of self-directedness have to teach us about how we hear the lordship dynamics of God? What do they teach us about loving our neighbor as we

---

159. Cohen and Johnson ("Religion and Well-Being," 14) say, "[m]easurements of individual happiness, life satisfaction, and subjective well-being may actually reflect the scientist's own values, cultural inputs, and religious views."

160. Shweder et al., "The Big Three of Morality," 119–72.

161. Cohen and Johnson ("Religion and Well-Being," 13) notes that "[s]hould priority be given to the assessment of individual well-being, the well-being of the community, or obedience to divine commands?"

love ourselves? What do they reveal to us about the life of sacrifice? What of the shape of *shalom*? My suspicion is that they have a role to play in helping us to understand liberation in a deeper way, particularly as it regards the liberation from the trauma of victimization manifested as the loss of self-love, the loss of a personal sense of power, and the loss of self-directedness. It is these losses that I believe Prosperity theologies have found a way to address with their relentless focus on breakthroughs and optimism regarding the Kingdom of God manifesting on the earth. This will be the core of my argument in the next chapter, uncovering the liberative elements of Prosperity theologies and demonstrating the deeper dimensions of their appeal to the poor.

Conclusion

In this chapter, we established the importance of formulating a theological view of human flourishing that resonates with ordinary views of human flourishing given the immanent frame of modern society. We then demonstrated that the biblical view of flourishing in both the Old and New Testaments could be best captured in the notion of *shalom*, which expressed the comprehensive nature of flourishing envisioned by the biblical writers. That still left us with questions about how relationship with God was vital to that flourishing, particularly in the dynamics of the lordship of God over humanity.

That brought us to the theological proposals for flourishing life from Jürgen Moltmann, Richard Bauckham, and Miroslav Volf. Moltmann's commitment to egalitarian mutuality and liberation is so important for addressing issues of social justice in the world. However, his rejection of the hierarchical language in Scripture and in the dynamics of the believer's relationship with God is hard to reconcile with contemporary biblical scholarship. If we can find a way to affirm the lordship of God while maintaining an egalitarian basis for justice-making in the world, we will have helpfully extended Moltmann's contribution to addressing the societal issues of human flourishing from a theo-centric point of view. We will explore this in detail in chapter 6 where we develop a *kenotic* model of God's relationality deriving from Prosperity theologies.

Richard Bauckham was able to restore a commitment to the lordship of God in a way that mitigated concerns about enabling an abusive patriarchy. He did this by framing obedience as a voluntary act flowing from responsive love to the Lord. Furthermore, that obedience was meant to free us from the compulsion to sin, so it was not an exploitative command. Rather, it was necessary to bring us into the sort of personal freedom that enables us to serve others in love. While I find Bauckham's proposal very commendable at every point, one perspective that could help to extend his insights even further comes from the experiences of the victims of sin. As valuable as being freed from the compulsion to sin is, it is equally important to address the freedom that people need from the victimizations caused by sin. We will address this by appealing to the liberative elements of Prosperity theologies that emphasize personal empowerment out of narratives of victimization in chapter four. This is also where we apply the insights of the behavioral sciences to our understanding of victimizations and of how Prosperity theologies might offer a surprisingly effective remedy for overcoming them.

Turning to the contribution of Miroslav Volf, we found an invitation to a sacramental life characterized by the cultivation of a mindfulness towards God in every moment and circumstance of life. Such a view could infuse the world with a deeper joy and meaning owing to the relational connection between the world and the Creator God. While I find this a beautiful approach to a devotional life, I do have some concerns that such a mindfulness can easily slip into a contentment with the current state of the world. To help avoid this misappropriation of mindfulness, we will build on Volf's proposal with the challenge to hold a proper tension between hunger for breakthrough and contentment in limitation in chapter 5.

Finally, our sampling of research from the behavioral sciences gave us many potential points of contact between theo-centric and humanistic views of flourishing life. We found resonance with Martin Seligman's desire to articulate what might constitute well-being from the standpoint of Psychology. That was further defined by Robert Cloninger and his identification of self-directedness, cooperativeness, and self-transcendence as the three qualities that were found to have the most correlation with subjective measurements of individual flourishing. Sociological studies from Harvard University and Brené Brown confirmed our suspicions that healthy social connections correlated with more happiness, healthiness, and longer life. Economist Daniel Sacks surprised us with his research on the correlation between upward mobility and exponentially greater reported well-being with no plateau effect at the higher ends of the spectrum. Yona Kifer and her colleagues connected greater well-being to people being given greater positions of power—interpreted as greater freedom to act in ways consistent with their true thoughts, beliefs, and values (authenticity). Amartya Sen spoke of flourishing as giving people resources that would allow them to attain the capabilities that they valued. And Martha Nussbaum and others sought to articulate what the most basic and common of those capabilities might be in order to minimally dignify human life (with due consideration to differences in cultural values as well).

All of these insights help to provide some concrete guidelines for what a humanistic understanding of human flourishing might be in the immanent frame. They will be important dialogue partners in the following chapters as I seek to articulate a responsible Prosperity theology that aligns with the biblical values for *shalom*, the theological dynamics of an obedient relationship to God, and a robust engagement with humanistic views of human flourishing informed by the behavioral sciences. This constructive theology of empowerment and abundance can then represent a theocentric affirmation of ordinary human flourishing in the immanent frame.

4

The Liberative Elements of Prosperity Theologies

Introduction

EVER SINCE THE PUBLICATION of Jürgen Moltmann's *Theology of Hope*, there has been a steadily growing chorus of voices in the theological movement known as "Liberation Theology" characterized by a prophetic call to the task of promoting the cause of liberation in society. This theological critique has taken many forms through the past forty years in its examination of racism, sexism, and classism throughout society and has become a hallmark of the contemporary turn to contextuality and concreteness in theology. Indeed, it is hard to imagine where contemporary theology would be without the deeply searching questions raised by these liberationists regarding the inherent weaknesses in traditional modes of theological reflection. Liberationists challenge us to go beyond rationalism and abstraction in our theology and instead ground it deeply in the concrete contexts of real life. They force us to recognize the structural dimensions of sin embedded in our traditions and to take action to remedy them. And they challenge us to imagine a world without oppression and to work to make that world a present reality. This corrective is a welcome one for contemporary theology and a milestone in the self-awareness of the theological enterprise.

In this chapter, I will explore the contributions of several prominent liberation theologians before drawing parallels showing how Prosperity theologies manifest many of these same liberative themes. In particular, I will explore how Prosperity theologies address the phenomenon of victimization and implicitly work to overcome the roots of victimization in people's lives. I will corroborate this by drawing connections between what Prosperity theologies are doing and the insights of the behavioral sciences. My goal is to argue that there are liberative elements in Prosperity theologies that account for its effectiveness in bringing about the uplift of the poor and that make it a valuable conversation partner in contemporary theology.

Orientation to Liberation Theology Themes

We begin with a brief history of key developments in Liberation theology from its origins in the work of Jürgen Moltmann to some of its major voices along the way. These voices include Gustavo Gutierrez and his Socio-Political Liberation, James Cone and his sensitivity to racial themes, and Elizabeth Johnson with her constructive approach to Feminist themes of Liberation.

Jürgen Moltmann and the Primacy of Eschatology in the Theological Task

One of the most fruitful theological projects in the past fifty years has surely been Jürgen Moltmann's imaginative revisioning of eschatology from an abstract reflection on last things into one of the primary reflections for the theological task.[162] Moltmann makes an important distinction between *futurum*, which sees the future developing out of processes in the present, and *adventus*, which understands the future as breaking into the present in such a way that the present is transformed by it.[163] According to this understanding, Moltmann believes that the Christian eschatological hope is not meant to be some pie-in-the-sky escapist dream for the eschaton. Rather, it is to be a living hope that empowers the church to contend for the concrete manifestation of the Kingdom realities here on earth in this present life. Likewise, instead of trying to recover some idealized form of Christianity in the historical context of the first-century Church, Moltmann finds the ideal form of Christianity in the eschatological vision it harbors for the coming Kingdom of God. It is this eschatological kingdom reality that the

---

162. See Moltmann's *Theology of Hope*.

163. The terminology of *futurum* and *adventus* is more clearly expressed in Moltmann, *Coming of God*, 25–26.

The Liberative Elements of Prosperity Theologies

Church is charged to manifest in present society. Thus, any present values that are not found in the eschaton can be set aside while values of the Kingdom that are not yet a present reality can be brought into the world now in anticipation of that eschaton. For instance, in the Kingdom of God, there is no Greek nor Jew, no slave nor free, no man nor woman, but all are one in Christ Jesus. If that is the case in the Christian eschatological future, why insist on maintaining these sorts of divisions in the contemporary moment? Why not rather challenge the church to bring more of the eschatological Kingdom to bear on the present world?[164]

The impact of Moltmann's theological vision has been nothing short of remarkable. Despite some concerns that Moltmann's views enable an idealistic and over-realized eschatology, his work has inspired many others to consider what it would take to more closely align theological reflection with the eschatological realities of the kingdom of God. More specifically, his egalitarian interpretation of the dynamics of kingdom life has been taken up by liberation theologians to critique racial, gender, class, and power disparities in societies around the world.

Gustavo Gutierrez and Socio-Political Liberation

Writing in the context of Latin America in the 1960s, where many military uprisings were taking place and the ill-effects of globalization were beginning to manifest in institutionalized poverty in the region, Gustavo Gutierrez and other Latin American Catholic leaders articulated the need for the church to identify with the poor classes of society and advocate for their liberation rather than protect their own elite status as friend to the political establishment. It was a fateful decision that would result in the martyrdom of several priests who stood with the poor against the political forces seeking to oppress them, but it sparked a theological movement that reverberated throughout the region and even came to influence many leaders of the larger Catholic church.

Embedded in this stance was the question of whether the church should "[p]ut its social weight behind social transformation in Latin America" or if it should maintain a strict separation of the church from political

---

164. Moltmann (*Trinity and the Kingdom*, xi–xii) is fond of saying that he opposes doing theology in such a way that it creates a fortress around historical traditions and dogmas. Rather, he wants to make "contributions" to the theological dialogue that promote critical thinking and encourage theology further towards eschatological realities.

engagement.¹⁶⁵ Gutierrez noted that in much of the history of the church, emphasis was placed on the contemplative life while social and political issues were often "[r]elegated to a lower plane."¹⁶⁶ Likewise, the history of theological reflection had been almost exclusively a rational affair seeking to understand the nature of ultimate reality or the workings of the two-natures of Christ. But such abstract theological reflection did not always engage the world and the lives of believers in the world. It did not have anything practical to say about how to deal with present injustices or how to challenge blatant abuses of power in concrete ways. Indeed, it almost justified a "world-flight" regarding the mundane workings of everyday life and society in favor of abstract contemplations undisturbed by the cares of the world. In the midst of the social struggles in Latin America in his day, Gutierrez came to believe that these approaches would no longer suffice and sought ways to enlist theology in the task of advocating for justice causes in society.

In order to connect theology with the social issues of his day, Gutierrez expanded the scope of what salvation could mean. Thus, in contrast to views that focused solely on the spiritual dimensions of salvation regarding life in the hereafter that were typically emphasized in the church, he argued that there should be a robust "this-worldly" dimension of salvation that transformed the present lives of believers and the societies in which they lived. "Salvation is not something other-worldly, in regard to which the present life is merely a test. Salvation—the communion of men with God and the communion of men among themselves—is something which embraces all human reality, transforms it, and leads it to its fullness in Christ."¹⁶⁷ And if salvation was to embrace all of human reality, then "[t]he struggle for a just society is in its own right very much a part of salvation history."¹⁶⁸

This expanded view of salvation allowed Gutierrez to challenge the church to highlight God's active involvement in history in making right the

---

165. Gutierrez, *Theology of Liberation*, 138.

166. Gutierrez (*Theology of Liberation*, 48–49) notes that "In the past, concern for social praxis in theological thought did not sufficiently take into account the political dimension . . . Stress was placed on private life and on the cultivation of private values; things political were relegated to a lower plane."

167. Gutierrez, *Theology of Liberation*, 151.

168. Gutierrez (*Theology of Liberation*, 168) believes that salvation should "embrace all men and the whole man." Gutierrez (*Theology of Liberation*, 177) also says, "Without liberating historical events, there would be no growth of the Kingdom."

The Liberative Elements of Prosperity Theologies

things that had gone wrong in society. Salvation became synonymous with liberation, which Gutierrez defined as "[l]iberation from all that limits or keeps man from self-fulfillment, liberation from all impediments to the exercise of his freedom."[169] And the fullness of that liberation was to be found in "[c]ommunion with God and with other men" amidst the struggle to overcome everything that hindered that real sense of communion among people.[170] This was a theology that was engaged, not disengaged; passionate, not forensic; political, not pietist. It was a theology that sought to make a difference in the world for the sake of God's kingdom on the earth.[171]

The recognition of the social and political dimensions of salvation led Gutierrez to identify the ways that sin could be institutionalized in oppressive social and political structures. Thus, in liberation theology the individual and private aspects of sin are set aside in order to bring greater attention to the collective dimensions of sin in society.[172] Gutierrez says, "Sin is evident in oppressive structures, in the exploitation of man by man, in the domination and slavery of peoples, races, and social classes."[173] Traditional theology's focus on individual guilt and justification had unintentionally masked these societal dimensions of sin. Liberation theology aimed to bring these societal dimensions of sin to the center of the theological discussion.

One of the key ways that liberation theology promoted this goal was to claim that Scripture reflected a preferential option for the poor, which meant that special consideration should be given to the needs of the poor. Gutierrez says, "The whole climate of the Gospel is a continual demand to subordinate economic needs to those of the deprived. Was not Christ's first preaching to 'proclaim the liberation of the oppressed?'"[174] Thus, Gutierrez believed that the church was called to solidarity with the poor in the

---

169. Gutierrez, *Theology of Liberation*, 27.

170. Gutierrez, *Theology of Liberation*, 36. Guttierez (*Theology of Liberation*, 48) also says, "The building of a just society means overcoming every obstacle to the creation of an authentic peace among people."

171. Gutierrez (*Theology of Liberation*, 275) notes that neutrality in the face of class struggles in society is not possible.

172. Gutierrez (*Theology of Liberation*, 175) notes that "[i]n the liberation approach sin is not considered as an individual, private, or merely interior reality ... Sin is regarded as a social, historical fact ... When it is considered in this way, the collective dimensions of sin are rediscovered."

173. Gutierrez, *Theology of Liberation*, 175.

174. Gutierrez, *Theology of Liberation*, 116.

form of social and political advocacy on their behalf and against the unjust and oppressive institutional factors facing the poor in society.[175] It was this advocacy for the poor that gave liberation theology its political expression.

The three key moves made by Gutierrez are all themes that are commonly found in various other expressions of liberation theology: (1) the commitment to concreteness in theology for the Christian life; (2) the attention given to the institutional dimensions of sin and salvation; and (3) the emphasis on the preferential option for the poor. For Gutierrez and Latin American liberation theologians, despite early concerns that their egalitarian values harbored an implicit Marxist worldview, their mature program contributed greatly to a recovery of the political dimensions of faith that has become an important part of contemporary constructive theology. Liberation theology helped to make the church more proactive in its political engagement for the purpose of advancing the liberation that comes in the Kingdom of God advancing on the earth.

James Cone and the Disruption of the Status Quo in Theology

One of the main insights of liberation theology has been its radical challenge to the structures of sin inherent in our society, and perhaps more disturbingly, in our very traditions themselves. That includes our theological traditions, which James Cone chastises for failing to speak out about the abuses of racism and slavery over the decades and even centuries they were tolerated in the Christianized world. How could theology have failed to address this grievous injustice? Unless . . . theology itself was racist.[176] This claim exposed the very contextuality of the theological tradition itself. It was a white, male, affluent, euro-centric, Christendom biased tradition—a far cry from the unattached, universal perspective it claimed to be. Thus, Cone's charge that theology is racist reverberates through the history of the church. Indeed, how could theology have been so blind to the dominating nature of its own narratives for so long?

---

175. "This solidarity means that we make ours their problems and their struggles, that we know how to speak with them. This has to be concretized in criticism of injustice and oppression, in the struggle against the intolerable situation which a poor person has to tolerate." See Second General Conference of Latin American Bishops, "Poverty of the Church."

176. Writing in a preface to a 1986 reprinting of his classic work, Cone (*Black Theology*, xviii) says, "I felt deeply that the time had come to expose white theology for what it was: a racist, theological justification of the status quo."

The Liberative Elements of Prosperity Theologies

Cone's charge that theology is racist is meant in two ways. First, it criticizes the way that our methods of theology have been abstract and do not engage in the workings of the world leaving injustices untouched. And second, it shows how traditional theology has always served to protect the status quo, in effect enabling abuses to continue unchecked as well. Thus, any claim that Scripture interprets itself is now suspect because this sort of talk usually leads to an affirmation of the status quo—the same status quo that silently endorsed all manner of racist, sexist, and classist abuse in the church for all these years. Something other than the status quo was needed if theology was to overcome this blindness.

For Cone, a true Christian theology would have identified with the plight of the oppressed and their fight for liberation and empowerment rather than preserving its own privilege by failing to challenge the status quo. He says, "There can be no Christian theology that is not identified unreservedly with those who are humiliated and abused."[177] The task of theology should be aimed squarely at the liberation of these marginalized ones. But this task to re-orient theology to serve the liberation of those who had been historically oppressed would be so disorienting that Cone believed it would be difficult for those who had been "oppressors" to understand the shape of a theology that arose from the oppressed. He says, "Not understanding what it means to be oppressed, the oppressor is in no position to understand the methods which the oppressed use in liberation. The logic of liberation is always incomprehensible to slave masters."[178] Indeed, Cone believed that the self-deception of "masters" was so deep that they often believed themselves to be acting in the best interests of all—including the slaves, when in actuality their stances effectively kept their slaves under oppression.[179]

One example of how Cone felt that the oppressors would not understand the methods of liberation for the oppressed was in the call to

---

177. Cone, *Black Theology*, 1. Cone (*Black Theology*, 3) also says, "In view of the biblical emphasis on liberation, it seems not only appropriate but necessary to define the Christian community as the community of the oppressed which joins Jesus Christ in his fight for the liberation of humankind."

178. Cone, *Black Theology*, 11. I find this point to be quite interesting and a possible reason why there is such a stark difference of opinion regarding the Prosperity movement between the theological establishment who disdain it and the poor who find it to be empowering. I will explore this at the end of this chapter.

179. Cone (*Black Theology*, 12) says, "Masters always pretend that they are not masters, insisting that they are only doing what is best for society as a whole, including the slaves."

self-giving love in accordance with the model of Christ's sacrifice. When this call is made with no reference to living in righteous relationships, it can effectively be used as a tool of continued oppression rather than of spiritual liberation. Imagine if an oppressor called upon the oppressed to lovingly surrender themselves to their masters as Christ had done for us. Such a call would entrap the oppressed in unjust social relationships with no theological justification to break free of those injustices. In just this sort of way, theology had been used to be complicit in the continued oppression of the marginalized. In Cone's view, this perspective of Christian self-giving love "[p]laces no obligation on white oppressors" and thus it reveals its inherent bias against the oppressed.[180]

Another way in which traditional theology would not understand the methods of liberation for the oppressed was in Cone's contention that a theology of the oppressed could not accept a view of God that approved of a divine purpose in human suffering. Traditional theology, in its intent to honor the sovereignty of God, tended to insist that all human suffering had its redemptive purpose in the plan of God. But for the oppressed, Cone insists that "Despite the emphasis on future redemption in present suffering, black theology cannot accept any view of God that even *indirectly* places divine approval on human suffering. The death and resurrection of Jesus does not mean that God promises us a future reality in order that we might tolerate present evil."[181] Cone is here pointing out the subtle ways that theology has been used to stifle the historical struggle against injustice in society. And any theological justification of embracing suffering for its spiritual benefits is suspect when seen from the perspective of the historically oppressed because it served to rob them of the will to resist injustices amongst them.

In contrast to the spiritualized view of suffering of traditional theology, Cone suggests that "[t]he suffering which is inseparable from the gospel . . . is suffering in the struggle for liberation."[182] He bases this on

---

180. Cone (*Black Theology*, 75) says, "By emphasizing the complete self-giving of God in Christ, without seeing also the content of righteousness, oppressors could then demand that the oppressed do likewise. If God freely enters into self-donation, then in order to be godlike we must give ourselves to our oppressors in like manner . . . This view of love places no obligation on white oppressors."

181. Cone, *Black Theology*, 85.

182. Cone (*Black Theology*, 86) says, "The suffering which is inseparable from the gospel is that style of existence that arises from a decision to *be* in spite of nonbeing. It is that type of suffering that is inseparable from freedom, the freedom that affirms black

The Liberative Elements of Prosperity Theologies

his conviction that the underlying theme of the gospel is for the liberation of the oppressed. Thus, even if suffering takes the form of a longing to be presently delivered from oppression, that is still better than a view that accepts suffering for the sake of future spiritual blessings beyond the concrete parameters of this-worldly life. Thus, a theology of suffering for the oppressed must be in the service of the liberation of the oppressed. And not just the liberation of our own insulated community, but the liberation of every person in every community because "[n]o one is free until all are free."[183]

A final example of how Cone believes that traditional theology cannot understand the methods of liberation employed by the oppressed is reflected in how Cone frames the issue of sin and repentance in traditional theology and among the oppressed. This is perhaps where Cone is most misunderstood because of the provocative language he employs. He says that "[s]in is whiteness—the desire of whites to play God in the realm of human affairs."[184] In contrast, the sin for black oppressed peoples is the "[l]oss of identity . . . accepting the world as it is by letting whites define black existence."[185] Of course, Cone is using "whiteness" as a euphemism for that traditional theology which had no words of critique in its silent endorsement of racism, classism, and slavery. And "blackness" is Cone's expression for a theology arising from the oppressed that is oriented towards the liberation of all.

What is more interesting here is Cone's recognition that different communities would have different sin-struggles based on an understanding of sin as that which obstructs wholeness in individuals and societies. Thus, for the oppressed black communities, traditional categories of sin and guilt needed to be re-formulated in light of their victimized status in society. Sin for the oppressed black person was not so much about committing offenses before God, but rather about allowing the sin perpetrated by others to rob them of their dignity and self-respect. While whites needed to repent for the oppression they put other people through, blacks needed to repent for relinquishing their identity to their oppressors.

---

liberation despite the white powers of evil. It is suffering in the struggle for liberation."

183. Cone (*Black Theology*, 92–93) says, "[h]uman existence must be explained as 'being in freedom,' which means rebellion against every form of slavery . . ."

184. Cone, *Black Theology*, 115.

185. Cone, *Black Theology*, 115.

The Empowering God

A natural consequence of this parsed understanding of sin and repentance was that Cone was now able to claim that "There is no use for a God who loves white oppressors *the same as* oppressed blacks."[186] While the overarching love of God was the same towards all people, the way that this love was expressed to oppressors could not be the same as the way that this love was expressed towards the victims of oppression. The love of God worked to compel the oppressors to give up their oppressive behaviors. That same love worked to affirm and empower the victims of oppression to call them back to dignity and a restored humanity. For Cone, this was one concrete expression of what it practically meant for liberation theologians to claim a preferential option for the poor. Thus, repentance for blacks was about gaining the courage to recover their dignity and self-respect—a far cry from traditional views which saw repentance as a necessary demonstration of contrition.

Cone develops many arguments to demonstrate the ways that traditional theology might have difficulty understanding the methods of liberation used by the oppressed, but the three that have been detailed here have particular relevance for our analysis of the Prosperity movement as a liberation theology. Before turning to that study, we will look at the contributions of feminist and post-colonial theologians to this conversation.

Elizabeth Johnson on Feminist Liberation

In detailing the problems of primarily androcentric images of God in traditional theology, Elizabeth Johnson points out that women have long lacked an equivalent access to gender-specific language of God oriented to their experience.[187] Classical theism imagines a God that is the Supreme Being who "made all things and rules all things." This rulership model of God was "[i]ntrinsically hierarchical whether the divine reign be accomplished through dominance or benevolence."[188] Even metaphysical descriptions of God portrayed God with an androcentric bias. God was equated with the "male principle" of spirit, reason, and act rather than the "female principle" of body, passion, and passivity.[189] Johnson associates these patterns of thinking with patriarchalism—the phenomenon of sexist social structures.

---

186. Cone, *Black Theology*, 74.
187. Johnson, *She Who Is*, 29.
188. Johnson, *She Who Is*, 20.
189. Johnson, *She Who Is*, 35.

The Liberative Elements of Prosperity Theologies

Historically, Johnson claims patriarchalism contributed to the oppression of women, whether that oppression was intended or not.

The fundamental problem patriarchalism reveals is the "[i]nability of a dominant group to deal with otherness, to acknowledge equal humanity and kinship with those who are different from themselves."[190] This dynamic of 'dominant' and 'marginalized' highlights Johnson's liberation perspective on the plight of women in the church. She says, "[e]xclusive, literal patriarchal speech about God is both oppressive and idolatrous. It functions to justify social structures of dominance/subordination and an androcentric world view inimical to the genuine and equal human dignity of women, while it simultaneously restricts the mystery of God."[191]

To counter this oppression, Johnson steers a careful balance between a "[r]everse sexism, which would place women in dominant positions to the diminishment of men, and a sameness, which would level out genuine variety and particularity, disrespecting uniqueness."[192] This is a key moderating dynamic in Johnson's thought that separates her position from those of her peers. Johnson proposes the need for a mutuality of images of God that affirms the vitality of both male and female metaphors of deity. This is a part of her larger move to engage in the "revolution in the idea of God" that is occurring in our day: moving towards an egalitarian vision of God who is "[t]he liberating God, the incarnational God, the relational God, the suffering God, the God who is future, and the unknown, hidden God of mystery."[193]

Rather than settle for merely giving "feminine" qualities to a still predominately "male" view of God or resorting to the common notion that the spirit represents the "feminine" dimension in the Trinity, Johnson insists on a fully articulated female dimension to each member of the Trinity—Father,

---

190. Johnson, *She Who Is*, 23. Johnson (*She Who Is*, 27) says, "The fundamental sin is exploitation, whether it be expressed in the domination of male over female, white over black, rich over poor, strong over weak, armed military over unarmed civilians, human beings over nature. These analogously abusive patterns interlock because they rest on the same base: a structure where an elite insists on its superiority and claims the right to exercise dominative power over all others considered subordinate, for its own benefit."

191. Johnson, *She Who Is*, 40. Johnson (*She Who Is*, 38) remarks, "As long as ultimate mystery is spoken about in exclusive and literal patriarchal terms, then persons fitting that description will continue to relate to others in a superior way."

192. Johnson, *She Who Is*, 32.

193. Johnson, *She Who Is*, 21.

Son, and Spirit.[194] The feminine dimension of the Spirit is generally acknowledged and is seen in the Spirit's activities in creating and sustaining new life. Similarly, the feminine dimension of the Father is recognized in the many biblical symbols for God that "[revolve] around women's experience of bearing, birthing, and nursing new human beings."[195] It is the feminine dimension of the Son that is most subtle and masterfully drawn out by Johnson.

Johnson associates the Son with the biblical "personification of God's presence and activity" in wisdom/Sophia. It is Sophia that "lures" people to life. It is Sophia that is perhaps "[a] female personification of God's own being in creative and saving involvement with the world."[196] And it is Sophia that is most closely aligned with early Christian Christology. Johnson details how the high Christology in the gospel of John "[p]resents the prehistory of Jesus as the story of Sophia: present 'in the beginning,' an active agent in creation, descending from heaven to pitch a tent among the people, rejected by some, giving life to those who seek, a radiant light that darkness cannot overcome (Jn 1:1–18)."[197] This identification of Christ with Sophia provides the feminine dimension to the Son that Johnson seeks.

To further support her Feminist reading of Scripture, Johnson appeals to the classical notion of the incomprehensibility of God. She states simply, "God's unlikeness to the corporal and spiritual finite world is total. Hence human beings simply cannot understand God."[198] As a result of this ultimate limitation in human knowledge of the divine, analogy presents itself as the proper category for speech about God. And owing to the inherent inability of any one metaphor to capture the full reality of God, a multiplicity of metaphors is the ideal way to draw nearer to the reality of God.[199] In a sense, because God is ultimately incomprehensible, this puts all metaphors

---

194. Johnson (*She Who Is*, 132) says, "I propose to keep the traditional language of Spirit and test whether it is capable of a feminist retrieval, not to the exclusion of the model of God as friend but toward the expansion of language."

195. Johnson, *She Who Is*, 100. Johnson (*She Who Is*, 54) points out that "If women are created in the image of God, then God can be spoken of in female metaphors in as full and as limited a way as God is imaged in male ones . . ."

196. These various insights can be found in Johnson, *She Who Is*, 91–94.

197. Johnson, *She Who Is*, 97.

198. Johnson, *She Who Is*, 105.

199. Johnson, *She Who Is*, 118. This is a theme that she shares with McFague (*Models of God*, 39–40) who also argues for a multiplicity of metaphors to express the ineffability of God.

The Liberative Elements of Prosperity Theologies

of God in a similar state of poverty in their ability to reflect God's reality. This allows Johnson to suggest that "[a]bsolutizing any particular expression as if it were adequate to divine reality is tantamount to a diminishment of truth about God."[200] Thus, female metaphors of God are necessary to supplement male metaphors of God in contributing to a fuller picture of Divine reality.

Beyond Johnson's attempt to broaden the conversation around an egalitarian vision of God, Johnson echoes James Cone's view of sin as that which obstructs wholeness by re-considering conversion in that light. If sin obstructs wholeness, then conversion entails the process of recovering wholeness, which Johnson understands as a process of empowerment for women who have experienced marginalization in society.[201] She suggests that "[c]onversion experienced not as giving up oneself but as tapping into the power of oneself simultaneously releases understanding of divine power not as dominating power-over but as the passionate ability to empower oneself and others."[202] For women, this conversion process involves (1) a coming to awareness of injustices suffered and a commitment to resist them; (2) a positive acknowledgment of their "beauty and power as active subjects in history"; and (3) a final acceptance of the "goodness of being a woman" in attitude and practice.[203] Put another way, conversion for women was about rediscovering their worth and their voice rather than some exercise in self-deprecation. Particularly because socialized self-deprecation had historically been a tool that the patriarchy had used to keep women in an oppressed social state,[204] Johnson's appropriation of female imagery of

---

200. Johnson, *She Who Is*, 112.

201. Johnson's (*She Who Is*, 30) view of the goal of feminist theology is that "It attempts new articulations of the norms and methods of theology itself and newly envisions Christian symbols and practices that would do justice to the full humanity of women as a key to a new whole."

202. Johnson, *She Who Is*, 67.

203. Johnson, *She Who Is*, 64.

204. Johnson (*She Who Is*, 64) says, "Analysis of women's experience is replete with the realization that within patriarchal systems women's primordial temptation is not to pride and self-assertion but rather to the lack of it, to diffuseness of personal center, overdependence on others for self-identity, drifting, and fear of recognizing one's own competence. In this situation grace comes to the sleeper not as the call to loss of self but as empowerment toward discovery of self and affirmation of one's strength, giftedness, and responsibility. Such is women's present experience of the perennial call to conversion. It involves a turning away from demeaning female identity toward new ownership of the female self as God's good gift."

The Empowering God

God in Scripture and tradition is her attempt at inspiring this conversion in the lives of oppressed women in the church and in society.

The Turn Towards Holistic Liberation

Having traced some of the major developments of Liberation theology through the years, we now turn to some contemporary approaches that aim at more holistic perspectives on Liberation theology that will help us to connect it with themes in Prosperity theologies. We will consider Miroslav Volf's provocative suggestion that a common thread exists between Pentecostal and Liberation theologies of a commitment to the materiality of salvation. Then we will reflect on the role of personal empowerment as a task of Liberation before suggesting that a theology of the sinned-against (victimization) is the prototype for all types of Liberation theologies.

Miroslav Volf on The Materiality of Salvation

The many insights of Liberation theology can be summed up in a relatively few key movements. First, it embraces a concrete and expanded view of salvation that centers on the recovery of justice in present life and community. Second, the understanding of sin is conditioned by this vision of justice such that the systemic aspects of sin that undermine justice are exposed. Third, these expanded views of salvation and sin entail a redefinition of the processes of repentance and conversion to serve the vision of present *shalom*. These key moves can themselves be represented by the overall theme of a value for the materiality of salvation, which is a phrase Miroslav Volf uses to highlight the commonalities between Liberation theologies and classical Pentecostal theologies.

Volf rightly points out that this pairing of Pentecostal theology and Liberation theology is unexpected because of: (1) the typical emphasis on the "transcendence" of God breaking into the world from above in Pentecostal theology vs. the "immanence" of God highlighted in Liberation theologies; (2) the common critique that Pentecostal theologies tend to be so attuned to individual spiritual experiences of grace and a flight from the world that they can miss the concrete issues of transformative social praxis that are one of the hallmarks of Liberation theologies; and (3) the fact that Pentecostals typically have held a vision for an eschatological *anihilatio*

The Liberative Elements of Prosperity Theologies

mundi whereas Liberationists hope for a transformation of the world.[205] But despite these differences, both Pentecostalism and Liberation theology attempt to recover the this-worldly dimensions of salvation in their own ways.

According to Volf, much of traditional theology has followed the distinction made by Martin Luther between the "inner man" and the "outer man" in his treatise on *The Freedom of a Christian*.[206] Luther understood the "outer man" to denote "[a] person with respect to his or her bodily existence in the world."[207] What the "inner man" represented was not entirely clear, but at the least it did not encompass bodily existence. For Luther, and much of Protestant theology after him, spiritual salvation was effective upon the "inner man" while leaving the "outer man" unmolested. This wasn't to say that salvation would have no material effect at all, but rather to emphasize that spiritual salvation was an internal matter independent of any outward manifestations of well-being or the lack of it. "The point Luther wanted to make is not that salvation has *nothing* to do with the bodily and earthly realm but that *no change for the better in that realm can be understood as an aspect of salvation itself.*"[208] In Volf's estimation, both Pentecostal and Liberation theologies mount some form of challenge to this soteriological division between the "inner" and "outer" man and attempt to explore the this-worldly manifestations of salvation more robustly.

While a few of the many key moves Liberation theologies have made to bridge this material gap have already been summarized above, Pentecostal theologies have typically done this by emphasizing divine healing either in the atonement or in a present manifestation of the eschatological kingdom.[209] Salvation, in this view, is not only a spiritual matter for the inner man, but carries promise for physical healing for the outer man in this life. But where Liberation theology has been criticized for focusing too much on socioeconomic and political manifestations of the kingdom of God to the neglect of individual spirituality, Pentecostal theologies have been challenged for their lack of socioeconomic and political engagement

---

205. Volf, "Materiality of Salvation," 447–48.

206. Volf, "Materiality of Salvation," 449–53. Cf. Martin Luther, "Freedom of a Christian," 261–316.

207. Volf, "Materiality of Salvation," 450.

208. Volf, "Materiality of Salvation," 453. Admittedly, there is a rich dialogue of diverging opinions on how to interpret the works of Luther.

209. Volf, "Materiality of Salvation," 457.

and for harboring an escapist view of the world. However, the Pentecostal theologies referenced by Volf represent classical streams of the movement and do not take into account the Prosperity theologies that have proliferated since the time of Volf's analysis. Is it possible that some of these new movements add another dimension to this study?

It is my proposal that Prosperity theologies represent a merging of the strengths of the classical Pentecostalism detailed by Volf with the expanded understanding of salvation found in the Liberation theologies explored above.[210] As such, some of these Prosperity theologies are perhaps better framed as nascent holistic liberation movements that mature the Pentecostal intuitions regarding the materiality of salvation into a full-fledged bio-psycho-social commitment to human flourishing joined together with a healthy spirituality of transcendence. In the remainder of this chapter, I will explore some of the ways this movement is developing and how it engages various dimensions of human flourishing as explored in the previous chapter of this study.

Personal Empowerment as a Task of Liberation Theology

When thinking about how the Prosperity movement can intersect with Liberation theology, I am often reminded of Paul's statements from the letter to the Philippians regarding being content in every circumstance whether in plenty or in want. Normally, I would find this exhortation to be wonderfully wise and welcome counsel in the midst of the changing fortunes of life. But would I feel differently about this message if it was spoken by a member of the socio-economic elite and I was living paycheck to paycheck trying to make ends meet? What about if a slave owner was to repeat this exhortation to his slaves? At what point would this exhortation cease being life-giving and become instead a tool of oppression entrapping people in cycles of poverty, disadvantage, and a resignation to fate? Learning to hear the liberative dimensions of the Prosperity message requires this sort of nuanced sensitivity to context and a discernment about whether a theological stance is actually being used to encourage kingdom values or if it is being used to oppose them.

In chapter 2 of this study I explored some of the differences between classical Pentecostalism with its ascetic values and Prosperity theologies

---

210. The Pentecostalism Volf speaks of is more representative of classical Pentecostalism as detailed in the second chapter of this work.

The Liberative Elements of Prosperity Theologies

with their embrace of a more consecrationist view of holiness. In short, the ascetic values of classical Pentecostalism lead to an understanding of holiness as separation from the mundane things of the world in order to emphasize the spiritual dimensions of salvation. That often limits the scope of God's salvific workings to the "inner man" as described by Luther, except where physical bodily healing is concerned.

In contrast, the consecrationist view of holiness held by some Prosperity theologies holds that anything in the world can be made holy if it is utilized for divine purposes. For these theologies, the belief that the promise of divine healing is secured in the atonement is expanded to recognize the fact that healing and prosperity are, in fact, multi-dimensional realities. In recent iterations, the wholeness won in Christ's atoning work goes beyond spiritual wholeness and bodily healing and now includes the healing of psychological wounds through mental and emotional healing as well.[211] Further, these movements have come to recognize the role that socio-economic factors play in health and well-being through a recognition of the crushing burden of debts and cycles of poverty inherited from generation to generation. The expanded understanding of healing in these movements thus begins to encompass every dimension that impacts the flourishing of life. It is merely semantic to recognize that this expanded view of divine healing is equivalent to a broadly expanded understanding of the this-worldly scope of salvation in these movements.

When the Prosperity movement is seen through this lens, its liberative dimensions begin to take shape. Divine healing and salvation have to do with setting people free from the physical, emotional, and socio-economic factors that keep them from experiencing fullness of life. Where the Prosperity movement still diverges from traditional Liberation theology is that rather than focus on the macro-political changes that might be required to address the obstacles to flourishing life in the community, the Prosperity movement instead focuses on the individual changes that are necessary to achieve personal breakthroughs in these areas. This is not to say that the Liberation theologies fail to address these personal dynamics as well since we have seen how Black and Feminist Liberationists speak of conversion as a recovery of personal voice and identity. Likewise, there are certainly streams in Prosperity theologies that are moving from the message of

---

211. This is commonly referred to as inner healing among practitioners and runs the gamut from basic crisis counseling to full blown exorcism-type deliverances. It is a field that could benefit from some moderating reflections by other theologians as well.

personal empowerment to one of social responsibility. But seen broadly, Liberation theologies emphasize the macro-political and systemic societal dimensions of sin while Prosperity theologies focus on personal empowerment and the micro-systemic dimensions of sin within individuals, families, and communities.

To put this distinction into clearer perspective, Latin American Liberation theologians have focused their efforts on identifying themselves with the plight of the poor and advocating for changes in public policy that could help alleviate their suffering. In contrast, Prosperity theologians focus on the individual mindsets that keep the poor trapped in personal and communal narratives of victimization. Those narratives might come from the patterns of poverty or abuse they have endured in their own families or even from the string of poor choices they might have made in their lives. Those narratives could also come from a systemic lack of opportunity due to the large-scale forces of globalization that effect their entire community. The difference between these approaches is in where the perceived power to change is located. For Latin American Liberationists, the power is often perceived to be in the hands of the elites and the marginalized are fighting to have a greater/equal share of that power. For Prosperity theologians, the power to change is always within the individuals themselves and the focus is on a personal transformation that results in new patterns of life that promote flourishing in themselves, their families, and their communities. It is from the proliferating of these personal empowerments/transformations that community practices can then begin to be transformed.[212]

Prosperity theologies place great emphasis on empowering believers to seek these personal breakthroughs towards flourishing. And while there is certainly room to question some of the motives and methods being used to accomplish this, the sociological impact of the Prosperity message amongst the poor, as noted by sociologist Peter Berger, bears witness to the fact that many are indeed experiencing uplift through this movement. For me, this speaks to the resonance of the personal empowerment aspect of the Prosperity message that evangelicals would do well to seek to understand

---

212. Another way that some Prosperity theologies help restore a sense of personal power for people over their circumstances is in the practice of a "negativity fast" where they abstain from complaints, criticisms, and disparaging remarks and thoughts in order to replace them with affirmations, encouragements, and compliments. This simple discipline is a part of creating a "culture of honor" that sees the best in self and others and is the heart of the kingdom culture that some iterations of these theologies seek to cultivate. See Silk, *Culture of Honor*, 160–61.

and perhaps even attempt to articulate in an evangelical voice. That is part of what I am attempting to do here.

Along these lines, to me the emphasis on health and prosperity in the atonement in Prosperity theologies is more palatably framed as a version of George E. Ladd's "already" and "not-yet" theology of the Kingdom as I mentioned in chapter 2. In this framework, the eschatological kingdom is both a present reality and a future promise. The million-dollar question is this: to what degree can we expect a present manifestation of the Kingdom? And to what degree must we be wary of an over-realized expectation of the eschatological kingdom? Navigating this distinction can result in a wide spectrum of opinion regarding the proper balance between the two. Prosperity theologies place a heavy priority on the "already" aspect of this duality in an effort to optimistically stretch the faith of the church regarding to what degree the manifestation of the eschatological Kingdom is possible in the here and now. And while some proponents cross the line to seemingly promote glib formulas regarding the practice of giving and the promise of breakthrough—practices which should certainly be critiqued and challenged—other iterations of the Prosperity message express a more moderated view on how to live with vibrant faith in the tension of this "already" and "not-yet" kingdom. This rendition of Prosperity theologies represents a view that, I believe, is fully compatible with the broader church, even if the optimism is much more pronounced.

I will explore how Prosperity theologies navigate this kingdom tension in more detail in the next chapter, but to give more substance to my claim that Prosperity theologies can be seen as an expression of Liberation theology, I want to move now towards a suggestion that the emphasis on the uplift of the poor in Prosperity theologies shares many points with the contemporary theology of the sinned-against. The theology of the sinned-against is, in my opinion, the broadest form of Liberation theology that seeks to do theology from the perspective of the victims of sin. In seeking to understand the phenomenon of victimization and what it looks like for someone to emerge from their narratives of victimization, I believe the theology of the sinned-against offers us insights into why the poor find the message of Prosperity theologies to be so personally empowering—certainly something more than the mere license for greed that some have suspected it to be.

THE EMPOWERING GOD

A Theology of the Sinned-Against

Liberation theologies thrived because they brought attention to the plight of the oppressed and marginalized in societies around the world. They highlighted the institutional and systemic expressions of sin in society and began to reflect on how this impacted the lives of the oppressed. And while that perspective has proven to be vitally important to the integrity of the theological task, one criticism of Liberation theology has been that it has focused on the systemic dimensions of sin at the expense of attending to its individual dimensions. That is where theologians who work on theology for the sinned-against succeed in bringing Liberation theology's attentiveness to the plight of the marginalized to the individual dynamics of sin and justice.

A theology for the sinned-against gets at the questions that haunt us most of all: in the words of Lisa Lampman and Michelle Shattuck, "[w]hat we all really want to know is what is in the heart of God—is He really good?"[213] How does God look upon the sin of the oppressors? How does He consider the pain of the oppressed? In the face of the evangelical message that we are all equally sinners in the eyes of God and that holding unforgiveness is tantamount to a rejection of the grace of God, how do we avoid silencing the voice of the oppressed?

Evangelicalism has often propagated a cheap and unilateral conception of justice that has failed on three counts. (1) It has failed to adequately reflect the profound goodness of God; (2) it has failed to address the specific needs of people who have been sinned against; and (3) it has failed to bring about real discipleship and the restoration of *shalom* in our communities of faith. That is why it is said that "[t]raditional Christianity has worked to release the offender from guilt while leaving the victim still hurting."[214] We have celebrated the sinner who comes to the Lord and has had his sins washed clean, but failed to remember the victims of his sin who must continue to live with the effects of his sin for the rest of their lives. Indeed, we have even criticized the wounded for harboring a victim-mentality—victim-shaming them into moving on without allowing them the necessary safety and counsel to process their pain and anger.

The sinned-against have a lot of questions in their hearts. They wonder where God was when they needed Him. They wonder if it was their sin that

---

213. Lampman and Shattuck, "Finding God," 14.
214. Zehr, "Restoring Justice," 136.

The Liberative Elements of Prosperity Theologies

brought evil upon their lives. They wonder if God is angry or unhappy with them. And everything they hear and read about Him comes through this lens of confusion and fear. So, it is important that a theology for the sinned-against begins by first seeking to understand in what ways God is actually good to the sinned-against. How does He really stand on their behalf?

A theology for the sinned-against addresses these questions by paying attention to the trialogue between God, the sinner, and the sinned-against throughout Scripture.[215] Reading Scripture from this perspective reveals that not only is the cry of the sinned-against important to God, but it is hard to avoid the conclusion that it is one of the *most* important things to Him. As Bryan Stone says, "[G]od is a God who takes sides, who works for human liberation and community and against oppression and slavery."[216] He takes sides to stand with the sinned-against and to put pressure on the sinners to right their wrongs. That is why Howard Zehr can say, "[G]od's heart is wounded by the hurt of the victim more than by the sinner's breaking of the law."[217] The sinned-against need to hear and understand this. God's anger is not directed *at* them. It is harnessed *for* them.

God's anger does have a restorative purpose, and He does punish sinners as a part of His effort to restore them to wholeness and community.[218] Thus His anger is primarily understood as the discipline of a Parent for his child. "As God does justice for victims . . . He does not give up on criminals . . . and even in punishment, God does not cease to extend grace . . . "[219] God's judgments are designed to stir sinners to repentance and to point

---

215. Brueggemann ("The Shrill Voice," 26–40) offers a helpful examination for us in his explanation of the 2-party narrative vs. the 3-party narrative. When Scripture is read as a 2-party narrative, we see how people can begin to read it as 'Quid Pro Quo' types of interaction. You sin, you get punished by God. You do well, you get blessed by God. But Scripture is not a 2-party narrative. Often it is a 3-party narrative where there is a person or group that is being oppressed, there is the oppressive enemy, and there is God the advocate who acts on behalf of the oppressed. We see this pattern repeated over and over in Scripture: Pharaoh, Israel, and God; Oppressive Elites, the poor, and the Advocating Prophets; the Lamenter, the Presumed offender, and God. If we insist on keeping it a 3-character plot—Sinner / Sinned-against / God the advocate—then it removes the element of Quid Pro Quo and puts it in the context of justice-making as restoring community wholeness and peace.

216. Stone, *Compassionate Ministry*, 57.

217. Zehr, "Restoring Justice," 136.

218. Wolterstorff ("Contours of Justice," 110) says, "I think it is starkly clear that the passages which speak of God's love of justice are not pointing to God's delight over the misery of those who are justly punished; God has no such delight."

219. Volf, "Original Crime," 33.

them in the direction of restoring wholeness in their relationship with the sinned-against. Understanding this leads us to a fully-orbed understanding of the advocacy of God, both for the rehabilitation of the sinner and for the restoration of the sinned-against. A true restoration of *shalom* in the community.

When we think about how people are made in the *imago Dei* to enjoy *shalom*, we can say that we are most authentically human and alive when we have *shalom* in ourselves and in our relationships with others. Sin, then "[i]s what robs human dignity to the extent that it distorts and hinders the creative exercise of our freedom. Sin dehumanizes."[220] Sin is not simply about right and wrong. It is about the natural tendency to dehumanize others and to be dehumanized by the sin of others. When we sin, it dehumanizes us because we become numb to the pain we are causing to others. When we are sinned against, it dehumanizes us because we are robbed of the ability to form trusting relationships as readily as before. "Dehumanization, as Paulo Freire admits, 'marks not only those whose humanity has been stolen, but also (though in a different way) those who have stolen it.'"[221]

Gregory Jones points out that there are two sides to sin. Systemic sin, which is often socio-culturally determined, and particular acts of sin. So, while it is important to deal with the specific instances of sin that break relationship and wholeness, it is also important for us to recognize and "unlearn" systemic sin and "re-learn" the ways of God.[222] In Jones's understanding, systemic sin is the cycle of violence. "[I]t reflects the inescapable networks of violence and diminution that separate us from one another and, most determinatively, from God."[223] This systemic sin is portrayed as being like addiction, which is a helpful analogy in that it gets us thinking along the lines of redemption as rescue and rehabilitation. This is especially useful because it "[a]llows us to move from punitive to therapeutic strategies of intervention."[224] Instead of thinking only about "sin-punishment," we can move to thinking about how to best restore *shalom* to everyone involved.

This leads us to the idea of God's justice and what it is really all about. Rather than what the images of vengeance and retribution painted on the

---

220. Stone, *Compassionate Ministry*, 88.
221. Stone, *Compassionate Ministry*, 102.
222. Jones, *Embodying Forgiveness*, 230.
223. Jones, *Embodying Forgiveness*, 86.
224. Myers, "Beyond the Addicts Excuse," 90–91.

The Liberative Elements of Prosperity Theologies

walls of Medieval Churches might indicate, God's justice is good. God's justice is desirable. God's justice is about restoring both the sinner and the sinned-against to *shalom* and authentic human relationships again. It is about the restoration to wholeness of a person—in mind, body, spirit, and sociality. It is about breaking the cycle of violence and healing the rifts of particular sins.[225]

God is in the business of re-humanizing people and their relationships with one another. And God calls each of us to pursue this in ourselves and for others too. "God commands us to be lovers and practitioners of justice as He is—and pronounces judgment on those of us who are not . . . how could God actively love justice and be indifferent to whether you and I do justice?"[226] So the Church is called to be a Justice-making, Justice-loving community and to diligently work towards the recovery of *shalom* in the lives of both sinners and the sinned-against.

Bryan Stone describes this as a "liberation community" that is not afraid to confront the unrepentant and to be a place of safety for the broken-hearted to find healing. "Liberation is best understood as a freedom from some injustice or captivity . . . freedom from oppression . . . best understood as any power or force that prevents a person from becoming fully human and thus fully reflective of the image of God."[227] We are to join God in the kingdom work of liberating those who have been de-humanized and helping them to recover their dignity as people made in the *imago Dei*.

To become that place of safety for the broken-hearted, a theology for the sinned-against calls the church to better understand the phenomenon of victimization and the process by which people can overcome it. Traditionally, the church has simply challenged victims to put their victimization behind them. But Marie Fortune points out that "[t]o suggest that if we don't think of ourselves as victims then we won't be victimized is a rhetorical trick that does not work. We ultimately don't have any choice about being a victim. That is what a victim is: someone who is deprived of her/his resources."[228] Instead, what the victim needs is to know the God of solidarity and rescue. The God who captures every tear in a bottle. The God who rises in indignation to stand by the side of the victimized when injustices

---

225. Stone, *Compassionate Ministry*, 84.
226. Wolterstorff, "Contours of Justice," 108.
227. Stone, *Compassionate Ministry*, 102.
228. Fortune, "The Conundrum of Sin," 134.

happen in their lives. This is a God who is safe and trustworthy. This is the God who is a true Friend. This is a God who understands their suffering.

Victimization entails the profound sense of a loss of personal power.[229] Encountering people who continually try to minimize the trauma of that experience only serves to exacerbate that sense of the loss of power. What the victim needs is not to simply buck up and move on. Rather, the first step in restoring some sense of personal power for the deeply traumatized is often a sense of validation that their inner turmoil is both recognized and warranted. This is the beginning of the process of empowerment that is needed to bring lasting wholeness to victimized souls. The theology of the sinned-against eliminates the problem of the impossibility of the victim in traditional theology and thus restores the voice of the oppressed beyond the categories of class, race, and gender discrimination. In that sense, it is the broadest Liberation theology, and thus, the most accessible.

Prosperity Theologies as an Overcoming of Narratives of Victimization

In this final section, we will develop the link between Liberation theologies and Prosperity theologies directly. This will center on the ways Prosperity theologies help to cultivate "good power" and generosity in the lives of their adherents that are the core of how they empower people to overcome their internal narratives of victimization. This is why a nuanced understanding of Prosperity theologies is able to appreciate the Liberative elements it contains that have allowed it to resonate so strongly with the poor despite scholarly objections to its theological constructions.

Prosperity Theologies and the Cultivation of Good Power

One of the most insidious problems of victimization is that it robs people of the sense that they have any power to change the circumstances of their lives. Indeed, the victimized often feel that they are at the mercy of other powers dictating the course of their everyday existence. If the first step in breaking this learned helplessness is the recovery of a sense that their voice is being heard and their pain is being validated, the process of overcoming

---

229. Regarding the way victimization disempowers victims and undermines their sense of personal agency, see Bondi, *To Pray and to Love*, 82. Cf. Elshtain, *Democracy on Trial*, 50.

their victimization ends only when they begin to believe that they have recovered the power to be an agent of change in their own lives again. This is what we can call "good" power and it is key in understanding why the permission to pursue flourishing life expressed in Prosperity theologies is such a vital message of empowerment to the victimized.

In this analysis, the poor are those who have lost this "good" power, which has many ramifications on how they are able or unable to achieve many of the milestones of what might generally be viewed as a flourishing life. To imagine the daily reality of someone who has completely lost this sense of personal power paints a dehumanizing picture with little space for joy, hope, or even dignity. Think of a young woman struggling with crippling depression who cannot find any source of motivation within herself to change her circumstances. Or the young man who has been traumatized by an abusive father who has developed an instinctual reaction of fear towards any and all social attachments. From this vantage, one could say that some baseline degree of personal pride would seem to be necessary for a healthy self-image. Some baseline of personal power and ambition might be necessary for a healthy engagement with the world. Some baseline of selfishness might be necessary for genuinely mutual connections with others. In extremis, all of these dynamics (pride, selfishness, ambition) have been the favorite targets of pastors and theologians for centuries. But when we step into the shoes of the poor and disempowered, it is hard not to agree with James Cone that they need a recovery of pride and identity and ambition for a brighter tomorrow.

The loss of personal power, whatever the causes of it might be, speaks to Robert Cloninger's concept of self-directedness as one of the key measurements of a flourishing life.[230] If we recall that self-directedness measures an individual's ability to define, set, and pursue meaningful goals, it is clear that those who experience a loss of personal power also experience a severe degradation to their degree of self-directedness. The way Prosperity theologies restore a healthy self-directedness in its adherents is by placing a strong emphasis on empowering people to take responsibility for their lives and their attitudes at all times. In this regard, the commonly derided "declarations" play a major role in the process of renewing the minds of believers through exercising their faith in speaking truths about the character of God and about His good plans for their lives.

---

230. Cloninger et al., "A Psychobiological Model," 975–90.

While it might be true that in some corners of the Prosperity movement, these declarations devolve to a "name it and claim it" superficiality, I would suggest that maturing strands of this movement understand this practice more as a communal process of discipleship—a learning to believe that God genuinely desires for believers to experience flourishing present life and *shalom*, and a commitment to restoring a sense of good power and self-directedness in each believer. For those of us raised in evangelical settings where our "declarations" often began with something along the lines of "I am a sinner and when I admit this I can begin to be reconciled to God," the positive and optimistic declarations made in Prosperity churches can often be quite jarring. It would not be uncommon to hear the enthusiastic declaration, "I am powerful! The way He made me is amazing!" This, of course, triggers suspicions of rampant narcissism and entitlement, but when we pause to imagine what this declaration is doing in the life of someone who has felt powerless their whole adult life, we can begin to see why this sort of positive declaration can be so very life-giving, transformative, and even necessary.

The practice of making these declarations has particular value in helping believers to overcome various manifestations of shame that might have kept them from appropriating this "good power" for themselves. Often the declarations are targeted against specific lies that Christians might believe about not being good enough in the eyes of God; not being beautiful enough to be loved by others; not being successful enough to be respected by their peers; or not being sociable enough to merit deep friendships.[231] These are manifestations of victimization insofar as they correlate with a sense of powerlessness to change these dynamics in one's life. Prosperity theologies seek to empower people who experience these traumas and insecurities so that they come to believe that God wants for their flourishing even more than they do and that they can be the agents of change to alter the path of their careers and relationships. There is no sulking away in one's past miseries here. Instead, there is an infusion of hope for a better future and the conviction that the power to effect that hopeful future lies close at hand.

This is not to say that everyone in Prosperity churches is a victim of shame or that they lack a healthy sense of self-directedness. This messaging is relevant even to those who have a healthy outlook to help them retain that health. But it does demonstrate the commitment in Prosperity churches to

---

231. Brown, *Gifts of Imperfection*, 19.

develop a healthy self-directedness in believers and that is why it has had a liberative effect, especially on the poor. If we recall the studies by Yona Kifer et al. on some of the positive effects of power allowing people to act more consistently with their authentic selves and to experience a greater degree of subjective well-being, we can affirm that the "good power" in the Prosperity movement aims at just this sort of personal empowerment and re-dignifying efficacy.[232] The secret here is that this sort of power is not a zero-sum game where "good power" is a limited commodity that comes at the expense of someone else losing power. Instead, the more people in the community that gain and exercise "good power," the healthier the overall community will be. This is the kind of empowerment that the Prosperity movement seeks.

Martha Nussbaum's list of basic capabilities that are necessary for dignified human life gives us one more way to frame exactly what "good power" is meant to enable.[233] A flourishing human life should be empowered to make informed choices to promote physical and mental health. It should be free to harness its abilities and resources to pursue goals and relationships that it deems worthwhile. It should enjoy some measure of control over its own material and political environment. And it should be free to imagine and sow into a future that is more hopeful than today. I believe that the maturing stream of Prosperity theologies aims to enable just such a vision for flourishing life and that a healthy engagement between Prosperity theologies and the broader church can help to promote just such a trajectory.

Generosity and the Enabling of Vulnerability

Alongside the message of personal empowerment, it is important to point out that most Prosperity churches place just as strong of an emphasis on the practice of generosity as they do on empowerment. And again, while some Prosperity proponents can be challenged for tying a believer's breakthrough directly to their level of generosity, best practices within the movement lean more towards the affirmation that "we are blessed to be a blessing unto others." Indeed, generosity is one of the most effective tools that re-establishes a sense of "good power" in people as it is a tangible expression that one has power if one is able to give something to another.

---

232. Yona Kifer et al., "The Good Life," 280–88.
233. Nussbaum, *Creating Capabilities*, 32–33.

The Empowering God

I remember hearing the testimony of a Holocaust survivor who had struggled for decades with a withering sense of powerlessness stemming from her experiences of humiliation and degradation in a concentration camp. What finally broke the narrative of victimization in her own life was the moment she decided to express forgiveness to the guards, officers, and doctors who had tormented her family so callously. When she spoke the words of forgiveness over them, it suddenly dawned upon her that here she had a power that they could never hope to steal away. She had the power to give forgiveness . . . or to withhold it. It was no one else's power. It was all her own. And that was the empowering moment that set her free from feeling that she was a powerless victim once and for all.

It is fascinating to think of the act of granting forgiveness as something so profoundly empowering. Indeed, it highlights the connection between acts of generosity and the harnessing of "good power" in the life of the believer. This is why I think it is important to hear the Prosperity movement's emphasis on empowerment in lock-step with its commitment to generosity to get an accurate reflection of what it aims to cultivate. Clearly, this is not an invitation to mere consumerism. Rather, it is an invitation to a personal empowerment through the cultivation of practices of generosity in every area of life.

Generosity as a theme in Prosperity churches goes beyond simple financial charity. It extends to attitudes to cultivate towards other people and, importantly, also towards oneself. Generosity towards others involves being gracious towards their missteps and being committed to "finding the gold" hidden in the midst of their brokenness.[234] Such an attitude takes an eschatological approach towards relating to others by choosing to see their future mature selves as a greater reality than their present immaturities might reflect. Relating to them on the basis of that future vision has the effect of calling them towards their full potential—in short, believing in them perhaps even before they have believed fully in themselves.

The effect of this sort of interpersonal generosity is the cultivation of a culture within the community where everyone begins to assume the best of others rather than the worst. Where giving trust is the natural behavior rather than harboring suspicion. Where it becomes easier to believe that tomorrow will be better than today than to be overcome by despair. When the entire community begins to reflect this broad generosity, then the very

---

234. This is a reflection of what Silk (*Culture of Honor*, 160) calls the culture of honor.

The Liberative Elements of Prosperity Theologies

culture itself disciples newcomers into this new and empowering way of life.

Just as important as the emphasis on interpersonal generosity is the messaging on the need for intrapersonal generosity, or, generosity towards oneself. This is obviously not about granting oneself carte blanche for a life of indulgence. It is instead, as sociologist Brené Brown has indicated, about having the compassion to treat oneself graciously regarding one's imperfections.[235] Being generous towards ourselves regarding our imperfections is the very environment needed to promote real vulnerability and authenticity.[236] And real vulnerability and authenticity are, of course, the bedrock of healthy and life-giving relationships with others. Being generous towards ourselves, then, is precisely the form of self-love that can help us to quiet the storms of shame that sabotage healthy connections in our lives.

Good Power and Civic Transformation

The priority placed on generosity in Prosperity churches is also behind their growing engagement in civic life and service to the larger community. It is a simple matter of "finding the gold" in people beyond the community of faith and working to broadly support the flourishing of community life and services for everyone. One of the recent ways that some Prosperity churches have begun to approach this task is by curtailing the practice of positioning the church as a prophetic voice of critique in the community. Instead, these churches see their ministry more in the vein of blessing and encouraging the seeds of what the Lord is doing in the community. In this way, the ethic of generosity is extended to the church's service to those outside of its walls.[237]

---

235. Brown, *Daring Greatly*, 34.

236. Brown (*Daring Greatly*, 33–34) says, "Vulnerability is the birthplace of love, belonging, joy, courage, empathy, and creativity."

237. Bethel Church in Redding, California under the leadership of pastor Bill Johnson is doing this in their outreach to serve the civic institutions of the city—even renting insolvent government buildings to use for their ministries in order to help support the local government. Likewise, the ministry of Rev. T. D. Jakes has long been engaged in investing extensively into the surrounding community with business ventures and community services. And the ministry of E. A. Adeboye at the Redeemed Christian Church of God in Nigeria has long been famous for providing the social services that the government has not been able to provide.

The Empowering God

While this engagement approach is quite different from the political critiques offered by many of the Liberation theologies, I do believe that their ultimate aims are still aligned. I find it helpful here to compare this with the ways that Christian missions engages a country that is closed to much of the world and that has been known to perpetrate human rights abuses among its citizenry. In this case, believers who choose to speak out about the human rights abuses are providing an important service by bringing awareness to the abuses and advocating for the victims within the country. But those same activists will likely be black-listed from visiting and engaging with the populace of that country themselves as a result of that activism. Meanwhile, believers who choose the engagement approach would have to intentionally set aside their prophetic critiques in order to gain the favor necessary to live amongst and work with the people in that country. In return, they would be able to spearhead efforts to bring humanitarian aid into the country and could be "cultural ambassadors" to help transform the image of foreigners from within the country itself—one relationship at a time.

Rather than insist that one of these methodologies is better than the other, I think a broader perspective understands that both approaches are useful in their different ways. It also recognizes that those involved in the activism will likely be unable to participate in the engagement efforts, and those committed to the engagement efforts will likely not be able to fully embrace prophetic activism. If we consider that many of the Liberation theologies express the activism and prophetic critique dimension of this duality, then we can say that maturing branches of Prosperity theologies tend to take up the responsibility of pastoral engagement in the civic life of the community. Yet both of these dimensions are integral elements of the work of promoting social justice in the community, each in their own way. As such, I believe it is appropriate to suggest that there is a shared ethic of social justice between these two movements despite their differing approaches to the issues.

One notable exception to the prophetic critique approach of many Liberation theologies is the work of Elizabeth Johnson who approaches her feminism in a constructive and reconciliatory spirit. Rather than call for a replacement of the traditional patriarchal images used in the church, she seeks to expand the theological vocabulary to include matriarchal images alongside the patriarchal ones.[238] She funds this by tapping resources

---

238. Johnson, *She Who Is*, 100.

The Liberative Elements of Prosperity Theologies

from the work of early church fathers and expanding the utility of their work for contemporary theology. I think this approach captures well the engagement approach of Prosperity theologies which seek to promote the flourishing of the entire city by partnering with government entities and public businesses to enhance the services offered to the community. Prosperity theologies also take a constructive and cooperative approach to promoting social justice, though not necessarily with the goal of fostering political equality for all. Rather, the goal seems to be to foster empowerment for all so that people can take full advantage of the opportunities that exist all around them, whatever those opportunities might be. And while empowering people to take advantage of opportunities can and should lead to advocacy for political equality, this is not necessarily the focus of the Prosperity movement's civic engagement.

Good Power and the Character of God

One final way in which Prosperity theologies resonate with Liberation theology is in its underlying program to reform the prevailing understanding regarding the character of God and His activity in the world. For Liberation theologians, God is the God of liberation who is actively engaged in history to work towards the liberation of all peoples of the earth. This is a challenge to the images of the unmoved Mover of traditional theology and that view's purported complicity in maintaining an unjust status quo. The God of Liberation is a God who takes sides and clearly stands on the side of the poor against their oppressors.

The Prosperity movement also embraces this message of a God who is actively committed to the flourishing of His creation and the overcoming of narratives of victimization in the lives of believers.[239] This is, after all, one of the key convictions required to restore a sense of personal agency to believers who have found themselves entrapped in patterns of victimization and powerlessness. It is in this light that the common refrain, "God is good, all the time; All the time, God is good" can be embraced. I will explore the root metaphor of God that arises out of the Prosperity movement in more detail in chapter 6, where I will attempt to bring it into conversation with a *kenotic* view of God's mode of relationality and with the Hospitable God movement. For the purposes of this present chapter, it is enough to note

---

239. Charry ("Literature as Scripture," 65–99) suggests that victims can be imprisoned within their own narratives of victimization.

that both the Prosperity movement and Liberation theology advocate for a vision of an active God committed to the liberation/flourishing of His creatures and creation. This shared vision further corroborates my contention that Prosperity theologies contain strong liberative elements and can be seen as a Liberation theology arising from within the Pentecostal stream.

Conclusion

We began this chapter exploring Gustavo Gutierrez's call for concreteness in theology with an expanded view of salvation that includes the rehabilitation of the material aspects of life alongside the spiritual. This led to a recognition of the institutional aspects of sin and an acknowledgement of the preferential option for the poor throughout Scripture. James Cone helped to further develop this liberative theme by pointing out the ways that our theological traditions themselves were contextual and biased towards the maintenance of the status quo—a status quo which unequally benefitted those in positions of privilege and power. He exposed how difficult it could be for those enjoying that privilege and power to understand the methods the oppressed might use for their own liberation. And he showed how things such as the call to selfless love or the exhortation to embrace suffering could be used to entrap the oppressed in cycles of poverty and disadvantage. We learned with Cone and Johnson to see sin as that which obstructs wholeness and came to understand how repentance for the oppressed might look like finding their voice and recovering their sense of dignity and self-respect again. Through this journey, we gained an appreciation for otherness and a fresh understanding of God and His liberative activity in the world.

I have tried to draw parallels between these themes from Liberation theology and Prosperity theologies in the framework of a theology for the sinned-against. While there is no political motivation in the Prosperity movement to advocate for equality for some particular social group, Prosperity theologies do address the underlying issue of empowerment for people who, for one reason or another, have lost or given up their personal agency. This is why I find it aligns well with the broad mission of the theology of the sinned-against, which also has no political agenda and simply seeks to address the phenomenon of victimization itself. The Prosperity movement does not ask what qualifies someone to be considered "oppressed" and instead broadly empowers its adherents to exercise "good

The Liberative Elements of Prosperity Theologies

power" and generosity to promote practices that enhance flourishing in their lives and in their communities. And while political transformation is not one of the primary aims of Prosperity theologies, its robust civic and business engagement in local communities does result in some political impact, though measuring that impact might not be as straightforward as it might be with Liberation theology.

Admittedly, the presence of bad actors and alternative streams within the Prosperity movement weighs down on its potential appeal to other diverse segments of the Church. That is why one the aims of this chapter was to bring the themes of the Prosperity movement into dialogue with other reformative movements in contemporary theology to illustrate its potential for fruitfully advancing Christian practices promoting human flourishing. This, I believe, has particular utility in the immanent frame that Charles Taylor has described where the Christian witness needs to engage meaningfully with themes of ordinary human flourishing if it is to be given a serious hearing in the coming decades.

It should be said that in no way does the Prosperity movement offer a replacement for the various Liberation theologies that have proliferated over the years. Each of these Liberation theologies is giving a voice to a social class that is under-represented in theology and we all benefit from learning how to listen to their lessons. It is entirely possible for Prosperity churches to advocate heroically for "good power" and generosity among its members while being blind to racist, sexist, and classist biases in their midst. To me, this is all the more reason why it is important to bring Prosperity theologies into the rich theological dialogue taking place in contemporary theology. That way, its particular brand of liberative advocacy can benefit other segments of the church, and other segments of the church can enrich its awareness and sensitivity to issues of diversity in society. I hope this study encourages just such a respectful engagement.

In this chapter, I have attempted to illuminate the positive convergences between Liberation theologies and Prosperity theologies. In doing so, I have intended to show how Prosperity theologies harbor a vision for human flourishing that really has the potential to engage the contemporary discussion on ordinary human flourishing with invigorating hope. But this positive vision for flourishing only represents one half of the necessary discussion. Theologians today are also asking how we are to understand flourishing in the context of the ordinary progression of life. Surely expectations of flourishing should be different for an adolescent then they would be for someone who has lived a rich life and is near the age when they might soon pass away. And what of the case of people who live with disabilities? What kind of flourishing might Prosperity theologies offer to such as these? And finally, what do Prosperity theologies have to say in the absence of traditional modes of flourishing? I will turn to offer perspectives from and for Prosperity theologies on these important questions in the next chapter.

5

Challenges to Flourishing Conceived of as Health and Prosperity

Introduction

In the previous chapter, I made the argument that Prosperity theologies can be understood as promoting human flourishing in the context of holistic liberation and I took pains to draw connections between these liberative themes and the behavioral sciences. This was an attempt to portray Prosperity theologies as an affirmation of ordinary human flourishing in the immanent frame. However, there are two further dimensions of flourishing life to consider that sometimes do not get enough emphasis in Prosperity theologies. They are (1) flourishing in the natural course of life and its progression, and (2) understanding how to engage the absence of traditional modes of flourishing in life. In this chapter, I will describe these two perspectives and attempt to construct a response to them using resources from Prosperity theologies. My goal is twofold. First, I want to broaden the conversation around human flourishing in Prosperity circles to include challenges to flourishing conceived of as health and prosperity. And second, I want to show that the ethic of hunger for breakthroughs deriving from Prosperity theologies should be balanced with an ethic of contentment in limitations to address a wider range of human experiences. My goal is to propose a maturing of Prosperity theologies to hold the tension between hungering for breakthroughs and being content in limitations. This is an important corrective for views that value only one side of this tension and thus offer an unbalanced perspective. Furthermore, I am proposing a shift from viewing flourishing as health and prosperity to viewing flourishing as empowerment to wholeness as a further maturing of Prosperity theology themes in light of this tension.

Flourishing in Light of Disability and Chronic Illness

To start this chapter, we will think about disability and what it might reveal to us about the nature of humanity created as *Imago Dei*. Then, we will consider how Prosperity theologies have (or have not) handled the issues of disability and chronic illness.

Disability and the *Imago Dei*

While the pursuit of flourishing life expressed as health and prosperity might seem to be a clear good when seen from the perspective of liberation theology, there are some ways that an emphasis on health and prosperity can be problematic if it is not developed in a properly comprehensive perspective. For instance, when speaking of flourishing life, how does this relate to theological understandings of the *Imago Dei*? Are people who experience challenges in health and prosperity somehow falling short of the *Imago Dei*? Is being healthy and prosperous what it means to flourish as the *Imago Dei*? Where is the line between health and prosperity functioning liberatively and where they might become corrosive or even oppressive towards liberative values? These sorts of questions expose how much more careful thought is needed in Prosperity theologies to bring their insights into the broader dialogue on human flourishing.

One of the main challenges to a conception of flourishing that is framed in terms of health and prosperity comes from the important tradition of post-holocaust theology and its defense of the dignity of all human life in the face of the Nazi program to de-humanize people with physical disabilities, mental disabilities, and purported moral disabilities (the Jews, according to Nazi propaganda). The Nazis targeted people whom they viewed as less than ideal specimens of health and wellness and assigned to them a lesser dignity based on that assessment. Such a practice highlights the dangers of locating human dignity in some substantive property or faculty of human life like reason, morality, or spirituality, all of which can be

Challenges to Flourishing Conceived of as Health and Prosperity

seen as particular manifestations of health.[240] To say that human dignity is reflected in rationality leaves room to imagine that people who are less capable of that rationality are less than flourishing human specimens in some fundamental way. Likewise, identifying human dignity with morality or spirituality suggests that people who exhibit less moral or spiritual character could be said to be less flourishing than those who were more moral or more spiritual. This is the type of thinking that enabled the atrocities that were committed by the Nazis against these people with "disabilities."

Veli-Matti Kärkkäinen says that the basis for human dignity must be in our understanding of the *Imago Dei*. He says, "While Christian theology should give full support to human attempts to establish human dignity on 'natural grounds,' particularly as it is affirmed by the United Nations, it also has to highlight the necessary reference to God . . . "[241] That "reference to God" is found in the various interpretations of the *Imago Dei* that have been proposed historically. Early reflections on the nature of the human distinctiveness that was found in the *Imago Dei* linked flourishing human life and the *Imago Dei* to a substantive aspect of humanity—most commonly either the faculty of reason, morality, or spirituality. Thus, for theologians from Augustine to Aquinas, something like reason was the uniquely human trait that was related to the *Imago Dei* and a flourishing life was thought of as one marked by reason and high rationality in submission to God. But we have already seen the dangers of such a view in the events of the Holocaust mentioned above.

Rather than associate the *Imago Dei* with some substantive faculty of humanity, other biblical scholars identified the *Imago Dei* with something functional—such as the role given to humanity in the creation narratives to steward creation responsibly.[242] In this conception, people align well with the *Imago Dei* when they function properly as stewards of creation. This was based on historical parallels in ancient Near Eastern documents where a monarch was identified as the "image" of their deity and delegated authority to rule. But this formulation also fails to avoid the problem of some people being more capable of fulfilling this stewardship role than others due to factors of intelligence, personality, available resources, or any

240. Yong (*Theology and Down Syndrome*, 172) provides a brief summary of these three substantive views of the *Imago Dei* in developing his theological anthropology in the light of disability.

241. Kärkkäinen, *CCTPW*, 3:285.

242. This is more common amongst Biblical scholars such as Richard Middleton (*The Liberating Image*, 43–91) than it is amongst theologians.

number of other such variables. How would such a view treat a person who was completely incapable of contributing responsibly to the stewardship of creation and instead lay in constant need of care from others? Would such a person have value if flourishing human life was equated with the level of one's stewardship of creation? Wouldn't this lead to the same sort of moral problems that the substantive views of the *Imago Dei* encountered?

Around the time of the Reformation, theologians began to shift towards relational approaches to the *Imago Dei* that focused not on a substantive or functional view of the *Imago Dei*, but rather on humanity's relationality with God.[243] Thus, for Calvin the *Imago Dei* spoke of humanity as the "mirror of divinity," and Luther pointed out that reason and will were only important to bring us into relationship with God.[244] In the nineteenth century, these views shifted again towards a dynamic view of the *Imago Dei* that highlighted the orientation towards growth of humanity in relationship with God. So, Mary Ann Donovan points out that humanity has been created with the "[c]apacity for growth that enables them to respond to God's invitations and come to maturity."[245] Joel Green speaks of this in terms of covenant saying,

> God's words affirm the creation of the human family in its relation to himself, as his counterpart, so that the nature of humanity derives from the human family's relatedness to God. The concept of the *imago Dei*, then, is fundamentally relational, or covenantal, and takes as its ground and focus the graciousness of God's own covenantal relations with humanity and the rest of creation . . . [G]enesis does not define humanity in essentialist terms but in relational, as Yahweh's partner, and with emphasis on the communal, intersexual character of personhood, the quality of care the human family is to exercise with regard to creation as God's representative, the importance of the human modeling of the personal character of God, and the unassailable vocation of humans to reflect among themselves God's own character.[246]

Placing this dynamic view of the *Imago Dei* in the language of covenant highlights that this relationality between God and humanity is not determined by a person's ability to relate back to God, but rather, it is based

---

243. Yong, *Theology and Down Syndrome*, 174.

244. For a summary of the historical development of these views of the *Imago Dei*, see Kärkkäinen, *CCTPW*, 3:274–84.

245. Donovan, *Guide to Irenaeus*, 129.

246. Green, *Body, Soul, and Human Life*, 63, 65.

Challenges to Flourishing Conceived of as Health and Prosperity

on God's action to relate to the person and draw them towards eschatological destiny. This is the how a dynamic/relational view of the *Imago Dei* can ensure that all human beings are given the dignity of being created in the *Imago Dei*—even those who are minimally able to reciprocate. This is the best foundation for ensuring that people with disabilities, chronic illnesses, or any other perceived limitations to ideals of flourishing will be treated with proper respect, mutuality, and dignity.

Veli-Matti Kärkkäinen suggests that the main views of the *Imago Dei*—structural, functional, relational, and dynamic—are best thought of as complementary to one another rather than as competing alternatives. After all, elements of each view contribute to a fuller understanding of the dynamic view of relatedness to God by covenant relationship. The shape, then, of the eschatological call in that dynamic view of the *Imago Dei* is for humanity to behold the glory of God fully revealed in Christ and be conformed to the image of Christ day by day until they grow to reflect that likeness.[247]

Another dimension of the Christological focus on the *Imago Dei* is that it allows humanity to find a point of relatability in the humanity of Christ from which to begin the process of growing in Christlikeness. Yet, if we consider this from the perspective of people with disabilities, it is not immediately clear how the experience of disability can find resonance in the life of Christ. If the experience of disability is to be normalized, then it is important to connect the experience of people with disabilities with the experience of Christ in His life and ministry. This is precisely what Nancy L. Eisland attempts to do in her classic work in this field, *The Disabled God*. Eisland's proposal suggests three ways that disability can be located in Christology: (1) In Christ's identification with broken humanity "in every respect," (2) in the persistence of scars on Christ's post-resurrection body dispelling any notions of perfection as some unblemished ideal, and (3) in the inclusive practice of the Eucharist where Christ's body is broken for the unity of the Church.[248] These reflections are meant to show that the experience of disability is integral to a fully formed understanding of Christ.

---

247. Kärkkäinen, *CCTPW*, 3:284.

248. There are many who both engage and challenge Eisland's (*The Disabled God*, 90) thesis, but the dialogue that she initiated has been fruitful for theological studies exploring disability—especially in recognizing the need and value of formulating a positive identification between the disabled experience and Christ as the prototype of the *Imago Dei*.

It is easy to understand the appeal for this type of Christological approach to the *Imago Dei* if we consider that people, those with disabilities in this case, desire to recognize something in Christ that is relatable to their own life experience. If Christ is *Imago Dei* only in His unblemished perfection, then it is difficult to see how humanity can retain the *Imago Dei* in its fallen state. But if Christ as *Imago Dei* includes temptation and the experience of marginalization and brokenness, then that can help to affirm the dignity of those who experience the same in their lives. This brings to mind the stirring testimony of Joni Eareckson Tada who experienced paralysis from the neck down after a diving accident in her youth. As she lay emotionally devastated in the hospital room unable to move her arms and legs, she heard Christ whisper to her: "I know what it is like not to be able to move my arms. I know what it is like not to be able to move my feet." That experience liberated her from seeing her disability as a limitation and allowed her to begin to use it as an opportunity to bring inspiration to others. So, a Christological approach to the *Imago Dei* that is inclusive of the experience of disability can help to dignify the self-identity of people with disabilities.

While it is valuable for people with disabilities to see how Christ himself identifies with the experience of marginalization and brokenness, the broadest approach to normalizing the experience of people with disabilities is to highlight the marginalization common to all humanity. To this end, Amos Yong takes Eisland's initiative a step further by proposing a "liberation theology of the cross" to flesh out how the life, ministry, and death of Christ all reflect a value for the marginalized and broken—which stretches to include all of sinful humanity, not just people with disabilities.[249] In this sense, we are all "people with disabilities" in some fundamental way by sin, yet we are valued enough to warrant the redemptive activity of the Triune God on our behalf. As such, people with disabilities can take comfort in the fact that their experience of marginalization is not a mark of shame, but rather, it is an impetus for the redeeming work of God on the earth. Thus, a Christological account of marginalization advocates for the common dignity of all marginalized peoples—including people with disabilities in our society.

Beyond this, Amos Yong offers a comprehensive hermeneutic of disability to help normalize the experience of impairment in our reading of Scripture. Yong first points out that the normative perspective regarding

---

249. Yong, *Theology and Down Syndrome*, 178.

Challenges to Flourishing Conceived of as Health and Prosperity

people with disabilities or illnesses in the Bible is that they must always be healed.[250] But such perspectives can function to oppress people with disabilities by stigmatizing them and missing the ways that they can experience vibrant life in the midst of their disabilities. As a result, Yong says, "Jesus the healer becomes an enigma rather than a source of hope."[251] People with disabilities are encouraged to see themselves as broken and in need of rescue rather than being empowered to be *Imago Dei* in the midst of their disabilities. Even the vision of a disability-free eschaton can be oppressive to the self-identities of people with disabilities.[252]

In response, Yong takes pains to demonstrate that there are moments in Scripture where people are welcomed into the Kingdom of Heaven without needing to be healed of their "conditions" as a pre-requisite. For example, Zacchaeus who was designated as "short" by the biblical writers did not need to be healed of that condition to experience the Kingdom of God.[253] Neither did the Ethiopian eunuch need to be made whole in body before his spirit could be illumined with the truth of the gospel. So, there is some room to imagine that the body of someone whose self-identity is healthy and entwined with the experience of disability may retain that physical limitation in the eschaton.[254]

Disability and Health and Prosperity Theologies

The reason these reflections on the *Imago Dei* and disability are important for a discussion of Prosperity theologies and human flourishing is twofold: (1) because chronic disability is not often openly discussed in Prosperity theologies leaving a lacuna in its messaging, and (2) because the lack of a dialogue around disability can default to an implicit (or even explicit in some cases) de-valuing of the disabled condition in these communities. To help broaden the applicability of Prosperity theology to every circumstance in life, including in chronic disability, these expanded discussions should be encouraged.

---

250. Yong, *Bible, Disability, and the Church*, 55.
251. Yong, *Bible, Disability, and the Church*, 60.
252. Yong, *Bible, Disability, and the Church*, 118.
253. Yong, *Bible, Disability, and the Church*, 67.
254. Yong (*Bible, Disability, and the Church*, 121) suggests that some disabilities are identity-constitutive.

It is not surprising that Prosperity theologies do not often engage the subject of what flourishing might look like in the context of chronic disability. After all, their focus is on empowering people to pursue greater measures of health and prosperity in their lives. Taking the time to articulate what flourishing might entail in the midst of chronic disability could appear to undermine that primary messaging or even interfere with the sort of faith commitments needed to achieve breakthroughs in these areas by accepting disability as something permanent. However, the problem with not engaging disability more comprehensively is that it leaves Prosperity theologies without the resources necessary to avoid devaluing the lives of the disabled people in their midst. And as we have seen with the substantive and functional conceptions of the *Imago Dei* that allow this same sort of devaluing of marginalized people, this can have dangerous moral implications for these communities in neglecting to protect the dignity and value of people with disabilities in society. At the very least, this can lead to unintentionally enabling societal elements that degrade the self-worth of those with disabilities. At the worst, this can lead to outright discrimination and injustice.

How might Prosperity theologies be complicit in devaluing the disabled? When flourishing is equated too closely with health and prosperity, it can lead to the marginalization of people who are not able to attain certain minimal levels of health and prosperity.[255] This is, of course, precisely the problem with the substantive and functional approaches to the *Imago Dei* where certain minimal standards of rationality or of competence in stewardship are used as the measure of flourishing life. In the absence of a developed theology of the *Imago Dei*, it is all too easy to default to these types of limited views of flourishing. Consequently, adding reflections on a dynamic/relational and Christological approach to the *Imago Dei* would be a positive development for a maturing Prosperity theology that is mindful of the life circumstances of the disabled.

Reflecting on the dynamic/relational conceptions of the *Imago Dei* can help to re-establish value for all who might be marginalized in Prosperity theologies because it focuses on the fact that God acts to draw each person into relationship with Himself instead of on measuring their flourishing according to some idealized standard of health or prosperity.[256] Any such

---

255. Kärkkäinen (*CCTPW*, 4:384) says, "Having been created in God's image, human personhood does not admit degrees."

256. This also aligns with the insights of Amartya Sen and his capabilities approach

Challenges to Flourishing Conceived of as Health and Prosperity

idealized standard of health or prosperity is bound to reflect some cultural bias and may even simply be a reflection of a particular theologian's own values and prejudices. This is highlighted when we remember the anthropological insights of Adam B. Cohen and Kathryn A. Johnson who found that ideas of well-being were often tied closely to a researcher's own personal values and cultural inputs.[257] Recognizing this perspectivalism doesn't mean that all formulations of well-being are suspect, but rather it means that many alternative formulations of well-being can be supported. Thus, a Prosperity theology framed with people with disabilities in mind can lead to a different conception of what a flourishing life can be and should be recognized as a valid context in which to imagine well-being.[258]

Framing Prosperity theology with people with disabilities in mind is further supported by the Christological reflections on the *Imago Dei* that identify the experience of marginalization as significant to the identity of Christ. This insight helps to normalize the experience of marginalization so that a view of flourishing that includes chronic disability can be affirmed as mentioned above. So, flourishing for people with mental disabilities might not look like the attainment of a higher IQ level. Rather, it might consist of enjoying and investing in the relationships one has been blessed with in life. Likewise, flourishing for those with physical disabilities might not be the recovery of a fully functioning body once again. Rather, it might look like coming to terms with limitations in one's body and not letting this prevent one's pursuit of dreams and ambitions in life.

Both of these examples can be aligned with Prosperity theology if we remember the liberative themes at its core. Prosperity, as we have seen in chapter 4, is about empowerment more than it is about physical health or material wealth. Health and wealth happen to be concrete ways that empowerment occurs for the poor who have been trapped in generational cycles of poverty, but Prosperity more broadly conceived is about a mode

---

to economic justice in his book, *Commodities and Capabilities*. Sen resisted the call to articulate universal basic capabilities because he was keen on preserving the fact that different people valued different capabilities.

257. Cohen and Johnson ("Religion and Well-Being," 14) remark that, "[M]easurements of individual happiness, life satisfaction, and subjective well-being may actually reflect the scientist's own values, cultural inputs, and religious views."

258. I have pointed to just such an approach in Amos Yong's (*The Bible, Disability, and the Church*, 55) hermeneutic of disability. In his book, *Crippled Grace*, Shane Clifton has also recently argued forcefully for this combining disabilities studies with virtue ethics to imagine what it means to flourish in the midst of disability.

of relating to God, oneself, others, and the world. It is about overcoming victim-narratives in every form that they occur in our lives and recovering that sense of "good power" where personal agency is affirmed and responsible living is cultivated. This can be done in many contexts of life and in the midst of many so-called limitations to mental or bodily health. Accordingly, I believe that the relational and Christological insights regarding the *Imago Dei* correspond well with a broadened view of flourishing conceived of as empowerment. Maturing Prosperity theologies would do well to bring greater emphasis to this correspondence by framing flourishing more consistently in the language of empowerment and by adopting a robust relational and Christological approach to the *Imago Dei*. This would be a positive step towards a Prosperity theology that is informed by the experience of disability.

Blind Spots in Prosperity Theology's Overcoming of Victimization Narratives

While the empowering form of Liberation of the Prosperity Movement's drive to overcome victimization is compelling in many regards, it does have some blind spots that should be addressed in any holistic view of human flourishing. Two that are addressed here include the commonly noted ambivalence of many Prosperity churches to issues of systemic societal victimization and the inherent insensitivity to the process of mourning and grieving that can arise in these environments.

Regarding the blind spot to legitimate societal victimizations: Considering the liberative themes at the core of Prosperity theologies begs the question of why these groups have not been at the forefront of championing other liberation theologies and social justice issues in society.[259] While this is certainly a complex matter with cultural and demographic issues at play, I do believe that one common factor may be in the Prosperity message of empowerment itself. My suspicion is that the rejection of victim-narratives creates a blind spot where legitimate societal victimization can be minimized along with the minimizing/overcoming of one's own victimizations.

---

259. This is a common critique (warranted or not) of Prosperity theologies in writings that have critically engaged their theological stances. They are often seen as an affirmation of rampant capitalism and greed with little to say to the social justice issues of the day. But this view has been challenged by Yong and Attanasi (*Pentecostalism and Prosperity*, 7).

After all, what room would there be to affirm societal victimization when the underlying message has consistently been to set aside any and all victimizations?

An example of just such a blind spot occurred in a Prosperity theology community in a predominately white middle-class area that did not understand the significance of a movement such as "Black Lives Matter."[260] Many prominent voices in this faith-community spoke out against the BLM movement and in support of police without having taken the time to listen and understand why these protests were taking place. While this is likely primarily a cultural/demographic issue since the lack of diversity in the area did not provide these leaders any window into the lived reality of the Black experience with law enforcement, that still did not excuse the lack of empathy and desire to seek understanding expressed here. In their responses to the BLM movement it was clear that the culture of rejecting victimizations in the faith community played a role in their inability to accept that the systemic victimization experienced by Black people might be of a different sort than the garden variety injustices people experience in their daily lives.

If the Prosperity message of empowerment contributed to allowing these leaders to dismiss the experience of systemic victimization here, then Prosperity theologies should learn from the marginalized in their midst to discern the difference between systemic and individualized forms of victimization.[261] And even in cases where the victimization can appear to be more individualized—such as in the "#metoo" movement calling attention to victims of sexual harassment (which is really also another subtle systemic problem)—Prosperity theologies need to be careful not to let the minimization of victimizations become a legitimation of victim-shaming, or, of blaming the victim for attracting the inappropriate behavior of men in positions of power rather than rebuking the harassing behavior itself.

---

260. In response to the BLM movement, many such communities proposed an "All Lives Matter" counter-movement to support the work of law enforcement. But such a response misses the point, articulated by a BLM activist, that in order for all lives to matter black lives need to matter as they were the ones most prominently under siege. This was not meant to minimize the lives of law enforcement officials in any way. Rather, it was meant to be heard as a call for genuine respect and mutuality for the black community to be treated equally by the law enforcement culture in America.

261. By individualized forms of victimization, I mean those forms of victimization that do not rise to the level of systemic abuses. For instance, overcoming a sense of victimization because Sally was not fair to you is different from victimization in the form of Jim Crow laws and racial discrimination.

Indeed, this same ministry referenced above often lectured women about dressing in a way that attracted unsavory men and then placed the blame for the consequences on the women, counseling them to take responsibility and be mindful of what they were "advertising." These types of examples represent a profoundly disempowering silencing of the victim and actually work to undermine the message of empowerment that Prosperity theologies seek to champion. Setting aside all victimizations can short-circuit the empowerment process if it is not done with sensitivity to the marginalized—especially in the case of systemic victimizations. Prosperity theologies should actively seek to cultivate this sensitivity in order to mature their message of empowerment to a broader and more diverse audience.

Regarding the blind spot to the legitimate processes of mourning and grieving: Another potential blind spot in Prosperity theologies can occur with regard to failing to understand the process that is required for people to properly mourn and grieve the losses that accompany victimization. This would be a failure to appreciate the nuances of a theology for the sinned-against. While the overall program of Prosperity theologies to help people overcome their personal victimization narratives is highly relevant and important, it is possible that too quick a rush to escape victimizations could short-circuit the healing process in unhealthy ways. Sometimes the process of overcoming victimization requires a season of mourning and grief. Sometimes it will involve permission to express anger at injustices that have been suffered. Coming to terms with loss is complicated by the fact that the loss often hits us in successive waves—or as another might say, we experience loss in pieces. There simply are times when walking out the front door with our most optimistic stance towards life is an act that undermines our real flourishing instead of promotes it. Prosperity theologies need to incorporate this sensitivity more intentionally as well.

In helping friends deal with deep personal loss in their lives, and in processing my own, I have often found Nicholas Wolterstorff's own journalistic account of dealing with the loss of his own son to offer the most effective comfort.[262] He details good days when the loss doesn't haunt him quite so much, and bad days when the pain is debilitating. Eventually, he meanders his way to the cross where he experiences more deeply than ever the Father God who knows what it is to lose His own Son. And though scars remain—deep scars—he is brought back to a place where he is ready to engage the world once again. Creating a space within the program of

---

262. See Wolterstorff's deeply personal reflections in *Lament for a Son*.

empowerment to affirm healthy grief and mourning is another task that Prosperity theologies would do well to embrace.

ORDINARY HUMAN FLOURISHING AND PROSPERITY THEOLOGIES

Having considered the way that dynamic/relational and Christological perspectives of the *Imago Dei* in conversation with perspectives from chronic disability help to broaden the scope of what flourishing can be and having considered what blind-spots might exist in Prosperity theologies, it is useful to also consider what contributions views of ordinary human flourishing can make to maturing Prosperity theologies. Ordinary human flourishing has to do with life lived in its normal everyday context and mindful of the natural progression of life through its stages from birth to adulthood and ultimately to death. What might flourishing look like apart from overarching meaning quests and goals that lie beyond the scope of this life? Are the goals of flourishing different in the different stages of life? Does a focus on ordinary human flourishing include some measure of health and prosperity? And if so, in what capacity? I hope to expand our discussion of challenges to viewing flourishing as health and prosperity by constructively incorporating the insights of these reflections towards a maturing Prosperity theology.

David Kelsey on the Value of the Quotidian

David Kelsey understands the difficulty and importance of the task to clarify a fundamentally immanent view of flourishing better than most. In light of the late modern suspicion that Christian faith seems to undermine this-worldly expressions of flourishing, Kelsey seeks to show that faith is integral to flourishing even from the perspective of earthly life.[263] Thus,

---

263. Kelsey ("On Human Flourishing," 1) says, "Christian theology has a large stake in making it clear that its affirmations about God and God's ways of relating to human beings underwrite human beings' flourishing. It has been especially important to emphasize this claim in the context of 'late modernity,' in which Friedrich Nietzsche is often cited as the most powerful spokesman for a widespread and deep suspicion that Christians magnify God and God's power and dominion by systematically minimizing human beings, making them small, weak, and servile—anything but flourishing... The challenge to Christian theology has been to develop conceptual and argumentative strategies by which to show that, properly understood, human flourishing is inseparable from

to ground a robustly immanent approach to theological anthropology, Kelsey explores alternative theological resources in Scripture beyond what has traditionally been used to fund a theology of creation. In contrast to theologians who base their creation theologies on the creation narratives in Genesis themselves, Kelsey examines the wisdom literature to extrapolate a creation theology that is firmly grounded in the lived context of everyday life. That everyday lived context is what Kelsey refers to as the quotidian, and it represents a challenge to views of creation that are grounded in anything but everyday finite reality. Thus, for Kelsey, "The quotidian is not denigrated. Its dignity lies, not in the fact that it inherently refers beyond itself to transcendent reality, nor in its having an ontological depth more meaningful than itself, but simply in being just what God creates in all its everydayness."[264]

The reason that Kelsey chooses the wisdom literature for his creation theology instead of the creation narratives is that he believes the creation narratives are written with a deliverance framework in mind and that this can distort their usefulness for a theological anthropology. In contrast, the wisdom literature is written "[r]esolutely within the framework of a theology of creation" and provides a more neutral account of humanity in creation.[265] Accordingly, a wisdom-based account of creation theology (1) lacks an account of cosmic origin, (2) does not talk about a fall from grace, (3) does not privilege an unseen spiritual reality over the physical reality, (4) does not emphasize eschatological hope over the present, (5) and does not focus on a teleological meaning to creation beyond simple concrete everydayness.[266] Each of these issues has historically been used to minimize the quotidian in some way. Instead, a wisdom-based account draws full attention to the reality of everyday life lived in vital relationship with God and works to resist any attempt to place meaning outside of this immanent context.

The significance of this focus on the quotidian is that it challenges conceptions of human flourishing that center on overarching meaning

---

God's active relating to human creatures such that their flourishing is always dependent upon God."

264. Kelsey, *EE*, 1:191.

265. Kelsey (*EE*, 1:189) says the wisdom literature is "[n]ot bent to the narrative of deliverance in Scripture." Whether or not we agree with this assessment, Kelsey's valuing of the quotidian is a useful recovery for thinking about human flourishing.

266. Kelsey, *EE*, 1:190–91.

Challenges to Flourishing Conceived of as Health and Prosperity

quests or meta-narratives.[267] "In this [wisdom-based] creation theology, God's relating to us as Creator gives us no theologically superior goal for our projects beyond the well-being of the quotidian."[268] Thus, having a successful career, achieving a certain level of self-actualization, or living "a life worth living" are all projects whose value is minimized in the framework of the quotidian. Kelsey points to the writer of Ecclesiastes where, "He regularly concludes with a recommendation that we focus our lives on the particularities of the everyday world, engaging in short-term projects whose goals are nothing more than our well-being in the practices that make up the well-being of the everyday world."[269] Thus, what does gives meaning to life is being related to God in the quotidian things like finding enjoyment in one's work, savoring the beauty and bounty of nature, and cherishing relationships. Indeed, Kelsey's view recalls the lessons of Brother Lawrence who practiced being mindful of the presence of God in the midst of his duties at the monastery washing the dishes and tending to the gardens.[270] Rather than find such chores mundane and beneath more noble "spiritual" pursuits, he found that doing them in relationship with God made them valuable experiences themselves. A focus on the quotidian would seem to have these same dynamics.

One of the reasons that Kelsey wants to minimize the role of large meta-projects as a source of meaning in life is that they do not typically deal with death as a natural part of everyday life. That means that from the perspective of these meta-projects, death is seen as ultimately undermining them and the sense of meaning that they impart to life. In contrast, a focus on the quotidian as the ground of a meaningful life affirms the role of death as a natural part of life. Kelsey calls this "dying life" in recognition of the fact that all of life is in the process of dying as a part of the natural progression of life in the quotidian.[271] Veli-Matti Kärkkäinen agrees, warning of

---

267. Kelsey (*EE*, 1:322) suggests that "[B]iblical wisdom's background creation theology undercuts all such totalizing views of history and their anthropological implications."

268. Kelsey, *EE*, 1:321. Likewise, Kelsey (*EE*, 1:324) says, "Personal bodies have a vocation in celebration of the quotidian for its own sake and not for the sake of any further goal."

269. Kelsey, *EE*, 1:326.

270. See Brother Lawrence's classic book, *The Practice of the Presence of God*.

271. Kelsey (*EE*, 1:327) says, "If life were made meaningful only by the actualization of some life-unifying project, even that of self-actualization, then death will inevitably undercut that meaning. In the context of this creation theology, death has its proper role in the quotidian. It is not inherently evil."

The Empowering God

the idolatry of everlasting health, fitness, beauty, and economic security in the modern worldview and reminding us that flourishing looks different in each season of life and there comes a time when flourishing looks like dying and diminishing well.[272] He says, "If life in the quotidian is the 'good' life, that means life in all its experiences, both in health and sickness can be a flourishing life."[273] Likewise Jürgen Moltmann says, "Only what can stand up to both health *and* sickness, and ultimately to living *and* dying, can count as a valid definition of what it means to be human."[274]

So, what is the standard of flourishing in the quotidian? Kelsey distinguishes between well-being, which he defines as a functional and self-referential notion that can be answered bio-psycho-socially, and flourishing, which he defines theo-centrically in terms of "[r]esponding appropriately to the triune God who has already related creatively to us."[275] Regarding the former, Kelsey says that wisdom literature clearly affirms that health is better than unhealth and that prosperity is better than impoverishment.[276] Thus, from a wisdom point of view, a case can be made for the benefits of practices and ideologies that promote better health and prosperity in the quotidian. But Kelsey understands flourishing to be distinct from health and prosperity in some fundamental way. Flourishing, conceived theo-centrically, is about displaying the glory of God.[277] This happens in two distinct modalities. First, humans are the glory of God by being living bodies in relationship with God. This can be as simple as affirming the intricate complexity of human physiology as an "impressive observable" of the glory of God.[278] Healthy or sick, every human being reflects this intricacy,

---

272. Kärkkäinen (*CCTPW*, 3:427) sees a focus on the quotidian to be a critique of the values of consumer society's ideals of "lasting fitness and beauty, economic security, and everlasting health."

273. Kärkkäinen, *Creation and Humanity*, 427.

274. Moltmann, *God in Creation*, 273.

275. Kelsey, *EE*, 1:328.

276. Kelsey (*EE*, 1:318) says, "Of course, a healthy human living body is preferable to an unhealthy one. For that matter, for any personal body, thriving in the sense of prospering is preferable to being impoverished . . . Wisdom literature cuts against any theological tendency to play down the importance of healthy and prosperous life."

277. Kelsey (*EE*, 1:317) points out that "Flourishing human bodies are not the glory of God because they are healthily flourishing; theologically speaking, they are deemed flourishing to the extent that even in extreme unhealth they are nonetheless in some mode (derivatively) the glory of God."

278. Kelsey (*EE*, 1:317) concludes that "Given that flourishing personal bodies are living bodies with a remarkably rich and complex array of types of powers, they are the

though each person reflects a different modality of it according to their capabilities.²⁷⁹ Second, humans are the glory of God "[t]o the extent that they take charge of themselves wisely for their own well-being and that of their proximate contexts."²⁸⁰

Kelsey believes that there are three dimensions to a wise human response to God that reflects responses to God's actions to create, to draw us to eschatological consummation, and to reconcile. Appropriate response to God's action to create is to express faith in God as the ground of our being and value.²⁸¹ This means locating our source of meaning, security, and significance in relationship with God rather than in anything else found in the world. Appropriate response to God's action to draw us to eschatological consummation is to engage in the cause of hope-filled liberation to counter unjust oppressions in our concrete contexts and more broadly in larger society.²⁸² And appropriate response to God's action to reconcile us is to be responsive in love back to God and in practical care for our neighbors.²⁸³ These three dimensions represent the "wise" responsive living in the quotidian that Kelsey claims best reflects the glory of God through our lives.

Wise Living in the Quotidian and the Ethic of Contentment

There are many resonances in Kelsey's proposals on understanding flourishing in terms of reflecting the glory of God and our previous discussion of the varying conceptions of the *Imago Dei*. For instance, to say that each person reflects a unique and intricate modality of the glory of God (in accordance with their capabilities) is to take a relational stance on a structural

---

glory of God in their own distinctive modes simply as living bodies creatively related to by God . . . If nothing else, the complex physiology of living human beings, as construed within their proximate and ultimate contexts, is in itself an 'impressive observable' expressive of God's glory."

279. Kelsey (*EE*, 1:318) says, "So long as they do physically live in virtue of God self-expressively relating to them, those suffering extreme unhealthy also are in their own ways the glory of God. The index of their flourishing as God's glory is not any sort of health, but simply the fact that God's creative relating to them is inherently self-expressive of God's own glory. In all the ambiguity of their dying lives, as God's creatures they express God's glory."

280. Kelsey, *EE*, 1:319.

281. Kelsey, "On Human Flourishing," 23–25.

282. Kelsey, "On Human Flourishing," 31.

283. Kelsey, "On Human Flourishing," 37.

conception of the *Imago Dei*. And while Kelsey's suggestion that we reflect the glory of God through wise action for the quotidian in our lived contexts is a functional take on the *Imago Dei*, when it is combined with his structural/relational reflections, his overall proposal is meant to affirm the equal dignity of every person regardless of levels of health, ability in stewardship or any other capabilities. So, Kelsey affirms our earlier conclusions regarding the importance of a dynamic/relational approach to the *Imago Dei* in order to counter any sense that people with disabilities or who are chronically ill are anything less than fully reflective of the *Imago Dei*.

What Kelsey adds to this discussion is a focus on the value of the quotidian for our understanding of a flourishing life. Embracing the quotidian teaches us to appreciate the natural progression of life through the various stages of health, sickness, and even the processes of dying. While other conceptions of flourishing might give in to an implicit denial of the role of death in the cycle of life, a value for the quotidian recognizes that death is a natural part of life and that there is such a thing as flourishing in the midst of the process of dying. Recognizing the quotidian also affirms the value of wise living towards a healthy and prosperous life in its everyday lived context while challenging the need for meta-projects to impart greater meaning to life beyond that found in the quotidian. Prosperity theologies could benefit from following Kelsey's lead in adopting elements of a creation theology that derives from the wisdom literature to fund their embrace of healthy and prosperous lifestyles.

At the heart of both the dynamic/relational approach to the *Imago Dei* in light of disability and the value for the quotidian in the wisdom literature is an underlying ethic of contentment that embraces one's present circumstances and limitations by affirming the dignity of disability and the significance of the quotidian. So, flourishing with disability is a matter of embracing the dignity of a life lived with disability. Flourishing in the twilight years of life means coming to terms with impending death and engaging the process of dying well. And flourishing in the quotidian means learning to be appreciative of the simple processes of daily life. These lessons are so valuable for a modern consumerist society that is programmed into discontent through advertising and impossible standards of health, beauty, and prosperity. They also offer a necessary counter-voice to Prosperity theologies that uncritically adopt these consumerist societal values without qualification. In this regard, an ethic of contentment can be seen as a vital part of any conception of a flourishing life.

Challenges to Flourishing Conceived of as Health and Prosperity

But one question that lingers regarding an ethic of contentment comes from our engagement with Liberation theology where James Cone taught us that to support the status quo was to fund the continued oppression of disempowered groups in society.[284] Does an ethic of contentment contain an inherent affirmation of the status quo? Does it leave societal oppressions unchallenged in the name of a heightened personal spirituality? If so, then an ethic of contentment alone is not enough. Kelsey seems to be aware of this potential lacuna in his proposal and attempts to address it with a call to hope-filled engagement with the cause of liberation.[285] However, it is not clear how this aligns with his focus on the quotidian and aversion for meta-projects in life. Isn't the work of liberation in many ways a disruption of the quotidian? Is there a greater meta-project in life than to participate in the process of the eschatological consummation of the Kingdom of God?

Still, Kelsey's contribution to an understanding of flourishing that is inclusive of the quotidian is an important perspective that Prosperity theologies should engage for their own enrichment. In the next section, I will turn to an exploration of what Prosperity theologies might contribute to these discussions on dealing with limitations to the ideals of flourishing and propose a blending of these contributions with perspectives on the *Imago Dei*, disability, and the quotidian to help articulate a mature Prosperity theology that is informed by both dimensions of this discussion.

PROSPERITY THEOLOGY IN LIGHT OF DISABILITY AND THE QUOTIDIAN

Having reflected on the challenges Prosperity theologies face in deepening their reflections on the issues of disability and chronic illness as well as the natural processes of grieving, aging, and death, this section considers how Prosperity theologies might better balance their hunger for breakthroughs with the need for contentment and peace. My suggestion is that these two ethics can both be held under a single ethic of empowerment.

---

284. See the preface to the 1986 reprinting of Cone's (*Black Theology of Liberation*, xviii) classic work.

285. See Kelsey's ("On Human Flourishing," 31) remarks on a response of hope to God's action to draw us to eschatological consummation.

The Empowering God

Prosperity Theologies and the Ethic of Hunger

When faced with the traditional challenges to flourishing represented by sickness, disability, cycles of poverty, and death, Prosperity theologies have typically taken a stand seeking to inspire people to pursue healing and establish practices that lead to prosperity in their lives. Indeed, one of the reasons for the widespread appeal of Prosperity theologies for the poor and suffering is that they continue to offer a message of tangible hope in the concrete circumstances that people face even when medicine and society fail them. In many ways, this can be understood to be in contrast to an ethic of contentment that focuses on helping people come to terms with limitations in their lives and learn to thrive in the midst of them. Prosperity theologies instead seek to cultivate an ethic of hunger that encourages people to contend for breakthroughs in their circumstances and refuses to accept a sense of finality in those circumstances, no matter how challenging or enduring they may be.

While we will explore whether such a strong emphasis on contending for breakthroughs is ultimately a healthy stance towards all scenarios later in this section, I want to first recognize the ways that this ethic of hunger has been valuable in challenging some perspectives that have undermined this-worldly views of flourishing in contemporary theology. We have already considered the ways that Prosperity theologies have a liberative dimension in how they empower people to greater measures of personal agency in chapter 4. Here I want to expand on how this manifests in specific challenges to some commonly held beliefs and values.

First, the ethic of hunger works against any tendency towards fatalism in the life of a believer. Whatever one's beliefs about the interactions between the sovereignty of God and the freedom of the will, most would reject any fatalistic conclusions about how believers should then live their lives. Fatalistic approaches to life give in to the inertia of circumstances based on a belief that if God wants something to happen, it will happen with or without our active participation. In contrast, an ethic of hunger encourages a deepened sense of responsibility in believers that challenges them to actively participate in establishing the blessings of Kingdom life and values in their communities. So, for example, rather than wait for God to do something about the divisive political climate in our country, believers would accept the responsibility to create an atmosphere of respect in their communities where dialogue and reconciliation could occur.

Challenges to Flourishing Conceived of as Health and Prosperity

Second, related to the above, the ethic of hunger works against any tendency to settle for the status quo in a believer's personal life as well as in the broader society. We have already established how the status quo often functions to uphold oppressive patterns in society that keep disadvantaged groups from flourishing. In an individual's personal life this status quo can take the form of inherited cycles of poverty, disempowering habits in social settings, or mental illnesses such as depression or emotional trauma. The ethic of hunger funds an internal motivation to overcome personal limiting factors as well as those in society. This is what fuels the setting aside of victimization narratives in one's personal life and affirms the right of every person to pursue a flourishing life. It reflects the vision of Irenaeus that "[h]uman beings fully alive are the glory of God" and raises questions for views that imagine that a limited and tightly controlled humanity is a flourishing humanity.[286]

Third, the ethic of hunger offers an important counter-perspective to the idea that sickness is ordained by God for the purpose of spiritually disciplining/benefitting the infirm. While anything that is brought before the Lord can certainly be transformed into a blessing by His grace, one of the drawbacks of believing that God ordains sickness for disciplinary purposes is that it suggests that seeking healing from infirmity could be an act of rebellion against the will of God. In contrast, the ethic of hunger encourages believers to vigorously pursue healing and wholeness over against any tendency to settle into a life identified by their sickness. The energy for this pursuit comes from the belief that sickness does not align with the promised realities of the eschatological kingdom of God. This gives believers an enhanced sense of confidence in their intercessions that as more of the Kingdom of God is made manifest on the earth, less sickness and infirmity will persist in people's lives.[287]

Fourth, the ethic of hunger can add diverse perspectives to the idea that self-sacrifice, suffering, and an ascetic lifestyle are the primary standard of a godly life. Throughout the history of the church, there have been many saints who have sacrificed, suffered, and set themselves apart from

---

286. Irenaeus, *Haer.* 4.34.5–7.

287. This is not meant to indicate an over-realized eschatology, but simply to reflect an optimistic expression of just how much of the Kingdom of God can be realized in this era. Prosperity theologies certainly err on the side of optimism in this regard. I am also sensitive to the fact that people with disabilities sometimes do not want to be seen as "handicapped" in any meaningful way. So, the obsessive desire for healing does not always apply to everyone whose lives might be limited in some way.

the world through ascetic pursuits who have lived exemplary lives and are rightly celebrated for their devotion. That devotion can even be considered an expression of an ethic of hunger for more awareness of the presence of God. But the Prosperity theology ethic of hunger centers around the manifestation of the kingdom of God upon the earth and the establishment of *shalom* throughout His creation. That *shalom* suggests that generosity, empathy, and consecrated work can also be a standard for a godly lifestyle that reflects kingdom flourishing and promotes *shalom* for all. Generosity is the "other-oriented" expression of sacrifice; empathy is the "other-oriented" expression of suffering; and consecrated work is the "other-oriented" expression of a set-apart lifestyle.[288]

The glamorization of the spiritual benefits of sickness, poverty and suffering represents one of the most significant theo-cultural resistances to the Prosperity theology focus on flourishing life.[289] But as I discussed in reflecting on ascetic views of flourishing in chapter 3, the immanent frame of modern society questions how faith in God can function for human flourishing in the concrete contexts of everyday lived life. In this context—where these ascetic values often fail to resonate—Prosperity theologies and their commitment to *shalom* can offer a fresh witness that embraces held-in-common ideas of well-being and flourishing life.

These few points are representative of the kinds of insights an ethic of hunger can contribute to support this-worldly views of flourishing in theology and spirituality. Taken together with the liberative dimensions of Prosperity theologies and their convergence with bio-psycho-social themes of human flourishing in contemporary behavioral science developed in chapter four, I believe Prosperity theologies already offer a viable and valuable contribution to contemporary theological reflection on human flourishing in the immanent frame. However, in light of the challenges to flourishing seen as health and prosperity discussed in the earlier sections of this chapter, I want to propose a way for Prosperity theologies to develop in a way that can incorporate these perspectives as well. The last section of this chapter will explore a proposal for what shape a maturing Prosperity theology might take that incorporates insights from both the ethic of contentment and the ethic of hunger.

---

288. I will develop the theological basis for the "other-oriented" dynamic of a spirituality grounded in *Imitatio Christi* in chapter 7 in a theology of abundance and overflow.

289. I use "theo-cultural" here to indicate cultural values that derive from theological stances and beliefs.

Challenges to Flourishing Conceived of as Health and Prosperity

The Balance of Contentment and Hunger in a Maturing Prosperity Theology

Having reviewed some of the benefits of an ethic of hunger that continually pushes the envelope of what measure of the kingdom of God we might experience while here on earth, it is clear that an ethic of hunger is an important aspect of a flourishing life in the immanent frame. At the same time, we have also reviewed how a focus on maximal health and prosperity can be problematic for people who suffer from chronic disabilities, illnesses, or some form of diminishing life. For people facing these realities, an ethic of contentment representing a dynamic/relational view of the *Imago Dei*, a recognition of legitimate victimizations and the processes of grieving, and an affirmation of the quotidian are equally important aspects of a flourishing life. The dilemma here is that these two orientations appear to conflict with one another leaving us to choose unsatisfactorily between them.

If we lean towards the ethic of hunger, it can leave the disabled and unhealed struggling to muster the faith for breakthrough year after year to the point of eventual discouragement and perhaps even bitterness and a threatened sense of self-worth. But if instead we lean towards the ethic of contentment, it leaves a different set of complications to address. Most notably, my own decades in pastoral ministry have borne out that the more I encourage an ethic of contentment in our community, the less breakthroughs we tend to see. Some will find this far preferable to the cultivation of disappointed hopes outlined above, but it is worth exploring if there is some way to reconcile both of these important dynamics together and reap the benefits that each provides.

Perhaps the best way to engage both the ethic of hunger and the ethic of contentment is to continually struggle to hold them together in tension. That might mean to embrace a life of settled peace and firm identity in the finished work of Christ as the steady foundation of one's contentment while also embracing the life of active faith and risk-taking hopefulness that hungers to expand the limits to how much of the kingdom of God it is possible to experience in this life.[290] Put on paper like this it doesn't appear to be difficult to hold this balance, but in lived experience this is certainly not always an easy tension to maintain. Think of a couple struggling to conceive. Where do they find a sense of contentment in the waiting? How

---

290. This is a lesson I learned from Pastor Bill Johnson of Bethel Church in Redding, California as he spoke about the importance of both hunger and contentment in the sometimes-long pursuit of personal healing.

do they keep trying for breakthrough after having their hopes dashed after each attempt? What kind of contentment will they hold onto on the day they realize their window has passed?

Theologically, at least, this tension is easier to affirm. A maturing Prosperity theology should continue to encourage the this-worldly pursuits of ordinary human flourishing (hunger) while incorporating other resources to affirm the quotidian, the natural progression of life and death, and the challenges to flourishing presented by disability and long-term illness (contentment). I want to review some of the insights we have developed through this chapter before offering a proposal for theological resources that can support just this sort of balanced and maturing Prosperity theology.

Prosperity theologies have championed the affirmation of this-worldly pursuits of ordinary human flourishing (health and prosperity) but have sometimes been lacking in responding appropriately to people with disabilities, chronic illnesses, and those in the twilight stages of life who might not ever achieve full health or prosperity. This lack is made more egregious in light of the marginalization and even outright discrimination these groups have experienced in recent history at the hands of those who would deny their human dignity. Something needs to be added to Prosperity theologies to broaden the applicability of their message to accommodate nuanced views of flourishing and protect the human rights of these vulnerable people groups.

One theological perspective that could help to fill this void is the dynamic/relational and Christological approach to the *Imago Dei*. Dynamic/relational and Christological approaches to the *Imago Dei* were crafted with these marginalized people in mind to affirm the value of every person regardless of their ability to achieve maximal health and prosperity or not. These views show us that flourishing might look different for people according to their life circumstances and present capabilities. For those with disabilities, part of flourishing might begin with a sense of contentment grounded in an acceptance of the permanence of their physical state. The acceptance of the permanence of a limited physical state is exactly where traditional Prosperity theologies have struggled and this is most clearly where the Prosperity ethic of hunger and the *Imago Dei* ethic of contentment clash. This is also where holding the tension that affirms both of these values shows its worth. Hungering for optimal health and prosperity while simultaneously being grounded in present contentment in limitation is precisely the shape of a maturing Prosperity theology.

Challenges to Flourishing Conceived of as Health and Prosperity

Another theological perspective that adds value to a maturing Prosperity theology is the affirmation of the quotidian in David Kelsey's wisdom literature-based creation theology.[291] Kelsey's affirmation of the quotidian is valuable to this discussion for a couple of reasons. First, it validates health and prosperity as legitimate measures of ordinary human flourishing. This helps to stave off critics who suggest that health and prosperity are simply expressions of unchecked consumerism. And second, it reminds us that death is also a part of the natural course of life's flourishing. Learning to be content in the context of dying life is an important theme to incorporate into a comprehensive view of ordinary flourishing. This represents a second expression of the ethic of contentment that helps to balance the Prosperity ethic of hunger.

Finally, if we add to these points the thought that the task of liberation at its most basic level is the empowerment of self and others to overcome narratives of victimization in order to pursue greater flourishing in life, it can allow us to see liberative action as a task in the quotidian and not necessarily as a meta-project outside of the scope of the quotidian.[292] That is due to the daily nature of a program of empowerment that seeks to transform and renew the mind in order to enable greater personal flourishing.

Understanding flourishing more broadly in this framework of empowerment/liberation instead of more narrowly as health and prosperity can provide a potentially broader basis for incorporating various nuanced views of flourishing under one paradigm. For instance, we can see how a disabled man finding contentment in the midst of his physical limitations can be an expression of empowerment. Likewise, someone learning that they do not need to stay trapped in a cycle of poverty but that they can hunger for a better future could also be an expression of empowerment. Thus, the ethic of contentment and the ethic of hunger can be held together

---

291. David Kelsey's (*EE*, 1:511) theo-centric conception of flourishing suggests that flourishing should be framed in terms of appropriate responses to God's actions to create, to draw to eschatological consummation, and to reconcile us. But he makes clear that this is not the same as well-being, which he defines as a self-referential bio-psycho-social view of humanity. I would offer some push-back to the idea that theo-centric flourishing and bio-centric well-being need be so starkly separated. Kelsey also never takes the time to connect his conception of well-being with resources in the behavioral sciences. I have attempted to do this in chapter 4 while discussing the parameters of the discussion on human flourishing in the immanent frame.

292. I develop this view of the basic task of liberation theology when I review contemporary theologies of the sinned-against in chapter 5. Also, see Marie Fortune, "The Conundrum of Sin," 134.

in a unified ethic of empowerment. The shape of a maturing Prosperity theology, then, is one of empowerment reflected in the held tension between hunger for breakthroughs and contentment in limitations.

Conclusion

We began this chapter by looking at the reasons why a view of flourishing as health and prosperity could marginalize people who were unable to achieve maximal health due to physical disabilities, mental disabilities, and chronic illnesses. In light of post-holocaust theologies, the danger of this inherent devaluation was in both the historical potential to be complicit in harm done to this people group as well as in the internal stigmatization that they carried in Prosperity-centric environments. This led us to a recognition that the inclusion of a theology of the *Imago Dei* could help Prosperity theologies to develop a broader vision of what shape flourishing life could take in light of the given capabilities and limitations that different people experienced. While structural and functional approaches to the *Imago Dei* were rejected for their failure to protect the dignity of the sick and disabled, dynamic/relational approaches to the *Imago Dei* showed promise as a safeguard for the human rights and dignity of all people, sick and disabled included.

To give the chronically sick and disabled a way to normalize their experience of limited life, we explored the contributions of Nancy Eisland and Amos Yong, who develop a Christological identification with the experience of limited life. This opened the way to begin exploring the question of what flourishing might look like in the context of chronic sickness or disability. As we expanded the discussion around flourishing, we came to see the value of understanding flourishing in the light of liberation and empowerment. Coming to terms with one's given limitations by expressing a contentment in the midst of them could now be affirmed as a legitimate expression of flourishing conceived of as empowerment.

To continue to broaden our examination of different contexts in which to imagine flourishing, we looked at the work of David Kelsey who developed a creation theology that was based in the wisdom-literature rather than in the creation accounts themselves. What he discerned in these writings was an affirmation of the processes of ordinary life that he referred to as the quotidian and a resistance to the idea that meta-projects were needed to give meaning to life. That affirmation of the quotidian came

Challenges to Flourishing Conceived of as Health and Prosperity

with an affirmation of the value of health and prosperity as a measure of ordinary flourishing in the quotidian. It also taught us to begin to think of dying life and how flourishing could look different in the various stages of life. This led us to recognize that there was a value in finding contentment and flourishing in the process of dying well beyond just continuing to press for optimal health.

In both the contexts of disability and of dying life we saw that an ethic of contentment was at work to dignify life in the face of its limitations. Accepting the finality of one's disability or life condition represented a major step in the shifting of perspectives on what would thereafter constitute a flourishing life. But this ethic of contentment was in direct opposition to the ethic of hunger at the heart of most Prosperity theologies—hunger to pursue growth and breakthroughs in ever higher degrees of health and prosperity. So, the question naturally arose of how these two competing ethics might be reconciled.

Taking a cue from pastoral practices in helping people to find contentment in Christ while stretching out in risk-taking faith to invite more of the breaking in of the kingdom of God in their lives and circumstances, we saw a way for the ethic of contentment and the ethic of hunger to be held together in a healthy tension. This is not unlike the tension between the "already" and the "not yet" in George Ladd's theology of the kingdom. And this tension is easier to hold when we frame flourishing not as health and prosperity, but rather as liberation and empowerment. Then we can see that both contentment and hunger are expressions of empowerment suggesting that an ethic of empowerment might best express the values of a maturing Prosperity theology that holds contentment and hunger in proper tension.

These efforts to expand the breadth of the flourishing envisioned in Prosperity theologies really build on the framing of Prosperity theologies as liberative in nature as I developed in chapter 4. That liberative value was established by relating the empowerment in Prosperity theologies to concepts of human flourishing developed in the behavioral sciences as shown in chapter 3. In the following chapter, I will explore what these insights on the liberative character of Prosperity theologies might mean for a reflection on theology-proper—a reflection on the nature and character of God. There, I hope to show how theo-centric formulations of flourishing life derived from Prosperity theologies can really be sensibly aligned with the values of ordinary human flourishing. This is part of my aim to show that a maturing Prosperity theology can thus be a fruitful dialogue partner for a contemporary society held in the immanent frame.

6

The Good, Hospitable, and Liberating God
A *Kenotic* Model of God

Introduction

HAVING EXPLORED THE INTERSECTION of the liberative dimensions of Prosperity theologies and insights from the behavioral sciences in chapter 4 and how these liberative themes could mature Prosperity theologies towards a healthy tension between an ethic of hunger and an ethic of contentment in chapter 5, I want to now turn to constructing a theo-centric model of human flourishing from the resources of Prosperity theologies.

At the heart of a theo-centric model of human flourishing is the question of what model of God drives its vision of the Christian life and how that differs from other prevalent models of God in contemporary theology. That leads naturally to questions of how such a model of God can underwrite the empowerment spirituality and embrace of immanent human flourishing that are so characteristic of Prosperity theologies. I aim to demonstrate that "the Good God" is the primary model of God in Prosperity theologies and that this represents a useful contribution to the diversity of models of God that have recently enriched this field of research. Then I will develop a constructive expansion of this model to continue my project to mature Prosperity theologies for broader engagement with contemporary theology and to encourage a deeper internal integration of its themes. My goal is to show that a maturing Prosperity theology can fund a theo-centric vision of human flourishing that embraces both the spiritual and material dimensions of salvation in the immanent frame. In other words, I want to show that following "the Good God," according to the vision of Prosperity theologies, results in tangible human flourishing broadly conceived in terms of empowerment that both Christians and Humanists can appreciate.

The Significance of Naming God as a Liberative Task of Theology

> With Ludwig Wittgenstein, feminists would say, "The limits of one's language are the limits of one's world," and with Martin Heidegger, "Language is the house of being."[293]

The importance of how we name God is brought out in nearly every form of liberation theology from Jürgen Moltmann challenging the impassibility of God to Gustavo Gutierrez reflecting on the God who stands with the poor. But nowhere is the task of challenging traditional ways of speaking of God more central than it is for women's theology. After all, the poor can target political oppressions and the racially discriminated-against can identify social oppressions, but for women, breaking the hold of patriarchy begins with our religious language itself, or lack thereof as we shall see. Accordingly, as we consider the justification for fresh religious language that arises from Prosperity theologies, it benefits us to learn what we can from women's perspectives.

Feminist theologian Sallie McFague helps to give us the language (and thereby the tools) to move beyond traditional predominately patriarchal religious language by pointing out the ways that this patriarchal language has exceeded its task. She says that recognizing God as "father" has become an entire patriarchal way of life that influences relationships between humanity and God, between men and women, and even in the modes of governance in the church and in the world.[294] Because of the pervasiveness of this model of God, McFague suggests that it has become, in some ways, an idol. "When a model becomes an idol, the hypothetical character of the model is forgotten and what ought to be seen as *one* way to understand our relationship with God has become identified as *the* way."[295] This idolatrous

---

293. McFague, *Metaphorical Theology*, 8.

294. McFague, *Metaphorical Theology*, 9.

295. McFague, *Metaphorical Theology*, 9. It should also be noted that for McFague (*Metaphorical Theology*, 23), a metaphor is an image of God (God is like a father), a model is a dominant metaphor (God as father).

The Good, Hospitable, and Liberating God

over-application of the model of God as father, she suggests, should be brought back to its proper dimensions.[296]

In addition to pointing out the ways that our models of God can become idols, McFague also says that a lack of feminine imagery for God can result in a lower self-image for women because of the absence of the ability for women to identify themselves with imagery of God. She says, "[t]he human images we choose for the divine influence the way we feel about ourselves, for these images are 'divinized' and hence raised in status. For instance, earthly kingship gains in importance when the image of king is applied to God."[297] Women lack these kinds of images of God and are further disadvantaged because of it.

While some theologians have responded to the abuse of patriarchal imagery of God and the lack of equivalent feminine imagery by calling for new imagery to replace traditional religious language, McFague and others have instead sought a middle way that seeks to preserve traditional religious language while challenging its idolatrous over-extension. They have suggested that we can only do justice to the complexity and multi-dimensionality of relationship with God by the proliferation of many metaphors and many models of the way that God relates to humanity—including the imagery of God as Father.[298] So to the imagery of the Fatherhood of God we might add other images such as Mother, Creator, Source, or Parent. This approach allows us to keep the traditional language intact while enriching it with new imagery to reflect the diversity of human experience in relationship with God.

Why is this relevant for our discussion of human flourishing? Because "[t]he way we model our relationship with God has significant impact on our understanding of human existence."[299] Or, to follow Wittgenstein quoted earlier—the limits of our language are the limits of our world. The language we use to speak of God is not neutral. Rather, "[t]here is an agenda

---

296. For those who challenge McFague's (*Metaphorical Theology*, 57–63, 120) adoption of metaphor in religious language, I refer you to her discussion of the way that using metaphor in theology is similar to the task we undertake when we interpret texts, drawing from Gadamer's "merging of horizons" and Ricouer's view of theology as a task of fresh interpretation. For a helpful summary of McFague's key methodological arguments, see Kärkkäinen (*CCTPW*, 2:318).

297. McFague, *Metaphorical Theology*, 10.

298. McFague, *Metaphorical Theology*, 20. Cf. Johnson, *She Who Is*, 21.

299. McFague, *Metaphorical Theology*, 181.

behind each metaphor employed."³⁰⁰ There is a relationship detailed in each metaphor that has direct implications to both our understanding of the nature of God and our vision for what human flourishing in relationship with God might be.³⁰¹ This is why when the poor name God as a Liberator it can have the effect of imparting a vision for a liberated life. Or when others name God as Master and Lord it can encourage a life of surrender and obedience. These are not necessarily conflicting perspectives, though theologians have certainly had differences of opinions about how they might be harmonized into a common vision of flourishing life.

Amidst the potential for an explosion of new imagery for relationship with God that arises from her proposal, McFague argues that there are "root metaphors" which are "[a] way of seeing "all that is" through a particular key concept."³⁰² Such root metaphors would have a much broader influence on conceptions of the dynamics of relationship with God and the visions of flourishing that derive from those ideas than other more circumstantial imagery of God. McFague claims that many such root metaphors have been advanced in the history of theology and offers this concise summary:

> The basic insight in Paul's theology is justification through grace by faith; in Augustine's, it is the radical dependence of all that is on God alone; in Aquinas's, it is the analogy of being in which each creature participates in and glorifies God through realizing its own proper finite end; in Martin Luther's, it is Paul's once again; in John Calvin's, it is the sovereignty of God over all that lives and breathes; in Friedrich Schleiermacher's, it is the feeling of absolute dependence on God; in Karl Barth's, it is the election of all to salvation in the election of Jesus Christ; in Paul Tillich's, it is the ultimate concern hidden in all penultimate concerns. Each of these is a translation of the relationship between the divine and the human projected in the parabolic stories of the kingdom and in Jesus as parable of God.³⁰³

So, what root metaphor does McFague endorse given her concerns about the idolatry of patriarchal imagery of God in the theological tradition? Following Jürgen Moltmann, she says that we should embrace a

---

300. Soskice, *Metaphor and Religious Language*, 62–63.

301. Kärkkäinen, *CCTPW*, 2:315.

302. McFague (*Metaphorical Theology*, 28) says that these root metaphors are "[t]he most basic assumption about the nature of the world or experience that we can make when we try to give a description of it."

303. McFague, *Metaphorical Theology*, 125–26.

The Good, Hospitable, and Liberating God

model of "God as Friend" as a way to balance maternal and paternal models of God with "[n]onfamilial, non-gender-related ones."[304] "The friend of God does not live any longer 'under God,' but with and in God. Such a person shares in the grief and the joy of God; such a person has become 'one' with God."[305] Imagery of God as a friend could help to undo some of the over-extended patriarchalism that has resulted from the traditional image of God as father by promoting an egalitarian vision of relationship with God that could be a model for egalitarian relationships throughout society. Furthermore, McFague applies the model of God as friend to our understanding of salvation saying that rather than promote a patriarchal view of God redeeming and protecting individuals, God as friend comes alongside humanity to partner with us in responsibly overcoming oppression in our lives.[306]

While it may seem that the hierarchical imagery supported by the model of God as Father and the egalitarian imagery supported by the model of God as Friend offer conflicting ways to imagine divine-human relationship, human-human relationship, and our models of governance in organizational settings, this is precisely where McFague finds value in the multiplicity of metaphors. Being able to biblically support both of these models allows for an egalitarian critique in cases where patriarchalism is seen to have over-reached. Similarly, a hierarchical critique can also be made in cases where egalitarian ideals may not always be the most appropriate, say for example, in the context of the organizational structure of a business.[307] Allowing for the multiplicity of metaphors gives theologians the flexibility to adapt different biblical values to an ever-changing cultural

---

304. McFague, *Metaphorical Theology*, 178.

305. Moltmann, "The Motherly Father," 55.

306. McFague (*Metaphorical Theology*, 188) says, "[t]he model of God as friend offers us a view of salvation substantially different from traditional views in which God redeems and protects individuals. Rather, it supports an 'adult' view of shared responsibility with God as our friend, identifying with us in our suffering and working with us toward overcoming the oppression brought about in large part by our own perversity and selfishness."

307. One of the assumptions being made in this discussion is that our models of God have some resonance with our views of life—in other words, our models of God can become our social programs. This is an oft challenged idea when Moltmann claims that the egalitarian model of the Trinity suggests an egalitarian social program, but if we simply say that our models of God inform our ideas of flourishing life, this somehow seems less controversial.

landscape and encourages more careful listening to under-represented and oppressed voices in the community.

One model that might take us another step forward comes from the contemporary study of the Trinity. While Jürgen Moltmann's vision of the mutuality of the members of the Trinity in *perichoretic* union has championed the mutual relationships at the heart of the Trinity for contemporary Liberation theology, it is perhaps Wolfhart Pannenberg's formulation that holds the most promise for our discussion here.[308] A full review of Pannenberg's Trinitarian proposal is beyond the scope of this present study but what is important for us is that he manages to construct a model of the Triune inter-relations that simultaneously supports the Monarchy of the Father and the mutuality of the Father, Son, and Spirit.[309] He says, "By their work the Son and Spirit serve the monarchy of the Father. Yet the Father does not have his kingdom or monarchy without the Son and Spirit, but only through them."[310] So, this model of the Trinity affirms both the traditional language of a hierarchy while also endorsing a vibrant egalitarianism in one package. This can allow an even stronger foundation from which to offer either hierarchical or egalitarian critique.

In this framework of an affirmation of the value of the multiplicity of metaphors for theological inquiry and societal practice, I want to introduce the model of "the Good God" as a contribution constructively derived from Prosperity theologies that holds the promise to advance a holistic vision for human flourishing in the immanent frame. I will then explore how this model interacts with recent models of the God of Liberation and the Hospitable God before concluding with some reflections on how this model might offer a fresh vision for Christian spirituality.

Prosperity Theologies and the Model of The Good God

Having made the case for the need for many models and metaphors of God, this section explores what might be the Prosperity theology contribution

---

308. For Moltmann's view, see *The Trinity and the Kingdom: The Doctrine of God*.

309. Pannenberg establishes Threeness through the relational idea of self-distinction and Oneness through a complex relational iteration of "essence" rather than a substance-oriented view of it. For a detailed exploration of Pannenberg's Trinitarian theology, see Veli-Matti Kärkkäinen (*The Trinity*, 123–50).

310. Pannenberg, *Systematic Theology*, 1:324.

to this dialogue. With its affirmation of ordinary goodness and flourishing, I propose that a *kenotic* model of the character of God aligns most closely with its value of empowerment.

An Affirmation of Ordinary Goodness

Every theological tradition affirms that God is good in some way or another. It is one of the most fundamental theological statements that one can make. So why should the goodness of God be claimed as the fresh contribution that Prosperity theologies make to the contemporary project of designating new metaphors for re-imagining God? What does Prosperity theology have to say about the goodness of God that is so different from what has been said throughout the history of the church?

I believe the difference is found in two dimensions. The first comes from the Prosperity theology affirmation of ordinary human flourishing where we hear unequivocally that God wants believers to flourish both in this life and the next. Even in the face of the challenges to flourishing reflected in sickness, suffering, and calamity, Prosperity theologies spend little time on elaborate theodicies or the ministries of comfort and consolation. Instead, they direct all their energies to positioning people for breakthrough. And a major component of that positioning of people for breakthrough is affirming to them that God has brought flourishing within the reach of faith.[311] The fact that Prosperity theologies have made ordinary human flourishing accessible and attainable for today is why I believe that they promote a tangible expression of the ordinary goodness of God.[312]

This affirmation of ordinary goodness is nothing more than an extension of the materiality of salvation in Prosperity theologies and reflects the fact that Prosperity theologies express one of the broadest affirmations of that materiality among contemporary theologies.[313] So, while contextualized

---

311. For Prosperity theologies, "taste and see that the Lord is good" becomes a mantra and there is an expectation that the many dimensions of *shalom*—the end of sickness, the end of suffering, the end of poverty, and the presence of flourishing—are within the reach of faith.

312. To show the importance of the theme of God's goodness for the development of Prosperity theology, Lewis Brogdon (*New Pentecostal Message*, 18–19) refers to Oral Roberts who framed Prosperity as a result of a right view of God in his book *God is a Good God*.

313. Prosperity theologies embrace both the liberative dimensions and the Pentecostal healing dimensions of the materiality of salvation and then add other dimensions to

Liberation theologies also advocate for the materiality of salvation primarily in working for the manifestation of justice in the world, Prosperity theologies broaden that advocacy to every dimension of life that is captured by the notion of *shalom*. This concreteness is what makes this ordinary view of goodness so visceral and relatable and is one of the key reasons why the Prosperity theology concept of the goodness of God "feels" like normal goodness and adds meaningfully to the theological discussion.[314]

So how did the Prosperity theology affirmation of materiality and ordinary goodness come about? If we remember the evolution of the four/five points of Pentecostalism we discussed in chapter 2 as they were adapted for Prosperity theologies, we can see how many of them contributed to the development of this robust view of the materiality of salvation. The most important development was the evolution of the belief that divine healing was made accessible through the atonement to the belief that all aspects of wholeness and *shalom* were made accessible through the atonement.[315] Then there was the shift in eschatology from an expectation of the world's destruction to a vision of the victorious church.[316] In this view, healing/*shalom* could be proleptic (anticipatory) expressions of the coming fullness of the Kingdom of God that could be accessed now by faith. Finally, the move away from the view of holiness as purification from the world and towards a view of holiness as consecration to the world also contributed to mitigating the stigma of materiality in Prosperity theologies.[317] Together, these three themes gave Prosperity theologies their broad embrace of materiality as a forum for the display of the ordinary goodness of God in the world.

---

it as well, such as personal empowerment and prosperity.

314. Beyond the theological arguments for this, one need only peruse the endless amount of Prosperity literature on the goodness of God. It saturates their declarations of faith and their songs of praise and constitutes a major portion of their inspirational writings. As a prime example, see Bill Johnson's book, *God is Good: He's Better Than You Think*.

315. As we covered in chapter 2, this doctrine of healing in the atonement has evolved to a more moderate view that the possibility of divine healing is made accessible through the atonement—reflecting the already/not yet tension of the Kingdom of God as expressed by George Ladd (*Theology*, 67).

316. On the recovery/use of the Latter Rain eschatology in Pentecostalism, see Peter Althouse, *Spirit of the Last Days*

317. Again, see chapter 2. The language of purification vs. consecration is from Yong (*IDC*, 172).

The Good, Hospitable, and Liberating God

The Kenotic Goodness of God

The second dimension that can differentiate the Prosperity theology view of God's goodness from tradition is a constructive one that I propose here. This one derives from the liberative elements of Prosperity theologies detailed in chapter 4 that highlight the activity of God to empower people out of the narratives of victimization in their lives. From this, we learn that God is committed to our empowerment as a basic component of our flourishing. This is interesting for two reasons: (1) It claims that God wants people to be empowered and not servile, and (2) it claims that God works for our flourishing rather than requiring us to work for His flourishing. This second point requires a good deal of theological sensitivity to avoid the erroneous conclusion that God is some sort of cosmic Santa Claus—something I will carefully develop in a theo-centric view of human flourishing that derives from Prosperity theologies. That said, I believe that both of these above claims can be supported in a *kenotic* approach to Christology that can provide theological nuance to Prosperity theologies and their embrace of the goodness of God.[318]

Rather than use *kenosis* (κένωσις) to refer to some ontological self-emptying as has been attempted in some misguided historical Christologies, I mean to use the term *kenosis* (κένωσις) to refer to a mode of relationality demonstrated in the life of Christ that also comes to characterize the relationality of the Father towards His creation.[319] In contemporary theology, this relational usage of *kenosis* (κένωσις) has typically been understood as a self-emptying or self-sacrificial act with the emphasis being on the self-denying elements of these formulations. I want to instead emphasize that the revelation of Christ's attitude and humility in Phil 2 is more profound than a simple disciplined self-abasement. Rather, *kenosis* (κένωσις) reflects a more fundamental "other-orientation" in which the motivation is not

---

318. Why look to Christ to reflect on the character of God? Because as Thomas Torrance (*Ground and Grammar*, 160) says, "Jesus Christ is . . . not a mere symbol, some representation of God detached from God, but God in his own Being and Act come among us, expressing in our human form the Word which he is eternally in himself, so that in our relations with Jesus Christ we have to do directly with the ultimate Reality of God."

319. "Your attitude should be the same as that of Christ Jesus: Who, being in very nature God, did not consider equality with God something to be grasped, but *made himself nothing*, taking *the very nature of a servant*, being made in human likeness. And being found in appearance as a man, he *humbled himself* and became obedient to death—even death on a cross!" Phil 2:5–8 (NIV, italics mine). See also "Anyone who has seen me has seen the Father" John 14:9 (NIV).

the humbling of the self but rather the flourishing of the other. Ironically, selfless action done for the humbling of the self is nothing more than a sophisticated form of self-centeredness. True selflessness is expressed in enabling and celebrating the flourishing of another. To put it in Walter Brueggemann's terms, God's self-regard and His other-regard are one and the same. His greatest joy (self-regard) is in the flourishing of His creation (other-regard).[320] When Prosperity theologies celebrate the goodness of God, it is this fundamental orientation towards the flourishing of His creation that they have in mind.

When I think about this "orientation towards the flourishing of another," I am often reminded of the story of Mike Grady, an accountant from Maitland, Florida, who was watching his twelve year old son playing in a mountain river during a family vacation.[321] When he saw his son get submerged in the rushing current he jumped into the icy waters to hold his son's head above water while others frantically tried to dislodge his son's foot from where it had gotten trapped in the rocks below. Mike positioned himself to shield his exhausted son from the onslaught of rushing water such that his own shirt was ripped right off his back. When rescuers were finally able to get a rope around his son thirty minutes later, Mike summoned all that was left of his strength to somehow lift his son up and out from the river. Moments after seeing his son reach safety, Mike Grady died in that river from exhaustion, hypothermia, and drowning. I want to honor his memory as an example of what "other-oriented" *kenosis* (κένωσις) can look like in practice. His whole attention was on ensuring the well-being of his son, not on thinking about the significance of his own sacrifice.

Clark Pinnock gives voice to the wonder of this truth when it is newly discovered: "How often have people been given the impression of God as a being exalting himself at our expense! God is not preoccupied with himself, not unable to give himself away. It is the essence of God that he go out from himself and overflow for the sake of the other."[322] Likewise Emil Brunner identifies this as the core truth of revelation: "Love is the movement which goes-out-of-oneself, which stoops down to that which is below: it is the

---

320. Brueggemann (*Theology of the Old Testament*, 303) unites Yhwh's "self-regard" and "other-regard" in the notion of Yhwh's righteousness. "Yahweh's righteousness entails governance of the world according to Yahweh's purposes, which are decreed at Sinai and which are assured in the very fabric of creation. The substance of that righteousness is the well-being of the world . . . "

321. Bianchi, "Mike Grady."

322. Pinnock, *Flame of Love*, 42–44.

The Good, Hospitable, and Liberating God

self-giving, the self-communication of God—and it is *this* which is His revelation."[323] And Graham Buxton chimes in saying, " . . . we do well to note that to penetrate the heart of God in communion with Him is to be grasped by his utter other-centeredness."[324]

These two dimensions—the clear affirmation that God wants people to flourish in both this life and the next and the *kenotic* orientation of God towards the flourishing of another—represent the main ideas behind the Prosperity theology affirmation of the ordinary goodness of God. I want to expand on these themes from Biblical and Theological perspectives before setting the model of the Good God in conversation with other contemporary efforts to expand the naming of God.

The Kenotic Goodness of God in Biblical and Theological Perspective

To further develop a *kenotic* model of the character of God, this section reviews relevant biblical and theological perspectives that corroborate this proposal. From looking at texts of the Triune God's self-revelation in Scripture to recognizing the link between holiness and goodness, Scripture is full of affirmations of the *kenotic* character of God and the mode of His lordship over creation. In this section, we will explore how *kenosis* relates to (1) our reading of the self-revelation of God in Scripture, (2) the connection between holiness and goodness, (3) the connection between goodness and justice, righteousness, and peace, (4) the loving-kindness of God, truthfulness, and the giving of the covenant, and (5) the compassion of God.

First, we will look at the ways that the *kenotic* character of Christ expressed in the Christ hymn of Phil 2 nuances our reading of the self-revelation of God in Scripture in Exod 34:6–7.

> The LORD, the LORD, a God merciful and gracious, slow to anger, and abounding in steadfast love and faithfulness, keeping steadfast love for thousands, forgiving iniquity and transgression and sin, but who will by no means clear the guilty, visiting the iniquity of the fathers on the children and the children's children, to the third and the fourth generation (Exod 34:6–7 ESV).

---

323. Brunner, *Christian Doctrine*, 187.
324. Buxton, *Dancing in the Dark*, 122.

The Empowering God

I have always found it fascinating that when Moses asks to see God's glory in Exod 34, God responds by saying that He will reveal His goodness to him. That suggests two things: (1) In some profound way, God's glory is expressed in His goodness rather than merely in His honor as some traditions have supposed, and (2) His goodness is expressed in His way of relating to people as His response to Moses makes clear. However, many have remarked at how the first half of this passage is difficult to reconcile with the language of the second half of the passage.[325] In particular, how are both halves of this passage meant to be reflective of the goodness of God?

I propose that one possible way to reconcile the two faces of this passage within a single conception of the goodness of God is found in the *kenotic* life of Christ, who is himself the living representation of the character hinted at in Exod 34.[326] We see in the life of Christ a similar sharp distinction between the way he addresses the broken and the way he addresses the religious leaders and Pharisees. Jesus is incredibly kind and affirming of the broken, even when they have no expectation of receiving mercy from him. In contrast, Jesus is often angry with the Pharisees and repeatedly uses a very confrontational tone with them. If we see this passage from the perspective of the *kenotic* orientation of Christ towards the flourishing of the other, we can imagine that to people whose primary limitation to flourishing is their shame, Jesus speaks in such a way as to lift that shame. Likewise, to people whose primary limitation to flourishing is their pride, Jesus speaks in such a way as to uproot that pride. Both shame and pride are manifestations of an inward turn towards self-orientation—one to brokenness and the other to arrogance. They each require a different prescription to return to a path that can result in a Christ-like orientation towards a life of enabling the flourishing of others. Thus, while God's actions in both situations might be starkly different, the "good" motivation to promote flourishing in both situations remains the same.

---

325. Brueggemann (*Theology of the Old Testament*, 270) notes that "[i]n the culmination of the formula in Ex. 34:7b, the statement does an abrupt about-face . . . I can find no evident way in which the two parts of this formulation can be readily and fully harmonized."

326. Bauckham (*Jesus and the God*, 55) says, "The last verses of the Prologue (Jn 1:14–18) claim that God, who has never been seen by human eyes, has been revealed in the human life of Jesus Christ, who reflects his Father's glory and is full of grace and truth. All these terms allude to the story of God's revelation of Himself to Moses in Ex. 33–34, in which the central Old Testament character description of God occurs." Cf. "Christ provided a visible embodiment of the self-revelation that God had already given Israel." (Goldingay, *OTT*, 2:19).

The Good, Hospitable, and Liberating God

In a similar way, the kindness of God towards the repentant in Exod 34:6 and the sternness of God towards the unrepentant in Exod 34:7b might be profitably seen in this *kenotic* light. God is committed to the flourishing of His children and gives to each what is needed to enable them to progress on the path of Christ-likeness—even if what is first needed is a step backwards before growth can take place. And as we will see, that Christ-likeness reflects a vision of human flourishing understood as the *kenotic* orientation towards enabling the flourishing of others both at an individual level and for the flourishing of the entire community.

Second, we explore how *kenosis* clarifies the connection between holiness and goodness. A *kenotic* understanding of the goodness of God gives added clarity to many themes that we find in Scripture relating to the ways of God. For instance, the theme of holiness is pivotal to an understanding of the nature of God and of the Spirit's work in the world. Daniel Migliore says, "Becoming holy or sanctified in the New Testament sense means being conformed to the image of Christ by the working of the Holy Spirit in our lives. The essential mark of this Christ-likeness is that free self-giving, other-regarding love that the New Testament calls agape."[327] Many conceptions of holiness that are not based in the revelation of God's *kenotic* orientation to the flourishing of His creation result in skewed ideas and misunderstandings that can hinder the purposes of God in people's lives rather than facilitate them. Applying divine *kenosis* (κένωσις) to the concept of Holiness, then, reveals the contours of "goodness" at the center of God's holiness.

In the acts of God throughout salvation history, the idea of holiness seems to carry the notion of being "set apart" for the purposes of God. This is observed in the various judges "set apart" to deliver Israel from her oppressors as well as in Israel itself being "set apart" in order to become a blessing to the nations.[328] But a more careful examination of the *kenotic* benevolence behind the call to be "set apart" begins to reveal that God desires people to be "set apart" not so that He can rule over them with an iron fist, but in order to lead them into the fullness of His good intentions for them. One way to conceive of this is to understand God's call to holiness as an invitation to wholeness (*shalom*). "Holiness is not flawlessness but the fulfillment of God's intention for us."[329] When people begin to realize that

---

327. Migliore, *Faith Seeking Understanding*, 178.
328. Callen, "The Context," 8.
329. Mannoia and Thorsen, eds., *The Holiness Manifesto*, 20.

the call to Holiness is not solely for God's sake but that it is God's provision for our wholeness and well-being, they will begin to discern the implicit connection between holiness and the goodness of God.

Abraham Heschel describes the Jewish understanding of God's goodness in this way: "To the Jewish mind, the understanding of God is not achieved by referring in a Greek way to timeless qualities of a Supreme Being, to ideas of goodness or perfection, but rather by sensing the living acts of His concern, to His dynamic attentiveness to man . . . God's goodness is not a cosmic force but a specific act of compassion."[330] Likewise, the people of God through history and believers today come to discover the goodness of God in His actions towards them. "How do we know He is good? His creation is good and what He does is good."[331]

As they followed Him in their early history, the people of Israel encountered many instances of His goodness. Jon Huntzinger notes how "Doing good for the people by leading them to a good land reflects the holy nature of God."[332] Likewise, "God's word—rules, commandments, and statutes—is good, allows for good judgment, and reveals the good nature of God."[333] God's benevolence extends into the New Testament where, "Jesus also is described as going about doing good. Peter is saying that Jesus is doing what God the Father has always been doing, and that is doing good."[334] What is seen here is that in all the instances when God's holy ways are illustrated, it is for the purpose of blessing His people. They are a reflection of His *kenotic* benevolence to lead his people into the fullness of all He created them to enjoy—union with Him (*theosis* [θέωσις]) overflowing into relationships of *shalom* with others.

Third, *kenosis* clarifies the connection between goodness and justice, righteousness, and peace. Understanding divine *kenosis* (κένωσις) allows the connection between God's goodness and His insistence on justice to be seen in proper context. Jon Huntzinger describes Biblical justice (*mishpat* [מִשְׁפָּט]) in this way, "Mishpat—'Justice'—is the idea that when there is a blessing, everybody within the community should be able to participate in that blessing in some way. When some are excluded, that angers God."[335]

---

330. Heschel, *God in Search*, 21.
331. Huntzinger, "Biblical Resources for Ministry."
332. Huntzinger, "Goodness and Worship," 34.
333. Huntzinger, "Goodness and Worship," 35.
334. Huntzinger, "School of Pastoral Nurture II."
335. Huntzinger, "Biblical Resources for Ministry."

The Good, Hospitable, and Liberating God

The neglect of the widow, the orphan, and the foreigners in their midst is the reason for many of the denunciations of Israel by the Hebrew Prophets. It is also at the heart of the disciplining of Egypt for its exploitation of Israel preceding the events of the Exodus.[336]

It is important to note that God's anger is not vented in a moment of irrationality. Even in His anger He is motivated by His goodness and *kenotic* orientation towards the flourishing of others. He is angry on behalf of the ones being kept from experiencing His goodness, justice, and *shalom*; the ones being kept from realizing His good and holy purposes for their lives. So, His anger towards the sinner is an expression of His passionate advocacy for the victims of sin.

God's anger is also a manifestation of divine pressure on the sinner to encourage them back towards repentance, restitution, and reconciliation with the sinned-against in order to restore *shalom* in the community. Thus, the spirit of justice is the desire for *shalom* for all and God's justice-making reflects His holiness in its commitment to bring all people in the community into that *shalom*.

This commitment to bring people into *shalom* is also at the heart of the Old Testament concept of righteousness (*sedaqa* [צְדָקָה]). John Goldingay defines righteousness as "[d]oing the right thing by someone in light of your relationship with them."[337] The pairing of justice (*mishpat* [מִשְׁפָּט]) and righteousness (*sedaqa* [צְדָקָה]) is one that is common in the Old Testament and can be understood to mean, "[t]he exercise of authority in a way that does right by people."[338] From this, we can see how righteousness flows into justice, especially in light of the *kenotic* benevolence at the heart of God. Righteousness is right action on behalf of another and it reveals that God's demands for righteousness are not the self-serving decrees people have imagined. Rather they express God's whole-hearted concern for the flourishing of all.

Fourth, *kenosis* is reflected in God's loving-kindness, truthfulness, and in the giving of the Covenant. As common as is the pairing of justice

---

336. Hans Urs von Balthasar (*Glory of the Lord*, 170) says, "[Mishpat is] ultimately the concern for what is right, right as a whole . . . It is never formal law, but is based in what is ethically right (cf. Gen. 18:19), and this in turn emerges irrefutably in concrete terms in the claim of the poor to what is right . . . *mishpat* is justice as the fruit of compassion, as grace (Is. 51:3, 8)."

337. Goldingay, *OTT*, 1:56.

338. Goldingay, *OTT*, 3:558. For more on Peace, Justice and Righteousness, see Walter Brueggemann's *Living Toward A Vision: Biblical Reflections on Shalom*.

The Empowering God

and righteousness in Scripture, Mic 6:8 also pairs justice with the covenant love of God. Regarding this passage in Micah, Goldingay notes that, "[t]his pairing suggests the exercise of authority in a way that expresses commitment to people . . . it is when Yhwh is acting in *mispat* and *sedaqa* or in *mispat* and *hesed* that Yhwh is most Godlike; they are the very expressions of Yhwh's holiness (Isa. 5:16). They are also thus the very expressions of Yhwh's goodness (Mk. 10:18)."[339]

The commitment of God to His people is normally understood in relation to His covenant (*berith* [בְּרִית]) with Israel. However, that covenant is qualified by the concept of loving-kindness (*hesed* [חֶסֶד]). These two ideas go hand in hand together so often in Scripture that they " . . . condition each other mutually . . . (Deut. 7:2, 12; 1 Kgs. 8:23; 2 Chr. 6:14; Neh. 1:9, 9:32)"[340] Balthasar even goes so far as to say, "On the level of human relationships, *chesed* constitutes the true substance of the covenant [*berith*]."[341]

What is important to understand is that God does not give loving-kindness (*hesed* [חֶסֶד]) because He is obligated by the covenant as if it was something against His will and nature to give. Rather, the loving-kindness (*hesed* [חֶסֶד]) that is already in God's nature is what motivates Him to express it in terms of giving the covenant. This is why, even when the covenant is broken on humanity's end, Deutero-Isaiah (40–55) depicts God forging a new covenant with humanity. The covenant is not ultimately what keeps God engaged with people. Rather, it is the loving-kindness (*hesed* [חֶסֶד]) behind the covenant that is the real substance of God's commitment to them.

John Goldingay helpfully expands our understanding of loving-kindness (*hesed* [חֶסֶד]):

> *Hesed*, often rendered as 'steadfast love,' suggests a practice of generosity or good will or beneficence that is extraordinary because it takes place either when there is no particular prior relationship between people and thus no obligation, or when there is a prior relationship but there is some reason why *hesed* could not be expected (for instance, because the other person has let you down). The nearest English word is *commitment*. It is the Hebrew equivalent

---

339. Goldingay, *OTT*, 3:558.
340. Balthasar, *Glory of the Lord*, 160.
341. Balthasar, *Glory of the Lord*, 159.

The Good, Hospitable, and Liberating God

of *agape* in the New Testament, *the love that can be thought of as a commitment of the will to the true good of another.*[342]

What is discovered in unprecedented depth in the New Testament revelation of Jesus is that this loving-kindness (*hesed* [חֶסֶד]) is not simply a willful act on the part of God, but that it is more fundamental to His nature. It is a fundamental aspect of God's nature to move with loving-kindness (*hesed* [חֶסֶד]) towards the other. It is a fundamental aspect of God's nature to be committed to the true good of the other. Loving-kindness (*hesed* [חֶסֶד]) is central to the Biblical understanding of the character of the Triune God and it dovetails nicely with the *kenotic* orientation of God towards the flourishing of the other that we developed above.

Loving-kindness (*hesed* [חֶסֶד]) is also closely aligned with the Hebrew idea of truthfulness (*emeth* [אֱמֶת]). Indeed, Balthasar notes that "*chesed* cannot be thought of without the idea of reliability and truthfulness (*emeth*)."[343] Truthfulness (*emeth* [אֱמֶת]), he says, "[e]xpresses the joy that comes from the fact that . . . there is no deceit: one takes hold of something firm, something that can give support, something valid and reliable; one can dare to enter into a relationship with it, one can count on it and depend on it."[344] In some sense, truthfulness (*emeth* [אֱמֶת]) encompasses the idea of 'integrity' and establishes that God's acts of loving-kindness (*hesed* [חֶסֶד]) are not alien to His character but are rather essential to it. He can be relied on to show loving-kindness (*hesed* [חֶסֶד]); a *kenotic* loving-kindness (*hesed* [חֶסֶד]) that is characteristic of the truth of His nature.

Fifth, *kenosis* is expressed as the compassion of God. Perhaps no Biblical concept better expresses the Triune God's mode of being than the notion of compassion (*rahamim* [רַחֲמִים]). The justification for this claim is that whereas it is possible to conceive of loving-kindness (*hesed* [חֶסֶד]) as primarily an act of commitment devoid of any contingent emotional element, that is not the case with the Biblical notion of compassion (*rahamim* [רַחֲמִים]). Likewise, the Triune God's granting of favor (*hen* [חֵן]) which can be understood as the giving of a "[k]indness to which no one may lay claim,"[345] similarly doesn't necessitate an emotional connection. However, compassion (*rahamim* [רַחֲמִים]), which is linked to a deep movement in the gut, conditions an understanding of loving-kindness (*hesed* [חֶסֶד]) and

---

342. Goldingay, *OTT*, 3:590 (italics mine). Cf. Goldingay, *OTT*, 1:56.
343. Balthasar, *Glory of the Lord*, 160.
344. Balthasar, *Glory of the Lord*, 173.
345. Balthasar, *Glory of the Lord*, 161.

favor (*hen* [חֵן]) to include an emotional dimension.³⁴⁶ Goldingay explains, "Compassion links naturally with commitment [*hesed*] (Ps. 103:4; Jer. 16:5; Zech. 7:9). Like commitment, compassion is an act of the will, but it is also more intrinsically an emotion. It suggests a feeling of pain at another person's actual or potential grievous misfortune . . . Compassion contrasts with mercy, which involves leniency but need not imply emotion."³⁴⁷

The practical expression of loving-kindness (*hesed* [חֶסֶד]), then, is compassion (*rahamim* [רַחֲמִים]); a fact that is most clearly demonstrated in the life and ministry of Christ.³⁴⁸ Loving-kindness (*hesed* [חֶסֶד]), conditioned by compassion (*rahamim* [רַחֲמִים]), is thus understood to carry an emotional component that indicates that the *kenotic* benevolence of the Triune God is not simply an emotionally detached commitment, but rather an emotionally engaged one between the Triune God and His people. The loving-kindness (*hesed* [חֶסֶד]) that underlies God's actions is one of great *pathos* as well as deep commitment to the flourishing of the other.

This exploration through some of the key Hebrew ideas used to characterize the activity of God affirms and adds texture to the *kenotic* orientation towards the flourishing of others that we identified in the life of Christ and gives depth to our understanding of the character of "the Good God." So, how might the model of the Good God that I propose is central to Prosperity theologies interact with other major themes in the contemporary project of re-imagining God? How might it inform a theo-centric view of human flourishing? We will explore these questions in the next sections of our study.

The Good God and the Contemporary Project of Naming God

Having established the basic contours of the Prosperity theology affirmation of the goodness of God, I want to consider how the model of the Good God can help to mitigate concerns about the patriarchal models of God

---

346. Coppes ("*Rahamim,*" 843) says, "*Rahamim* can refer to the seat of one's emotions (Gen. 43:30) or the expression of one's deep emotion (1 Kgs 3:26)."

347. Goldingay, *OTT*, 3:592.

348. Stoebe ("Rahum," 1230) says, "One should note that most passages [with *rahamim*] involve a close connection with *hesed* . . . If *hesed* is singular and the two terms constitute a unit, *hesed* precedes *rahamim* (Ps. 103:4; Jer. 16:5; Hos. 2:21; Zech. 7:9;cf. Dan 1:9) . . . This observation suggests that *rahamim* itself has now taken on the character of a concrete demonstration understood as the effluence of a *hesed* attitude."

The Good, Hospitable, and Liberating God

used most commonly in tradition. Then I will explore how this model of the Good God interacts with other root metaphors that are common in the contemporary project of re-imagining God such as the God of Liberation and the Hospitable God.

The Good God as a Supra-Adjective for Traditional Models of God

The promise of the Prosperity theology model of the Good God in relation to the traditional patriarchal models of God is that by using the qualification of "good" we can turn traditional models of hierarchy upside down. So, the model of God as Father becomes good Father who is oriented towards the flourishing of His children. Likewise, the model of God as King becomes good King who exercises His power and authority for the benefit of His people. Even the model of God as Lord can become good Lord who seeks the loyalty of His subjects in order to better protect them from harm and danger. These "qualified" models of God better align with the dynamics of the Kingdom of God reflected in the life and ministry of Christ where the last shall be first and the greatest among you shall be the one who serves.[349]

This way of "qualifying" the hierarchical language of God in tradition mitigates the need to eliminate hierarchical religious language because the mode of that relationality has now been shifted towards the language of empowerment and benevolence rather than domination and narcissism. It also avoids resorting to a straight egalitarianism that is difficult to support in a biblical model of divine-human relationality. Finally, it avoids the problem of jumbling together many competing and sometimes even contradictory metaphors where it is not always entirely clear which metaphor should prevail as a model in any particular social dynamic. While there are other benefits to the proliferation of metaphors of God, such as the ability to affirm the equal value of women's identity granted by equivalent feminine imaging of God, the use of qualifying language provides another angle from which to challenge the improper application of biblical models of God to the social dynamics at work in our culture. Sadly, in our present culture, we even have to qualify our use of the imagery of mother to that of good Mother to ensure that this imagery retains its benevolent connotations.

---

349. Matt 29:30; 23:11.

Liberation and The Hospitable God

Turning to the contemporary project of re-imagining God, there are two prevailing models that I want to further engage in this study.[350] The first is from Liberation theology with its model of the egalitarian God of justice. The second is from the Hospitable God movement with its model of the hospitable God of welcome. I have already discussed the vision of Liberation theology extensively in chapter 4 of this study where I identified three of its key movements: (1) the expanded view of salvation that embraces concrete justice-making in this life, (2) the challenge to the systemic forces of sin that undermine that justice, and (3) the recognition of some of the personal effects of systemic sin.[351] These ideas center around the restoration of egalitarian justice in the world in accordance with a vision where "[t]here is neither Jew nor Greek, there is neither slave nor free, there is no male and female, for you are all one in Christ Jesus."[352]

The hospitable God movement builds on this with an ethic of hospitality that aims to eliminate all forms of violence in the encounter between persons who are different from one another.[353] Letty Russell has written of hospitality as "[t]he practice of God's welcome reaching out across difference to participate in God's actions bringing justice and healing in our world of crisis and our fear of the ones we call 'other.'"[354] At heart, this is about learning to appreciate a "unity without uniformity" such that people who are of different backgrounds, political persuasions, or religious convictions can live together in harmony in the midst of their differences.[355] This avoids the "colonialist" tendencies to see those who are different as either a threat to be dominated or as "[a] form of charity or entertainment" to be treated patronizingly. Instead it seeks to build harmonious partnerships

---

350. Newlands and Smith (*Hospitable God*, 8) say, "What sort of God is the God of Jesus Christ? Not a God of tribal partiality, hate, discrimination, punishment and the like. Such imagery in relation to God has been operative in all the major religious traditions. Against this there is a persistent tradition in Christianity and in other major religions that there is a God of love, compassion, justice and fairness, forgiveness and reconciliation. There is an urgent need to encourage all of us to re-imagine this God, and to use all the imagery and imagination at our disposal to do so."

351. See opening paragraph on "Materiality of Salvation" in chapter 4.

352. Gal 3:28 (ESV).

353. For more on this "elimination of violence" aspect of hospitality, see Kärkkäinen's (*CCTPW*, 2:310–39) chapter on "Divine Hospitality."

354. Russell, *Just Hospitality*, 53.

355. Russell, *Just Hospitality*, 65.

among those who are different based on a mutual sense of respect and hospitality.[356] Clearly, this remains an urgent task in society as those who are perceived as different are often demonized and discriminated-against with ever-increasing frequency.[357]

Lucien Richard writes that "Hospitality to the stranger demands sacrifice: to surrender our biases: to make the interests, joys and sorrows of the stranger our own. As such, hospitality to the stranger is subversive by nature, threatening to the existing powers."[358] George Newlands and Allen Smith concur, suggesting that hospitality involves a generosity in looking at strange cultures with a positive appreciation for their beliefs and an openness to learn from them.[359] As such, they rightly believe that hospitality is a matter of vital importance for the creation of a humane society.[360]

While the hospitable God movement reflects an effort to put into practice the unconditional love of God, there are things that it simply cannot embrace. For instance, violence, coercion, manipulation, neglecting the marginalized, and oppression towards others represent things that are incompatible with the orientation towards hospitality. Newlands and Smith suggest that when confronted by people who act in these ways, there might still be dialogue, but there will be no agreement that allows those practices to continue. Thus, "[h]ospitality is a challenge as much as a willingness to embrace."[361] It is a challenge to all the ways of relating that undermine genuine mutuality and respect. It is an embrace of the beauty of difference and the humility to be made a learner again in the presence of that difference.

---

356. Russell, *Just Hospitality*, 82.

357. Russell (*Just Hospitality*, 82–84) sees this call to hospitality as having four interwoven biblical aspects: (1) The unexpected presence of God that can manifest in our random acts of hospitality, (2) solidarity with the marginalized who struggle for empowerment, dignity and fullness of life, (3) living in harmony with others despite our differences, and (4) the creation of a community that acts hospitably towards others.

358. Richard, *Living The Hospitality*, 21.

359. Newlands and Smith (*Hospitable God*, 19) say, "Generosity in a Christian context involves a commitment to giving, unconditionally and with an emphasis on those who are most in need. It also means an intellectual generosity, a willingness to look for the best interpretations of strange cultures and beliefs and to be open to learn from them."

360. Newlands and Smith, *Hospitable God*, 7.

361. Newlands and Smith, *Hospitable God*, 19.

The Good, Hospitable and Liberating God

Rather than make a claim that either the model of the egalitarian God of justice in Liberation theology, or the hospitable God of welcome in the Hospitable God movement, or the good God of empowerment in Prosperity theology can stand alone as the one model to rule them all, I want to instead suggest that each of these models represents a key dimension of *shalom* that can only be fully appreciated by holding all three of these models together. So, I propose that a model of the Good, Hospitable, and Liberating God best captures the dynamics of the three main dimensions of human flourishing represented by the Hebrew notion of *shalom*—the personal, the interpersonal, and the societal. And while these three models each have a slightly different understanding of the mode of relationality of the Triune God, these models can still be reconciled under the *kenotic* vision of the relationality of God as I will detail below. Taken together then, these models can more comprehensively reflect the *kenotic* orientation towards the flourishing of His creation that marks the divine-human relationship and underwrites the affirmation of ecological flourishing as well.

If we think about Prosperity theologies and their focus on personal empowerment out of narratives of victimization, it is possible to imagine that apart from hospitality and a concern for societal justice, this can lead to a self-assertiveness that borders on narcissism. This is why some have been critical of popular psychology and the message "I'll make a champion out of you."[362] If the attitude is "I'm going to do what I want. I'm going to say what I say. Don't anyone try to shut me down," then it's easy to see how this can result in a dismissal of others and a flouting of societal justice. But as we have discussed in our exploration of the liberative elements of Prosperity theologies, there is a real need for the affirmation of self-worth in individuals who have been stripped of it their entire lives. A certain base affirmation of self-worth is actually necessary before people are able to see value in others in a healthy and mutual way. A certain base of healthy self-worth is also necessary so that people can say "justice for all" instead of "justice for me." This contribution to personal empowerment and the cultivation of a healthy sense of self-worth is what Prosperity theologies safeguard in the larger picture of comprehensive *shalom*.

It is also important to consider that personal empowerment and a concern for systemic justice without a value for others who are different

---

362. See Volf (*A Public Faith*, 12) for this critique.

The Good, Hospitable, and Liberating God

from yourself can lead to fighting for the rights of your own social clique over-against all others. "Justice for me and those like me!" it says. And everyone else doesn't much matter. That sort of narrowness is what is behind racial, political, religious, and sexual divisions of every kind. Likewise, personal empowerment combined with a value for others without an acknowledgement of systemic sin can lead to a naivety about the social advantages/disadvantages that factor into the personal development of people who come from disadvantaged backgrounds. This is similar to the difficult reality many Black Americans feel when told that their disadvantaged status is due to their own "poor" choices with no recognition of the historical context of their circumstances. This is why empowerment should always be paired with hospitality and justice in an affirmation of human flourishing.

Turning now to the role of hospitality in the larger picture of *shalom*, we have already developed the way that the Hospitable God movement advocates for a sense of value for those who are different from ourselves. Indeed, this movement makes difference something to be celebrated and embraced rather than devalued and excluded. But when placed apart from personal empowerment, this value for others can become a form of idolatry—looking to others for the strength, affirmation, and empowerment that one cannot find in oneself. In other circumstances, it can manifest as a lack of proper self-care in the name of compassionate action towards others, which could lead to burn-out. It can even enable an avoidance of having to face issues of personal brokenness in the name of having to tend to the needs of others. But the value for others only comes into proper perspective in the context of a healthy value for the self. After all, we are exhorted to love others as we love ourselves.[363]

Receiving genuine and respectful hospitality from others can also result in a disempowering dynamic, even when the other has our empowerment and affirmation in mind. This is because the point of real empowerment is that it must arise from within the individual him/herself. They must overcome their own narratives of victimization—no one can do this on their behalf without undermining their growth and development. Even if *we* don't harbor any colonialist view of others as "charity cases" or "entertainment," they might still receive it as charity and remain disempowered in themselves.[364] This is why it is important to supplement a vision for hospitality with a vision for proper empowerment.

---

363. Mark 12:31.
364. Russell, *Just Hospitality*, 82.

Finally, while the Hospitable God movement does acknowledge the need for solidarity with the marginalized, it is a hard thing to recognize the ways that we ourselves contribute to the systemic oppression of others. Thus, while a value for others and respect for their differences are important foundations for learning to listen well, overcoming our blind spots may often require the kind of stark calls for systemic justice that arise from Liberation theologies. In short, we should never underestimate our ability to live unaware of our own biases. The louder the voices for justice can be, the better chance that we will awaken from our slumber.

Earlier we discussed how traditional Liberation theologies focus our attention on countering the systemic effects of sin in society. Some Liberation theologies even bring attention to the personal effects of systemic sin. When victimization occurs at the systemic level, it needs to be countered at the systemic level to eliminate its effects on the entire culture. However, dealing with these systemic issues can have some unintended consequences that undermine the flourishing we are trying to achieve. For instance, challenging the systemic issues that lead to poverty and disenfranchisement by advocating for political and economic reforms is certainly a fundamental and necessary task of justice-making in the world. However, without a sensitivity to the dynamics of personal empowerment, it is entirely possible to address systemic victimization while leaving personal internal narratives of victimization untouched. So, while I may fight for a change to the laws that restrict my ability to break out of poverty, I might harbor the belief that I am a victim to these laws and that my life can only be improved when these laws are changed. This locates the power to change outside of myself—which is profoundly disempowering in its own way. Prosperity theologies act to confront these sorts of internal victim-narratives and relocate the power to change within the victim him/herself.

One more factor to consider is that the emphasis on systemic justice-making separated from a value for those who are different from ourselves can lead to a marketplace of competing justice-causes that are each fighting for a piece of a shrinking pie of resources. Hospitality teaches us how to make appropriate compromises along the way so that all of these justice-causes can co-exist in harmony.

The Good, Hospitable, and Liberating God

Empowerment, Hospitality, and Liberation as Peace, Righteousness, and Justice

If we remember our discussion of the way peace, righteousness and justice coincide in the biblical understanding of *shalom*, we can see why these categories of empowerment, hospitality, and justice also intermingle in a more comprehensive view of wholeness.[365] Each of these deals with the phenomenon of victimization in a different dimension. Empowerment (intrapersonal *shalom*) deals with victimization within oneself manifested in limiting narratives of victimization that we internalize and believe. Hospitality (interpersonal *shalom* and righteousness) speaks to the victimization of others who are different from ourselves through conscious and subconscious bias and the failure to learn from the perspectives of others. And justice (systemic *shalom*) addresses victimization at a societal level that traps entire people groups in systemic manifestations of oppression. Thus, a model of the Good God of empowerment, the Hospitable God of welcome, and the Liberating God of justice speaks most broadly and clearly to a comprehensive vision of human flourishing in the immanent frame that addresses all three dimensions of victimization that we experience. And while each of these models contains hints of the others, the distinct challenges raised by each form of victimization affirms that holding these three models in tension together is a more effective way to overcome those challenges than privileging one model alone.

But, how are we to reconcile the different views of the relationality of God held by each of these views? After all, the Good God derives from a *kenotic* other-oriented understanding of the relationality of God; the Hospitable God arises from the self-giving unconditional love of God; and the Liberating God arises from an egalitarian social model of the Trinity. For this task, I propose that the *kenotic* understanding of the relationality of God has the potential to encompass the important dimensions of all of these views and should be adopted as the unifying model of God's relationality for this hybrid metaphor of the Good, Hospitable, and Liberating God.

In regards to the model of the Hospitable God, a *kenotic* understanding of the love of God is perhaps an even better fit than a focus on self-giving unconditional love. After all, a *kenotic* orientation to the flourishing of another is nearly an exact definition of what it means to be hospitable. Besides this, I have already discussed how being "oriented to the flourishing

---

365. Goldingay, *OTT*, 3:558.

of another" is a better translation of *kenosis* (κένωσις) than "self-giving" because self-giving can imply a focus on one's own sacrifice rather than on the need of another. Again, not very hospitable.

As for the egalitarianism that derives from a social model of the Trinity, without getting into the muddy waters of the debates about the appropriateness of using intra-Trinitarian *perichoresis* (περιχώρησις) as a model for a social program, I'd like to propose an alternative way to affirm these goals that Liberation theology sets out to achieve.[366] I have already shown how using the supra-adjective "good" offers a different way to reform the traditional patriarchal religious language in a way that undermines abusive expressions of hierarchy and replaces them with an "upside-down" servant-hood understanding of Lordship. So, if the greatest is the one who serves, then the Lord is the one who serves most profoundly. Isn't this the meaning of Jesus washing his disciples' feet and responding to Peter's protests by saying, "Unless I wash you, you have no part with me"?[367] I.e.—Unless you allow me to serve you, you have no understanding of what I've come to reveal about the Father and His Kingdom. I have translated this servant-heartedness as the *kenotic* commitment of the Lord to promote the flourishing of His creation—again to emphasize that the motivation is the need of the other rather than the self-sacrifice in the act of being a servant. So, this *kenotic* orientation succeeds in offering a critique of the prevailing abuses of hierarchy.

But how can a *kenotic* view of God's mode of relating lead to egalitarianism among people—the second task of Liberation theologies? I propose that the goal of flourishing relationships is a mutual hospitality towards one another. A mutual *kenosis* (κένωσις) where each person is oriented to promote the flourishing of the other. It is an ideal that is certainly hard to reach and maintain in reality, but as a vision for truly egalitarian relationships, I cannot think of a more generous egalitarianism. Imagine, as a contrast, an egalitarianism where each person is constantly making sure their own rights are defended at all times. This is what an egalitarianism looks like that is grounded in the affirmation of the sanctity of the autonomous self. But a *kenotic* egalitarianism where each person lives oriented in hospitality towards the other—now that sounds divine.[368]

---

366. As an example of a view opposed to the use of the Trinity as a social program, see Husbands ("The Trinity is *Not* Our Social Program," 121–22).

367. John 13:8 (NIV).

368. Pun intended.

The Good, Hospitable, and Liberating God

In relationships, the goal of other-oriented hospitality is not to end up creating a co-dependent relationship on the one hand or to be a narcissist on the other. If I allow the other person to lose their identity in me, that is co-dependency where I am enabling the other person's perpetual immaturity and dependence. If I lose my identity in serving them, that is a sophisticated form of narcissism where I am focused on my own self-sacrifice and self-erasure.[369] Neither of these can lead to healthy mutual relationships. This is why I have said throughout this study that a certain baseline level of self-love/wholeness is required to have genuinely mutual *kenotic* relationships. One that refuses co-dependency and self-erasure. The goal is to be empowered to become a whole person oneself and to empower others to become whole people themselves too.[370] Ultimately that looks like them being empowered to enter into mutual relationships of hospitality of their own.

Think of how this qualifies male headship in the family. Men, according to *kenotic* egalitarianism, have the responsibility of being the first to show hospitality, i.e.—the responsibility of bending first in an argument; the responsibility of listening first towards a reconciliation. But if that hospitality is not reciprocated, it can devolve again to autonomous selves defending their own territory.[371] Alternatively, if one party always gives hospitality to the other ad infinitum and the other remains an autonomous self, it can result in an abusive relationship between them. That is why egalitarian mutuality is the true end goal of *kenotic* relationships. And, ironically, why *kenotic* relationships are probably the best way to achieve truly egalitarian relationships.

All of that to say, the *kenotic* model of God's relationality can support the egalitarian values needed for the justice-making of Liberation theology. So, having established that the *kenotic* model of God's relationality can support the model of the Good God, the Hospitable God, and the Liberating

---

369. Miroslav Volf (*After Our Likeness*, 67) has suggested that some have taken the concept of *kenosis* to an extreme to suggest that in authentic personhood there is no "self" that remains. There is only the movement of pure relation 'from' and 'towards' the other. I also question this interpretation of *kenosis*, especially as it relates to the self-erasure of identity of Christians to form the "single subject" of the universal church.

370. I will talk about how this is sourced in God in the section on a Theology of Abundance.

371. This is certainly not to say that women cannot initiate hospitality—and probably in most relationships, they do—but God makes this a responsibility and requirement for men. I will refrain from speculating as to why.

God, we can embrace this hybrid model and its comprehensive vision of human flourishing in the immanent frame as the expression of the *kenotic* orientation of God for the flourishing of others.[372]

The Good, Hospitable, and Liberating God and Theo-Centric Flourishing in the Immanent Frame

Finally, we come full circle back to the subject of how a theo-centric view of flourishing that arises from the Prosperity theology convictions regarding the goodness of God can correspond with a view of ordinary human flourishing in the immanent frame. In various places throughout this study I have detailed how this immanent focus came to prominence in the Prosperity tradition through its view of healing as wholeness, embrace of a victorious eschatology, and understanding of holiness as consecrated materiality. This, combined with its singular focus on positioning people for maximal faith and breakthrough in this life, naturally led to a view of *shalom* that converged at many points with the immanent frame of modern society. These liberative elements were detailed in chapter 4 of this study and emphasized the theme of empowerment to overcome the narratives of victimization in a believer's life.

In this chapter I identified the model of the Good God as the primary metaphor of God that arises from Prosperity theologies and proposed a hybrid model of the Good, Hospitable, and Liberating God as a comprehensive metaphor to address the three forms of victimization that need to be overcome for comprehensive *shalom* to arise. The task that remains is to articulate how this model of the Good, Hospitable, and Liberating God conditions our understanding of the Lordship demands of God expressed in the calls to obedience, discipleship, repentance, and forgiveness and then to show how this results in a theology of abundance regarding the Christian life. I hope to show how these calls can be framed to promote ordinary human flourishing in keeping with the *kenotic* orientation of God and a comprehensive vision of *shalom* as empowerment, hospitality, and liberation.

---

372. Beyond the *kenosis* of the Son (Phil 2:5–8), we can recognize the *kenosis* of the Father who 'so loved the world that He gave . . .' (John 3:16) And we can recognize the *kenosis* of the Spirit who 'does not speak on his own,' but only what he hears (John 16:13). So, *kenosis* can denote the mode of relationality characteristic of each of the members of the Trinity.

The Good, Hospitable, and Liberating God

Theo-Centric Flourishing and the Benevolent Lordship of the Triune God

In chapter 3, we looked at theological proposals for flourishing life from Jürgen Moltmann, Richard Bauckham, and Miroslav Volf. There, we saw the value of Moltmann's commitment to egalitarian mutuality and liberation but could not follow him in rejecting the hierarchical language in Scripture and in the believer's relationship with God. We wondered if there was a way to keep his egalitarian values in the framework of a hierarchical relationality. We have established that here in the *kenotic* model of God's relationality.

Next, we considered Bauckham's qualification of Moltmann's views and appreciated his sensitive take on obedience to the Lord being responsive love meant to free us from the compulsion to sin. That freedom was then meant to be a freedom *for* others, not a freedom *from* others. While there was much to like in Bauckham's proposal, we wondered how it might apply to people who had been victims of sin and were carrying deep brokenness as a result. We addressed that with the liberative elements of Prosperity theologies that emphasize personal empowerment out of narratives of victimization in chapter 4.

Finally, we heard Miroslav Volf's call to a sacramental life of mindfulness and the cultivation of the virtue needed to achieve it.[373] The life that goes well, that is lived well, and that is pleasurable boils down to one thing that is within our control—to live our lives in mindfulness of God and others and to find pleasure in doing so. We have built on this with the challenge to hold a proper tension between hunger for breakthrough and contentment in limitation in chapter five.

So, what do we gain with these various qualifications? We establish the *kenotic* orientation towards the flourishing of the other as the mode of the Triune God's relationality; we extend the task of liberation to include every form of victimization, intrapersonal, interpersonal, and systemic; and we find a responsible way to encourage the pursuit of breakthroughs in life while holding onto contentment in relationship with God. In other words, we discover that God wants us to flourish! And that this involves being freed from every form of victimization and receiving the permission to

---

373. Volf (*Flourishing*, 206) says, "[t]he right kind of love for the right kind of God bathes our world in the light of transcendent glory and turns it into a theater of joy."

pursue breakthroughs in every area of life by faith. This is the promise held by a mature expression of Prosperity theology for the immanent frame.

On Obedience and Discipleship in Kenotic Perspective

In light of this mature expression of Prosperity theology, I want to offer some reflections on how this qualifies the way we understand various dimensions of the Christian life. Hans Urs von Balthasar, in reflecting on theological anthropology, notes that "One becomes a true human person . . . when one is able to relate to the Father in the way the incarnate Son relates to the Father, and that relation takes the form of obedient response."[374] John Goldingay and Walter Brueggemann agree, saying "Israel's crucial mode of engagement with Yahweh is by obedience."[375] Taking seriously this element of divine lordship over humanity, it is then left to work out how to reconcile this with the revelation of the Triune God's persistent *kenotic* "other-regard." The obvious implication is that as He is committed to people's flourishing, their wisest course of action is in trusting obedience. If His highest delight is in seeing people into *shalom*, they can delight in surrendering to His rule trusting that it is for their flourishing. Bauckham captures the profundity of this revelation in saying, "[The Triune God's] self-giving in abasement and service ensures that his sovereignty over all things is also a form of his self-giving."[376] He rules with the flourishing of others in mind.

What might this benevolent rule of God mean for the high call to discipleship? The call to discipleship has sometimes been understood as somewhat exclusive and elitist. The impression is that those who are unwilling to adhere to the high discipleship standards of Christ are deemed to be unworthy of God's acceptance and favor. But a *kenotic* paradigm of God's relationality helps to reveal God's "other-orientation" in the call to discipleship as well. Perhaps discipleship can then be likened to an invitation to a program of rehabilitation where the addiction is to sin and to our chosen coping mechanisms for dealing with victimization. For instance, how else might God remove pride and fear from our hearts? If our commitment to the process of rehabilitation is weak, then as soon as God begins to provoke our pride, we will abandon the process with our pride intact. As

---

374. For a summary of Balthasar's Theological Anthropology, see Aristotle Papanikolaou, "Person, *Kenosis* and Abuse," 49.

375. Goldingay, *OTT*, 3:181.

376. Bauckham, *Jesus and the God*, 45.

soon as God begins to touch our fears, we will run back to our unhealthy coping patterns more full of fear than ever. The high commitment level required by God is so that we allow His Spirit to complete its purifying work of removing the compulsions to sin and the narratives of victimization from our lives.

If you tell me to lie down so you can cut open my arm I will either run away in terror or punch you in the face. If you tell me to lie down so you can cut open my arm to remove a dangerous infection, then as painful as that process will be, I won't move a muscle—because I know it is for my flourishing. This should be the context in which the call to discipleship is heard. This is different from Bauckham's view that obedience is a manifestation of responsive love to God. This is claiming that because God is oriented to our flourishing, obedience to Him is vital to our own ordinary human flourishing.

On Repentance and Forgiveness in Kenotic Perspective

Another way that *kenosis* (κένωσις) changes the way we hear God is in the call to repentance. One of the common effects of a repeated pattern of sin is that it "sears the conscience" and progressively de-sensitizes a person to that sin. Think of a young man who numbs his loneliness by inflicting self-harm. Then over some time that ceases to bring relief and so he moves on to harming animals. And the pattern repeats until he finds he feels nothing committing violence against people. We have heard that the call to repentance is meant to demonstrate the authenticity of our remorse. But if we consider this call from the perspective of the *kenotic* "other-regard" of God, we can also see something important for our own ordinary flourishing in this call. Just as sin de-sensitizes our conscience to the brokenness caused by our sin, repentance re-sensitizes us to the consequences of our sins. The deeper the repentance, the more our consciences are restored. So, a program of regular repentance—the quick acknowledgement of our mistakes—can help to keep our consciences sensitive to the movements of the Spirit alerting us to ways that we might be being inhospitable towards others. In other words, repentance can be a healthy part of ordinary flourishing.

Finally, the flip side of repentance is the practice of offering forgiveness. I have already written about how giving forgiveness can be part of the recovery of "good power" for the victims of sin who feel that their power over their lives has been taken from them. Forgiveness is one of the expressions of "good power" that can never be taken away by another. With that in mind, how might we hear the call to forgiveness that Jesus gives? What I hear is that to hold onto unforgiveness requires holding onto victimization narratives as well. And so long as we hold onto victimization narratives, we will be profoundly disempowered in those areas of our lives that they touch. This is one reason why the regular practice of forgiveness is empowering because it restores a sense of personal agency to the victims of sin. When Jesus calls us to a life of forgiveness, he is calling us to a life of overcoming victimization—even when what happened to us was not anyone's fault in particular.[377] The life that practices forgiveness is the life that is free of the narratives of victimization.[378] The life that is adept at blaming is a life drowned in narratives of victimization. This is why the call to forgiveness is also vital to our ordinary flourishing.

It is not for believers to decide who is a real victim and who is not. Victims are identified by whomever displays the symptoms of victimization. And everyone does in some measure and in particular areas of their lives. Broadly applied, the life of forgiveness—of overcoming our victimization narratives—ensures that we never cease to flourish, no matter the circumstances of our lives. Thus, it is not the absence of sin alone that leads to *shalom*.[379] It is the presence of forgiving life that provides the best evidence of human flourishing.

On Christian Freedom in Light of Kenotic Relationality

As we come to the close of this study, I want to return now to consider how a *kenotic* view of God's relationality influences how we understand Christian freedom. With Richard Bauckham I agree that the biblical view of Christian freedom involves a submission to the lordship of God motivated by responsive love where that freedom is not meant to be freedom *from* others, but rather a freedom *for* others to serve them in love.[380] And I

---

377. This overcoming of victimization is what allows for the will to embrace described by Volf (*Exclusion & Embrace*, 105).

378. This addresses Volf's (*Exclusion & Embrace*, 103) legitimate concerns about using the language of oppressor/victim. After all, "[e]ach party will find good reasons for claiming the higher moral ground of a victim." My point is that using the language of victimization is useful only when you are exhorting everyone to relinquish their victimizations. Otherwise, it is actually disempowering.

379. Plantinga Jr., *Breviary of Sin*, 7–27.

380. Bauckham, *Crisis of Freedom*, 68.

The Good, Hospitable, and Liberating God

agree that this submission to God results in our deliverance from the "compulsion to sin" so that we can be freed to love others well.[381] However, I have pointed out that this view misses the fact that God doesn't just deliver us from the "compulsion to sin," but also delivers us from the residue of the sins that have been committed against us—the narratives of victimization that can so thoroughly suffocate our lives.

If we take seriously the "other side of sin," then it becomes clear that a part of becoming freed to love others well is being restored to a healthy sense of self-worth and empowerment to the "good power" of personal agency again. This is where I think Bauckham's resistance to an autonomous view of the self misses the phenomenon of victimization and why it is vital to "humanity made whole" to express some healthy form of autonomy. In this regard, I appreciate the point that Jürgen Moltmann and Hannah Arendt are making that Christian freedom should have a component where freedom is defined as the ability to begin something new—such as a new stance towards life, or a new decision to give forgiveness to our oppressors.[382] At heart, this is about restoring a healthy sense of "good power" to people so that they can be capable of genuinely mutual relationships in their lives again.[383]

In the *kenotic* view of mutual relationships there is a balance between healthy self-care and healthy orientation to the flourishing of others. God is committed to our flourishing to wholeness so that we can overflow to being committed to the flourishing of others too. This is not self-erasure, losing our identity completely in the other; and it is not co-dependency, allowing others to remain immature in their dependence upon us. Rather, it is liberation from our own narratives of victimization and then becoming passionate about helping others to be liberated from their narratives of victimization. The only caveat is that while we can point the way, others can only be liberated if they walk the path of liberation themselves. That is why empowerment and some measure of autonomy is a key part of liberation. We simply cannot give empowerment to others. They must grasp it

---

381. Bauckham, *Crisis of Freedom*, 17.

382. Moltmann (*LGFL*, 110) is referencing Hannah Arendt's (*Vita Activa*, 168) work.

383. Bauckham's fear of autonomy is that it will lead to consumerism or the idea that others are a limitation to our own freedom/power. But in the case of overcoming victimization, it might really be true that others are limiting our own freedom/power in unhealthy ways. That is why healthy autonomy must be a part of a balanced view of freedom.

for themselves for it to be meaningful in overcoming their own ontological victimization.

Miroslav Volf spoke of freedom as the ancient idea of disciplining oneself so that one could achieve the freedom of mastery in a particular field. He spoke of it as mindfulness of God so that we could enjoy the world as a theater of His glory.[384] I would say another discipline to learn would be the discipline to be made whole so that we could be a part of God's growing *shalom* in the world. We spread wholeness by being whole ourselves. A *kenotic* view of God's relationality envisions everyone living empowered, hospitable, and liberating lives that reflect the *shalom* of God at every level of human life. That is the picture of a healthy balance between self-care and the care of others.

I have proposed the model of the Good God because I believe that it is the underlying theological affirmation that lies behind many of the other commitments in Prosperity theologies. In particular, it is the primary metaphor of God that adherents of Prosperity theologies cling to in order to realize the empowering dimensions of the Prosperity message. To believe that God wants to transform our lives and communities towards the promised *shalom* of heaven right now can only work in a model of the goodness of God. But this simple notion stood in need of deeper development to showcase its full radical potential. That is why I have devoted this chapter to extending it by rooting it in a *kenotic* view of the character of God that more fully captures the Biblical nuances of divine self-revelation.

I have further developed this *kenotic* model of the Good God to include hospitality and liberation in order to mature Prosperity theologies beyond its blind spots and to point to how a robust vision of the Good God who seeks the flourishing of all creation could fund a theo-centric understanding of the lordship of God that could align with humanistic views of human flourishing—an important apologetic task in contemporary theology. Part of this was my attempt to bring Prosperity theology out of the theological doghouse and into legitimate contemporary theological dialogues on a wide variety of themes. Another part of it was to try to point the way to how Prosperity theologies might mature going into the future. That is what I will address in the next and final chapter of this study.

---

384. Volf, *Flourishing*, 206.

The Good, Hospitable, and Liberating God

Conclusion

In this chapter, I wanted to establish the basis for exploring new metaphors of God to frame why I believed that the model of the Good God that arises from Prosperity theologies could make a meaningful contribution to the field. To say that "the Good God" is the best model of God to represent Prosperity theologies is, of course, my own opinion. However, I feel confident that this model reflects the key values of Prosperity theologies as reflected in many songs, books, and themes that suggest that this is so. In particular, the themes of the affirmation that God wants believers to experience ordinary human flourishing both in this life and the next, as well as the focus on the *kenotic* orientation of God towards our flourishing, further establishes the validity of naming "the Good God" as the model best reflective of Prosperity theologies.

Having identified this model, I drew attention to the biblical support for an emphasis on Goodness through looking at the relationships between Hebraic ideas of holiness; peace, justice, and righteousness; loving-kindness, truthfulness and covenant; and divine compassion. This led to the suggestion that using "good" as a supra-adjective of the traditional language for God could provide another way to challenge the abuses of patriarchalism without abandoning the traditional language.

In trying to place the model of the Good God amongst other contemporary efforts to re-imagine God, such as the Hospitable God movement and Liberation theology, I pointed out that each of these models represented a different dimension of overcoming victimization narratives. The Good God of empowerment addressed the overcoming of intrapersonal victimizations; the Hospitable God of welcome focused on overcoming interpersonal victimizations; and the Liberating God of justice spoke to the systemic victimizations in society. These needed to be harmonized in order to provide a better unified front to address comprehensive victimizations for the sake of promoting human flourishing. That is why I took up the task of expanding my vision of the *kenotic* orientation of God to be able to apply to the model of the Hospitable God and the Liberating God as well.

The connection between *kenosis* (κένωσις) and the Hospitable God was easy and natural. But demonstrating how a *kenotic* orientation could support the egalitarian values needed for Liberation theology required a bit more creative development. In the end, I drew the connection by showing that the goal of *kenotic* relationships is egalitarian mutuality—and not an egalitarianism of two autonomous selves, but rather an egalitarianism of two hospitable selves. Thus, I demonstrated that the *kenotic* orientation of God could fund the hybrid model of the Good, Hospitable, and Liberating God that affirmed every dimension of ordinary human flourishing.

The last section allowed me to summarize the various ways that Prosperity theologies have affirmed ordinary human flourishing from its liberative elements, its tension between hunger and contentment, and its *kenotic* model of God's relationality. I developed the implications of this for the Christian understanding of obedience, discipleship, repentance, and forgiveness to show how each of these dynamics actually can be understood to promote ordinary human flourishing rather than restrict it. Though many further tasks of development for this *kenotic* model of God could also be addressed, this marks the end of this study into the liberative elements of Prosperity theologies that affirm ordinary human flourishing in the immanent frame of modern society.

The ultimate expression of *shalom* would manifest when the *kenotic* orientation of God is finally reflected in the entire community. So, believers living empowered lives that are oriented to empowering others would help them to (1) overcome their own victimization narratives, (2) learn the practices of hospitality, and (3) eliminate the systemic roots of sin in society. Such a community would embrace the task of the *kenotic* stewardship of creation to extend *shalomic*-living to the whole of God's creation.

Conclusion

7
Conclusion
Towards a Theology of Empowerment and Abundance

A Theology of Empowerment and Abundance

THE THEMES THAT ARISE from maturing strands of Prosperity theology combined with the *kenotic* model of the relationality of God lead to the rough contours of a constructive theology of empowerment and abundance. The three ways that I want to talk about this here are (1) in the affirmation of empowerment, (2) in living from abundance and overflow, and (3) in living for abundance and overflow.

The Affirmation of Empowerment

It is certainly worth noting that theologians have not always seen the value of personal empowerment, sometimes even deriding the idea that God would bring out our best life now (referring to the popular title by Pastor Joel Osteen). There has been in theology a lingering fear that this would result in a self-oriented "me-first" quasi-spirituality—a far cry from the self-sacrifice modeled by Christ, they might say. But having looked at the liberative elements of Prosperity theologies from the perspective of helping people to overcome the narratives of victimization that have piled up in their lives, we have shown that some of this self-oriented "me-first" attitude can actually be a healthy part of the process of recovering an empowered and healthy self-image. The fact that it is an open question whether theologians believe God wants us to be empowered in this way or not is one of the reasons that I believe seeing the model of Christ's *kenosis* (κένωσις) as "self-sacrifice" has been so harmful to the lives of struggling believers for so long. In contrast, if the model of Christ's *kenosis* (κένωσις) is "other-orientation" towards enabling our flourishing, then we have room to affirm that some forms of empowerment are good—even essential—for authentic human dignity.

I remember hearing of a young mother driving her children to church one day. From the back seat her daughter exclaimed proudly, "Look mom! I put on my seatbelt all by myself!" To which her devout mother replied, "Now now, we don't brag on ourselves dear." That kind of fear of any hint of self-promotion and pride misses the ways that God wants to bring about healthy empowerment at every level of our lives. There are certainly some unhealthy forms of self-promotion. After all, the self-nature that constantly puts self above others is one of the primary manifestations of sin. But that is only half of the picture. Drawing on the example of Christ I used to describe *kenosis* (κένωσις) earlier, when our primary "self" problem is pride, then God will rebuke that pride to help us move towards true flourishing. But when our primary "self" problem is shame, then God will build us up with unexpected kindness and affirmation to move us towards true flourishing. We would do well to learn to better discern where the line is between healthy self-expression and unhealthy self-expression.

Healthy empowerment is about overcoming victimizations so that we can enter into hospitable relationships at every level of our lives. So personal empowerment is to recover in us a healthy sense of self-directedness that we can be the agents of change in our circumstances by the power of the Spirit. Interpersonal empowerment is about learning when and how to speak up for ourselves when we are being silenced or abused in manipulative relationships. And societal empowerment is about recognizing and challenging the systemic roots that disempower people and rob them of their equal dignity. Some theologians love the issues of societal empowerment, but not the issues of personal and interpersonal empowerment. That is short-sighted. Empowerment and flourishing should be affirmed at all three levels for healthy relationships to be possible at all.

We have already established that relationship with the *kenotic* God is the basis for the call to discipleship as rehabilitation from pride and fear, the call to a lifestyle of forgiveness as overcoming narratives of victimization, and the call to repentance as re-sensitizing our consciences for hospitable

Conclusion

relationships. These are reflective of key steps towards real empowerment to "good power" in believer's lives that God intends for everyone.

In Living FROM Abundance and Overflow

One of the undeveloped ideas that comes from the *kenosis* (κένωσις) model of God is that God creates out of the super-abundance within himself. So even after creating the vastness of the universe, God never lacks in abundance within himself. Neither was God lonely and in need of creation for company. But out of His nature of generosity, He created. Out of His super-abundance, He created. This, I believe offers an alternative way to envision what generosity is supposed to look like in the believer's life as well.

The vision of generosity that comes from a view of *kenosis* (κένωσις) as self-sacrifice pictures a generosity that flows out of lack—a self-sacrificing generosity. And while that sort of giving is commended by Jesus in the story of the widow's mite (Luke 21), I'm not sure that it should be normative of all giving in the Kingdom of God. Let me explain. If we always give out of our lack, it will lead either to burnout or to the exhaustion of our resources. Think of overfishing the sea or overharvesting the land. The sea and land might be able to sustain that sort of giving out of lack for a short amount of time, but if that practice is not curtailed, soon the resource will collapse and cease to be a resource for us and all future generations. A far better model is sustainable farming or fishing where the land and sea give out of the over-abundance of resources such that they are always being replenished for each new season. That, to me, is a picture of what sustainable generosity in the soul is supposed to look like under normal Kingdom circumstances.

While a *kenotic* view of generosity as orientation to the flourishing of another can also be interpreted to support sacrificial giving, in the framework of the generosity of God giving out of His super-abundance, the *kenotic* view can also support a view of generosity where we are meant to give out of abundance as well. The difference is that our internal resources of generosity are very limited and need to be constantly replenished by God's generosity towards us. The key to sustainable giving, then, is a spirituality of overflow that derives from a theology of abundance.

A spirituality of overflow begins with encounters with God's generous love for us and wholehearted commitment to our flourishing to *shalom* (wholeness in every dimension of life). That leads to a responsive love back to Him demonstrated by our willingness to accept the calls to wholeness represented in repentance (re-sensitizing our consciences towards hospitality to others), a lifestyle of forgiveness (overcoming our internal narratives of victimization), the challenges of discipleship (confronting the fears and pride that sabotage our relationships), and the vision of *shalom* for all. This program of empowerment imparts a healthy sense of self-worth and self-love in us and works to remove all of our internal barriers to healthy engagement with others. And out of that healthy self-love and experience of the generous commitment of God towards us for our flourishing, we begin to overflow with hospitality towards others once again. In short, the healthy self in healthy relationship with God seeks to share that health with others.

Picture for a moment how surprised we would be if we arrived at heaven's gates and the first thing that we encountered was Jesus with a towel slung over his shoulder kneeling down to wash our feet. What would we say if we reached out to serve God only for Him to stop us and say, "Let me serve you first." Would not such an encounter with God inspire us to respond in generosity to God and others out of joy and inspiration rather than a sense of duty? That is the cascading overflow created by the *kenotic* orientation of God towards the flourishing of others. The reason for the centrality of celebratory worship in Prosperity circles is to catch a glimpse of that divine generosity once again so that it can be deposited in our hearts to reinvigorate joyful generosity towards others.

In Living FOR Abundance and Overflow

Perhaps the most significant recovery of Prosperity theologies is in affirming the comprehensive materiality of the *shalom* that God desires to bring into the lives of His people. No longer is salvation relegated primarily to the spiritual dimension, but its ramifications for every area of present life are now being explored. This makes it clear that the fundamental purpose of the Kingdom of God/reign of God is not to establish loyalty throughout the earth or even submission to His will. Rather, it is to promote wholeness in every individual, in every relationship and in every system of the world. And this is why the intuitions of Prosperity theologies can speak so fluently to the topics of ordinary human flourishing in the immanent frame.

Of course, we recognize that this future *shalom* can only partially be realized here and that the most responsible attitude to cultivate towards it is in holding the tension between hungering for breakthroughs of that *shalom*

Conclusion

into our lives and finding contentment in our limitations as we await the final unveiling of the Kingdom of God. But as Moltmann and the Liberation theologians have shown us, a vision of the victory of *shalom* and the super-abundance of heaven in the eschaton is not just a wishful dream. Rather, that vision is a roadmap and a resource for present victorious living. It changes the way we pray with an awareness of the abundant resources in heaven that are right now within the reach of faith. It changes the way we worship to shift atmospheres towards active faith and a celebration of the unabashed goodness of the abundant life God intends for all. It changes the way we steward our gifts and talents to maximize our impact in welcoming the *shalom* of the Kingdom into every level of society to combat systemic obstacles to wholeness. And it changes the way we approach our relationships to dignify others before they feel dignified themselves, and to find ways to actively encourage the flourishing of all those around us.

As a final reflection for this study, I offer the following thought: What if building the Kingdom of God on the earth required more feasting and less fasting? More celebration and less consternation? Might that better capture the spirit of the *shalom* of which we speak? My prayer for you who have taken the time to work your way through this study is that you will experience the *shalom* of God breaking into your own heart and restoring in you a healthy self-worth, planting in you a vision for hospitable egalitarian relationships with your loved ones, and inspiring in you a compassion for those who are being hindered from experiencing that *shalom* for themselves. May God bless you as you shine your light on the world.

For Further Study

In concluding, I propose three areas where this research can be naturally expanded: (1) in deepening the connections between research in the behavioral and medical sciences with the theology of empowerment and abundance to further define our understanding of healthy self-expression and behavioral science perspectives on flourishing life; (2) to explore the differences between scarcity-based thinking and abundance-based thinking to position the church at the forefront of creative justice-making promoting the *shalom* of all; and (3) to consider how a theology of empowerment and abundance in a *kenotic* model of God's relationality can provide a fresh paradigm for Christian political engagement with the world.

Deepening Links to the Behavioral and Medical Sciences

In this study we have just scratched the surface of the types of synergies that can be developed between theology and the behavioral and medical sciences in an affirmation of ordinary human flourishing and *shalom*. From Robert Cloninger's Temperament and Character Inventory to Amartya Sen's capabilities approach to economic justice, we have already seen many ways that this dialogue develops and clarifies both fields. To this we could add studies such as Robert Ornstein and David Sobel's research on the medical benefits of pleasure, purpose, meaning, fun, and laughter.[385] Similarly, a recent study by Andrew Steptoe, Jane Wardle, and Michael Marmot explores how measurements of happiness correlate with markers of biological health. Researchers have long known that depression and stress correlate with higher incidences of heart disease and type II diabetes. What was novel was that higher reported levels of happiness and well-being also correlated with lower heart rates and lower levels of stress hormone in participant's bodies. In other words, actively improving the subjective well-being of patients had a therapeutic effect on their biological health.[386] This illustrates how a theological engagement with humanistic research on human flourishing quite literally has life and death stakes. These types of studies have to do with the field of proper self-care that should be a critical part of a lifelong discipleship program that aims for community *shalom*. Additionally, we could incorporate the research of Joel Fuhrman on the effects of nutrition on the healthy functioning of the body—in particular, the strengthening of the immune system.[387] The whole idea of finding ways to activate the natural healing processes of the body should be a field where Christians demonstrate clear leadership by developing a theology of healing based in a theology of creation.

Another clear connection is the significance of a theology of empowerment and abundance on a Christian view of mental health.[388] In my twenty years of ministry experience in pastoral counseling, the encounters that still haunt me were with individuals with PTSD due to traumatic experiences they had suffered that I could not help. Despite my best efforts to follow

---

385. See Ornstein and Sobel's work, *Healthy Pleasures: Discover the Proven Medical Benefits of Pleasure and Live a Longer, Healthier Life*.

386. Steptoe et al., "Positive Affect," 6508–12.

387. See Fuhrman, *Eat to Live: The Amazing Nutrient-Rich Program for Fast and Sustained Weight Loss*.

388. See Fayard, et al. on *A Christian Worldview and Mental Health*.

Conclusion

my training to help them to face the source of their fear and pain, I found that the more I tried to get them to engage their traumatic experiences, the more they were triggered into dissociative defense mechanisms. When the only tool you have in your toolkit is a hammer, everything looks like a nail. And I hammered away at their refusal to face the roots of their pain to no avail. Years later, I met one of them who had found help elsewhere and largely recovered. When I asked them what worked, they told me about a combination of psychiatric drugs to reduce neurotransmitter responses that helped to mitigate the intensity of their fight and flight reactions and about eye movement desensitization and reprocessing therapies that helped to reduce the association of their "triggers" with negative emotions. These therapies allowed them to remain calm enough to actually work through their fears and their pain and find gradual recovery. This again expands the way we think about empowerment and what the process of bringing an individual to a healthy self-image can entail. More studies like this would be valuable for both theological and pastoral reasons.

Scarcity-Thinking vs. Abundance-Thinking

Thomas Homer-Dixon has helped to start the conversation on the role scarcity can play in contributing to violence in the world.[389] He says that "[s]carcity of renewable resources—or what I call environmental scarcity—can contribute to civil violence, including insurgencies and ethnic clashes."[390] Brueggeman speaks of scarcity as something that was exploited by Pharaoh to his own economic gain at the expense of the people of Israel.[391] Recent research on the phenomenon of scarcity found that people who experienced the stress of scarcity in their lives whether from lack of money, time, companionship, or food suffered a reduced cognitive rationality to the tune of an equivalent 13 point reduction in IQ.[392] When there are not enough resources to meet the need, we become less rational and less able to step back to see the bigger picture. Scarcity, it seems, brings out the worst tendencies in us to hoard and deny resources to others to ensure our own advantage and survival. But the theology of abundance holds that a world of scarcity was never the intention of the Creator God, and neither was it ever meant

---

389. See Homer-Dixon, *The Environment, Scarcity, and Violence*.
390. Homer-Dixon, *The Environment*, 177.
391. Brueggeman, "The Liturgy of Abundance," 42–47.
392. Mani et al., "Poverty Impedes Cognitive Function," 976–80.

to be the ultimate end of the world. Instead, in a world of *shalom*, scarcity has been defeated by abundance and generosity in keeping with the *kenotic* character of God.

So how might believers best promote the proliferation of abundance throughout the earth? Beyond prayers and active faith to welcome proleptic experiences of the Kingdom of God in our present circumstances, I think that the work of promoting abundance throughout the world is a task for spirit-empowered imagination and creativity. This can work in parallel with an initiative for justly distributing scarce resources to all those in need, but it represents a different focus aimed at undermining the very causes of that scarcity in the world. So, for example, to address the unequal access to education in the world, creative entrepreneurs are envisioning a network of satellites around the entire planet that can provide equal access to the internet to every child in the world. Coupled with means of accessing the internet and online educational programs from the best universities in the world, this can revolutionize the problem of the scarcity of education in the poor countries of the world.

Another exciting and creative solution to some of the most vexing problems in the world comes from blockchain technology and its potential to disrupt many established industries and social systems. For example, the unhackable nature of the ledger technology behind blockchain can be used to create a voting system that eliminates the possibility of election fraud. Imagine the impact that this could have in countries rife with corruption. A scarcity-mentality would simply try to manage the corruption with the best methods currently available. The abundance-mentality actively seeks to creatively eliminate the root of the problem so there is no corruption to manage—at least in this part of the voting process. This might sound like it is just an affirmation of ingenuity and entrepreneurial spirit. But my point is that it should be the church that is leading the way in this sort of spirit-empowered ingenuity. This is why a theology of ingenuity and creativity based in a theology of abundance would be an invigorating extension of this study.

Another way that the mentality of scarcity expresses itself is seen in the tragic phenomenon of abortion in America today. There was a young mother who found out that she was pregnant at a time in her life when her family was experiencing financial insecurity and her relationship with her husband had subsequently been strained. He was out of town on a business trip and she knew that if he found out about the pregnancy it would make

Conclusion

domestic matters even more stressful. So, she felt trapped and as though she had to choose between saving her marriage or keeping the child. She made the difficult decision to have an abortion alone and under great stress. When her husband returned home, he happily shared the news that he had received a promotion at work and that their financial plight would now be relieved. But the news was devastating to the young mother because she realized that she had ended the life of her child for nothing. She had been trapped in a circumstance of threatened scarcity and it had caused her to make a decision that would grieve her for years to come. I wonder whether she would have made such a decision if she had not been experiencing such a threat of scarcity. What if she had had the assurance that resources would be available to her to help raise the child? Would it have changed how she might have made that decision that day? What if organizations that are pro-life focused more attention on providing such resources to women who are likewise under threatened scarcity? Might it give these young mothers the support they need to make a decision to preserve the life of their child instead? How many women who choose to have abortions do so under a similar threatened scarcity? When believers are narrowly fixated on the passage of anti-abortion legislation in their pro-life crusades, they might miss the more practical ways that a culture that values life could be cultivated in their local communities. Whether the laws change or not, the deeper issues of scarcity behind many abortions is something that can be positively addressed in communities right now.

Andrew Yang, a Democratic Presidential candidate during the 2020 election cycle, has spoken out about the stranglehold that this mentality of scarcity has had on many families in America. The financial insecurity that they are experiencing in the midst of accelerating job losses due to automation and a growing sense that the economy is not working for them have contributed to this widespread sense of scarcity across the nation. That has led to increased tribalism, racial tension, and indifference to issues such as climate change because it is hard to care about the penguins in Antarctica when you are struggling to figure out how you will pay your rent this month. Mr. Yang's proposed solution is to offer a universal basic income to all Americans over the age of 18 to help "take the financial boot off of their necks" and ease the transition during this fourth industrial revolution.

This universal basic income would effect many changes in how we perceive work and value in modern society. For starters, it would finally recognize the work being done by caregivers at home. And it would value the work of artists and culture creators more than the market system currently does. As more and more automation takes hold of the economy, people will have to replace the value they found in work with other ways to contribute meaningfully to society. But at the least, a universal basic income would value human life simply for being—a stark contrast to the utilitarian value of human life assigned by market economies. I think the recognition of the scarcity problem and the creative problem-solving demonstrated by Mr. Yang is a good example of the sort of approach a mindset of abundance would promote. The resources to solve the problems the world is facing are all out there ready to be marshalled to the cause. They just require some inspired imagination to unlock.

A Kenotic Theology of Political and Civic Engagement

This same spirit of ingenuity should apply to a *kenotic* theology of political and civic engagement as I have already alluded to above. From a broader perspective, this follows the two main movements of the exilic politics of John Howard Yoder which advocates for (1) the church as an alternative social group within society, and (2) the church seeking the welfare of the city in which it lives.[393] Contrast this with the Dominion theology popular in some Christian groups that attempts to either exercise a Christian form of government by electing Christian leaders into office, or that develops an entirely separate "alternative polis" with its own social services competing with governmental services.[394] Such an attempt to force "Christian" values on the society for people who don't necessarily share those values is colonialistic and misunderstands or ignores the roots of the issues—namely that this clash of values might not be most effectively addressed through heavy-handed policy changes. And the attempt to create a separated ideal Christian society abandons those who are excluded from that "Christian" alternative city. Yoder's exilic politics allows the church to be distinctive in its values and practices within the city while being charged to seek the welfare of the city as "good guests" in that city.

---

393. Yoder, *The Politics of Jesus*, 111. Cf. Yoder, *The Jewish-Christian Schism*, 193. I am aware that the scandals involving Yoder regarding long-running patterns of sexual harassment of young women compromises his credibility in ethics in certain respects. So, I engage his perspectives here with some reservations and mainly to propose a way to go beyond them.

394. Smith, "Politics and Economics," 184.

Conclusion

A *kenotic* theology of political and civic engagement extends what Yoder has proposed in that seeking the welfare of the city is not merely a "task" of the church, but rather it is the church living out its identity as the people who experience the *shalom* of God in their own lives and who have a resulting overflow of generosity for the *shalom* of the world. We do not serve the city because we are directed to do so. It is a natural overflow of a life that is rooted in the generosity of God who is passionate about our flourishing in every dimension of life. Thus, wisdom plays a central role in our methods of evangelism and witness to the city—when people see the wisdom of our lives in our flourishing in every dimension of life, they will seek out the church to be discipled into that wisdom and relationship with the God who is committed to their flourishing. When people see how we cultivate successful relationships of mutual trust and respect, they will come to learn how to cultivate that in their own families. When people see believers practice healthy conflict resolution habits, they will come to learn how to implement those in their relationships with their loved ones. In short, when people see believers flourishing in life, they will be drawn to the wisdom of life lived well and come to learn the values and beliefs that underwrite that wisdom.

In politics today, we are often forced to make an artificial choice between justice for the unborn on the one hand vs. justice for the poor, the abused, and the immigrants on the other. Yet somehow, we must rediscover how to make a choice for the Kingdom of God and for all of these justice issues over and against either of these inadequate options. That choice to stand for all justice issues is rooted in our commitment to the *shalom* of our communities—but the political sphere is not the only way to make this stand . . . perhaps not even the most appropriate way. The role that the church could play in our communities is to initiate creative ways to subvert the problems at the root of these justice issues in our society. The example of providing resources for newborn care to pregnant mothers who may feel the threatened scarcity that I detailed above is one way this could be done. Similar initiatives that identify and address the root problems facing the poor, abused, and immigrants in our communities would also help. Positioning the church as a reservoir of wisdom and resources for flourishing life in the community allows the church to serve everyone in the community irrespective of political differences that may persist.

Such a stance of the church in the city also allows for the church not to feel threatened by advances in science or technology or even the humanities.

Indeed, the *kenotic* theology of engagement actively seeks to learn from every science and from every culture to try to discern in those advances fresh ways to promote the flourishing of all. This is why the *kenotic* theology of political and civic engagement should be characterized by a spirit of ingenuity that seeks creative new solutions to societal issues that can work to promote the flourishing of all. Developing this *kenotic* political theology is an important future task for a theology of empowerment and abundance.

Surely, there are many more ways that this research can be extended to fully engage the many dimensions of *shalom*. If we want a theological vision of human flourishing that resonates with the immanent frame of modern society, we must continue to evolve our understandings of ordinary human flourishing to correlate with the best of the modern sciences and humanities. It is one of the key tasks of modern theology to interpret this proliferation of information into a coherent affirmation of a Christian view of flourishing in vital relationship with God. I remain excited to see this conversation deepen and unfold.

Bibliography

Adeboye, Olufanke. "'Arrowhead' of Nigerian Pentecostalism: The Redeemed Christian Church of God, 1952–2005." *Pnuema* 29 (2007) 24–58.
Albrecht, Daniel E., and Evan B. Howard. "Pentecostal Spirituality." In *The Cambridge Companion to Pentecostalism*, edited by Cecil M. Robeck Jr. and Amos Yong, 235–53. Cambridge: Cambridge University Press, 2014.
Althouse, Peter. *Spirit of the Last Days: Pentecostal Eschatology in Conversation with Jürgen Moltmann*. New York: Bloomsbury Academic, 2003.
Archer, Kenneth J. *A Pentecostal Hermeneutic: Spirit, Scripture and Community*. Cleveland, TN: Center for Pentecostal Theology, 2009.
Arendt, Hannah. *Vita Activa oder vom tätigen Leben*. Stuttgart: Kohlhammer, 1960.
Balthasar, Hans Urs Von. *The Glory of the Lord, A Theological Aesthetics, vol. VI: Theology: The Old Covenant*, edited by John Riches. Translated by Erasmo Leiva-Merikakis and Brian McNeil. Edinburgh: T. & T. Clark, 1983.
Barron, Bruce. *The Health and Wealth Gospel: What's Going on Today in a Movement that has Shaped the Faith of Millions?* Downers Grove, IL: Intervarsity, 1987.
Bauckham, Richard. *God and the Crisis of Freedom: Biblical and Contemporary Perspectives*. Louisville: Westminster John Knox, 2002.
———. *Jesus and the God of Israel: God Crucified and other Studies on the New Testament's Christology of Divine Identity*. Grand Rapids: Eerdmans, 2008.
Beeley, Christopher A. "Christ and Human Flourishing in Patristic Theology." Paper presented at the Yale Center for Faith and Culture Consultation on Christ and Human Flourishing, New Haven, CT, December, 2014.
Berger, Peter. "Pennies From Heaven." *The Wall Street Journal*, October 24, 2008. http://www.wsj.com/articles/SB122479455028963963.
Berry, Malinda. "Mission of God: Message of Shalom." In *Anabaptist Visions for the New Millenium*, edited by Dale Schrag and James Juhnke, 167–73. Scottdale, PA: Herald, 2000.
Bianchi, Mike. "Little League Dad Mike Grady Gave His All to Save Life of 12-year-Old Son." *Orlando Sentinel*, July 3, 2009. http://articles.orlandosentinel.com/2009-07-03/sports/bianchi_1_mike-grady-tony-dungy-two-sons.
Bloom, Paul. *How Pleasure Work: The New Science of Why We Like What We Like*. New York: Norton, 2010.

Bibliography

Bondi, Roberta C. *To Pray and to Love*. Minneapolis: Fortress, 1991.

Bowler, Kate. *Blessed: A History of the American Prosperity Gospel*. Oxford: Oxford University Press, 2013.

Bowman, Robert M. *The Word-Faith Controversy: Understanding the Health and Wealth Gospel*. Grand Rapids: Baker, 2001.

Brother Lawrence. *The Practice of the Presence of God*. Translated by John J. Delaney. New York: Image, 1977.

Brown, Brené. *Daring Greatly: How the Courage to Be Vulnerable Transforms the Way We Live, Love, Parent, and Lead*. New York: Avery, 2012.

———. *The Gifts of Imperfection: Let Go of Who You Think You're Supposed to Be and Embrace Who You Are*. Center City, MN: Hazelden, 2010.

Brueggeman, Walter. "The Liturgy of Abundance, the Myth of Scarcity." *Christian Century* 116.10 (1999) 42–47.

———. *Living Toward A Vision: Biblical Reflections on Shalom*, 2nd edition. New York: United Church, 1982.

———. "The Shrill Voice of the Wounded Party." In *The Other Side of Sin*, edited by Andrew S. Park and Susan L. Nelson, 26–40. Albany: State University of New York Press, 2001.

———. *Theology of the Old Testament: Testimony, Dispute, Advocacy*. Minneapolis: Fortress, 1997.

Brunner, Emil. *The Christian Doctrine of God*. Translated by Olive Wyon. Cambridge: James Clarke & Co., 2002.

Buxton, Graham. *Dancing in the Dark*. Waynesboro, GA: Paternoster, 2001.

Callen, Barry. "The Context: Past and Present." In *The Holiness Manifesto*, edited by Kevin Mannoia and Don Thorsen, 8–17. Grand Rapids: Eerdmans, 2008.

Carter, Robert K. *The Atonement for Sin and Sickness; or, a Full Salvation for Soul and Body*. Boston: Willard Tract Repository, 1884.

Cartledge, Mark. "Pentecostal Theology." In *The Cambridge Companion to Pentecostalism*, edited by Cecil M. Robeck Jr. and Amos Yong, 254–72. Cambridge: Cambridge University Press, 2014.

Chan, Simon. *Pentecostal Theology and the Christian Spiritual Tradition*. Eugene, OR: Wipf & Stock, 2000.

Charry, Ellen T. "Literature as Scripture: Privileged Reading in Current Religious Reflection." *Soundings* 74 (1991) 65–99.

Childs, Brevard S. *Old Testament Theology in a Canonical Context*. Philadelphia: Fortress, 1985.

Cho, David Y. *Five-Fold Gospel and Three-Fold Blessing*. Seoul: Young San Publishing, 1983.

———. *Salvation, Health and Prosperity. Our Threefold Blessings in Christ*. Altamonte Springs: Creation House, 1987.

Clark, Mathew S., and Henry L. Lederle. *What is Distinctive About Pentecostal Theology*. Muckleneuk: South Africa, 1989.

Clifton, Shane. *Crippled Grace: Disability, Virtue Ethics, and the Good Life*. Waco, TX: Baylor University Press, 2018.

Cloninger, C. Robert. *Feeling Good: The Science of Well-Being*. Oxford: Oxford University Press, 2004.

———. "Spirituality and the Science of Feeling Good." *Southern Medical Journal* 100 (2007) 740–43.

Bibliography

Cloninger, C. Robert, et al. "A Psychobiological Model of Temperament and Character." *Archives of General Psychiatry* 50 (1993) 975–90.

Cohen, Adam B., and Kathryn A. Johnson. "Religion and Well-Being." Paper presented at the Yale Center for Faith and Culture Consultation on Happiness and Human Flourishing, New Haven, CT, December 9–10, 2011.

Cohen, Michael M. Interview by Author. Bennington College, June 15, 2016.

Cone, James H. *A Black Theology of Liberation: Fortieth Anniversary Edition*. New York: Orbis, 2013.

Copan, Paul. *Is God a Moral Monster? Making Sense of the Old Testament God*. Grand Rapids: Baker, 2011.

Coppes, Leonard J. "Rahamim." In *Theological Wordbook of the Old Testament*, edited by Laird Harris et al., 841–43. Chicago: Moody, 1980.

Cox, Harvey. *Fire from Heaven: The Rise of Pentecostal Spirituality and the Reshaping of Religion in the Twenty-First Century*. Reading, MA: Addison-Wesley, 1995.

Dabney, Lyle D. "Saul's Armor: The Problem and the Promise of Pentecostal Theology Today." *Pneuma* 23 (2001) 115–46.

Daniels III, David D. "North American Pentecostalism." In *The Cambridge Companion to Pentecostalism*, edited by Cecil M. Robeck Jr. and Amos Yong, 73–92. Cambridge: Cambridge University Press, 2014.

Dayton, Donald. *Theological Roots of Pentecostalism*. Grand Rapids: Baker Academic, 1987.

Del Colle, Ralph. "Aesthetics and Pathos in the Vision of God: A Catholic-Pentecostal Encounter." *Pneuma* 26 (2004) 107–10.

Diener, Ed, et al. "Personality, Culture, and Subjective Well-Being: Emotional and Cognitive Evaluations of Life." *Annual Review of Psychology* 54 (2003) 403–25.

Donovan, Mary Ann. *One Right Reading? A Guide to Irenaeus*. Collegeville, MN: Liturgical, 1997.

Dréze, Jean, and Amartya Sen. *An Uncertain Glory: India and its Contradictions*. Princeton: Princeton University Press, 2013.

Droogers, André. "The Cultural Dimension of Pentecostalism." In *The Cambridge Companion to Pentecostalism*, edited by Cecil M. Robeck Jr. and Amos Yong, 195–214. Cambridge: Cambridge University Press, 2014.

Ehrenreich, Barbara. *Bright-Sided: How Positive Thinking is Undermining America*. New York: Metropolitan, 2009.

Eisland, Nancy L. *The Disabled God: Toward a Liberation Theology of Disability*. Nashville: Abingdon, 1994.

Elshtain, Jean Bethke. *Democracy on Trial*. New York: Basic, 1995.

———. "Three Meditations on Human Flourishing." Paper presented at the Yale Center for Faith and Culture Consultation on God's Power and Human Flourishing, New Haven, CT, May 23–24, 2008.

Ervin, Howard. "Hermeneutics: A Pentecostal Option." *Pneuma* 3 (1981) 11–25.

Farley, Wendy. "Reforming Desire: A Theology of the Incarnation." Paper presented at the Yale Center for Faith and Culture Consultation on Desire and Human Flourishing, New Haven, CT, December 10–11, 2010.

Faupel, William D. *The Everlasting Gospel: The Significance of Eschatology in the Development of Pentecostal Thought*. Sheffield: Sheffield Academic, 1996.

Fayard, Carlos, et al. *A Christian Worldview and Mental Health: A Seventh-day Adventist Perspective*. Berrien Springs, MI: Andrews University Press, 2011.

Bibliography

Fee, Gordon D. *The Disease of the Health and Wealth Gospels.* Beverly, MA: Frontline, 1985.

Ford, David F. "God's Power and Human Flourishing: A Biblical Inquiry After Charles Taylor's *A Secular Age.*" Paper presented at the Yale Center for Faith and Culture Consultation on God's Power and Human Flourishing, New Haven, CT, May 23–24, 2008.

Fortune, Marie. "The Conundrum of Sin, Sex, Violence, and Theodicy." In *The Other Side of Sin,* edited by Andrew S. Park and Susan L. Nelson, 123–42. Albany: State University of New York Press, 2001.

Fuhrman, Joel. *Eat to Live: The Amazing Nutrient-Rich Program for Fast and Sustained Weight Loss,* revised edition. New York: Hachette, 2011.

Gabriel, Andrew K. *The Lord is the Spirit: The Holy Spirit and the Divine Attributes.* Eugene, OR: Pickwick, 2011.

Green, Joel B. *Body, Soul, and Human Life: The Nature of Humanity in the Bible.* Grand Rapids: Baker Academic, 2008.

Gutierrez, Gustavo. *A Theology of Liberation: History, Politics, and Salvation,* edited by Caridad Inda and John Eagleson. Translated by Caridad Inda and John Eagleson. New York: Orbis, 1973.

Harell Jr., David Edwin. *Oral Roberts: An American Life.* Bloomington: Indiana University Press, 1985.

Herdt, Jennifer A. "Desire for the Common Good: A Defense of Eudaimonism." Paper presented at the Yale Center for Faith and Culture Consultation on Desire and Human Flourishing, New Haven, CT, December 10–11, 2010.

Heschel, Abraham. *God in Search of Man.* New York: Farrar, Straus and Giroux, 1983.

Hollenweger, Walter J. *Pentecostalism: Origins and Developments Worldwide.* Grand Rapids: Baker Academic, 1997.

Horn, J. N. *From Rags to Riches: An Analysis of the Faith Movement and Its Relationship to the Classical Pentecostal Movement.* Pretoria: University of South Africa, 1989.

Homer-Dixon, Thomas F. *The Environment, Scarcity, and Violence.* Princeton: Princeton University Press, 1999.

Huntzinger, Jon D. "Biblical Resources for Ministry." Lecture given at The King's College and Seminary, Van Nuys, CA, June 2008.

———. "Goodness and Worship: A Perspective on Old Testament Holiness." In *The Holiness Manifesto,* edited by Kevin Mannoia and Don Thorsen, 29–37. Grand Rapids: Eerdmans, 2008.

———. "The Jack W. Hayford School of Pastoral Nurture, Consultation II." Lecture given at The King's College and Seminary, Van Nuys, CA, October 2008.

Husbands, Mark. "The Trinity is *Not* Our Social Program." In *Trinitarian Theology for the Church,* edited by Daniel Treier and David Lauber, 120–41. Downers Grove, IL: InterVarsity, 2009.

Johnson, Bill. *God is Good: He's Better Than You Think.* Shippensburg, PA: Destiny Image, 2016.

Johnson, Elizabeth A. *She Who Is: The Mystery of God in Feminist Theological Discourse.* New York: Crossroad, 2001.

Johnson, Luke Timothy. "Jesus Among the Philosophers: Ancient Conceptions of Happiness." Paper presented at the Yale Center for Faith and Culture Consultation on Happiness and Human Flourishing, New Haven, CT, December 9–10, 2011.

Jones, James W. *The Spirit and the World.* New York: Hawthorn, 1975.

Bibliography

Jones, L. Gregory. *Embodying Forgiveness: A Theological Analysis.* Grand Rapids: Eerdmans, 1995.

Kärkkäinen, Veli-Matti. "David's Sling: The Promise and the Problem of Pentecostal Theology Today: A Response to D. Lyle Dabney." *Pneuma* 23 (2001) 147–52.

———. "Pentecostal Mission and Encounter with Religions." In *The Cambridge Companion to Pentecostalism*, edited by Cecil M. Robeck Jr. and Amos Yong, 294–312. Cambridge: Cambridge University Press, 2014.

———. *The Trinity: Global Perspectives.* Louisville: Westminster John Knox, 2007.

Keller, Catherine. "Folding Power." Paper presented at the Yale Center for Faith and Culture Consultation on Good Power—Divine and Human, New Haven, CT, October 5–6, 2007.

Kelsey, David H. "On Human Flourishing: A Theocentric Perspective." Paper presented at the Yale Center for Faith and Culture Consultation on God's Power and Human Flourishing, New Haven, CT, May 23–24, 2008.

Kifer, Yona, et al. "The Good Life and the Powerful: The Experience of Power and Authenticity Enhances Subjective Well-Being." *Psychological Science* 24 (2013) 280–88.

Kross, Ethan, et al. "Social Rejection Shares Somatosensory Representations with Physical Pain." *Proceedings of the National Academy of Sciences* 108 (2011) 6270–75.

Ladd, George E. *The Gospel of the Kingdom.* Grand Rapids: Eerdmans, 1995.

———. *A Theology of the New Testament*, edited by Donald A. Hagner. Revised edition. Grand Rapids: Eerdmans, 1993.

Lamb, David T. *God Behaving Badly: Is the God of the Old Testament Angry, Sexist and Racist?* Downers Grove, IL: IVP, 2011.

Lampman, Lisa B., and Michelle D. Shattuck. "Finding God in the Wake of Crime: Answers to Hard Questions." In *God and the Victim*, edited by Lisa B. Lampman and Michelle D. Shattuck, 1–16. Grand Rapids: Eerdmans, 1999.

Land, Steven J. *Pentecostal Spirituality: A Passion for the Kingdom.* Sheffield: Sheffield Academic, 1993.

Lee, Shayne. *T. D. Jakes: America's New Preacher.* New York: New York University Press, 2005.

———. "Prosperity Theology: T. D. Jakes and the Gospel of the Almighty Dollar." *Crosscurrents* 52 (2007) 227–36.

Lewis, Charles. "Divine Goodness and Worship Worthiness." *International Journal for Philosophy of Religion* 14 (1983) 143–58.

Luther, Martin. "The Freedom of a Christian." In *Three Treatises*, revised by Harold J. Grimm, 261–316. Translated by W. A. Lambert. Philadelphia: Fortress, 1970.

Ma, Wonsuk. "Asian Pentecostalism in Context." In *The Cambridge Companion to Pentecostalism*, edited by Cecil M. Robeck Jr. and Amos Yong, 152–71. Cambridge: Cambridge University Press, 2014.

Macchia, Frank. D. *Baptized in the Spirit: A Global Pentecostal Theology.* Grand Rapids: Zondervan, 2006.

———. *Justified in the Spirit: Creation, Redemption, and the Triune God.* Grand Rapids: Eerdmans, 2010.

———. "A North American Response." *Journal of Pentecostal Theology* 2.4 (1994) 25–33.

Mani, Anandi, et al. "Poverty Impedes Cognitive Function." *Science* 341 (2013) 976–80.

Mannoia, Kevin, and Don Thorsen, eds. *The Holiness Manifesto.* Grand Rapids: Eerdmans, 2008.

Bibliography

McClymond, Michael J. "Charismatic Renewal and Neo-Pentecostalism: From North American Origins to Global Permutations." In *The Cambridge Companion to Pentecostalism*, edited by Cecil M. Robeck Jr. and Amos Yong, 31–51. Cambridge: Cambridge University Press, 2014.

Menzies, William W., and Robert P. Menzies. *Spirit and Power: Foundations of Pentecostal Experience*. Grand Rapids: Zondervan, 2000.

McConnell, D. R. *A Different Gospel: A Historical and Biblical Analysis of the Modern Faith Movement*. Peabody, MA: Hendrickson, 1988.

McFague, Sallie. *Metaphorical Theology: Models of God in Religious Language*. Minneapolis: Fortress, 1982.

———. *Models of God: Theology for an Ecological, Nuclear Age*. Minneapolis: Fortress, 1987.

Middleton, J. Richard, *The Liberating Image: The Imago Dei in Genesis 1*. Grand Rapids: Brazos, 2005.

Migliore, Daniel. *Faith Seeking Understanding: An Introduction to Christian Theology*. Grand Rapids: Eerdmans, 1991.

Moltmann, Jürgen. "Christianity: A Religion of Joy." In *Joy and Human Flourishing: Essays on Theology, Culture, and the Good Life*, edited by Miroslav Volf and Justin E. Crisp, 1–16. Minneapolis: Fortress, 2015.

———. *The Coming of God: Christian Eschatology*. Translated by Margaret Kohl. Minneapolis: Fortress, 1996.

———. *The Crucified God: The Cross of Christ as the Foundation and Criticism of Christian Theology*. Translated by R. A. Wilson and John Bowden. New York: Harper & Row, 1974.

———. *God in Creation: A New Theology of Creation and the Spirit of God*. Translated by Margaret Kohl. Minneapolis: Fortress, 1993.

———. "The Motherly Father: Is Trinitarian Patripassionism Replacing Theological Patriarchalism?" In *God as Father?*, edited by Johannes-Baptist Metz and Edward Schillebeeckx, 51–56. New York: Seabury, 1981.

———. *The Spirit of Life: A Universal Affirmation*. Translated by Margaret Kohl. Minneapolis: Fortress, 1992.

———. *The Trinity and the Kingdom: Doctrine of God*. Translated by Margaret Kohl. Minneapolis: Fortress, 1993.

———. *Theology of Hope: On the Ground and the Implications of a Christian Eschatology*. Translated by James W. Leitch. Minneapolis: Fortress, 1993.

Moschella, Mary Clark. "Calling and Compassion: Elements of Joy in Lived Practices of Care." In *Joy and Human Flourishing: Essays on Theology, Culture, and the Good Life*, edited by Miroslav Volf and Justin E. Crisp, 97–126. Minneapolis: Fortress, 2015.

Murphy, Nancy. *Bodies and Souls, or Spirited Bodies?* Cambridge: Cambridge University Press, 2006.

Myers, Ched. "Beyond 'the Addict's Excuse': Sin, Public Addiction, and Ecclesial Recovery." In *The Other Side of Sin*, edited by Andrew S. Park and Susan L. Nelson, 87–108. Albany: State University of New York Press, 2001.

Myland, D. Wesley. *The Latter Rain Covenant and Pentecostal Power*. Chicago: Evangel, 1910.

Neff, Kristen. "Self-Compassion: An Alternative Conceptualization of a Healthy Attitude Toward Oneself." *Self and Identity* 2 (2003) 85–101.

Bibliography

Newlands, George and Smith, Allen. *Hospitable God: The Transformative Dream*. Burlington, VT: Ashgate, 2010.

Nichols, David. "The Search for a Pentecostal Structure in Systematic Theology." *Pneuma* 6 (1984) 57–76.

Nussbaum, Martha. *Creating Capabilities: The Human Development Approach*. Cambridge, MA: Belknap, 2011.

Nwankwo, Lawrence. "'You Have Received the Spirit of Power . . .' (2 Tim. 1:7). Reviewing the Prosperity Message in the Light of a Theology of Empowerment." *Journal of the European Pentecostal Theological Association* 22 (2002) 56–77.

Omenyo, Cephas N. "African Pentecostalism." In *The Cambridge Companion to Pentecostalism*, edited by Cecil M. Robeck Jr. and Amos Yong, 132–51. Cambridge: Cambridge University Press, 2014.

Ornstein, Robert E., and David S. Sobel. *Healthy Pleasures: Discover the Proven Medical Benefits of Pleasure and Live a Longer, Healthier Life*. Woburn, MA: Perseus, 1989.

Osteen, Joel. *Your Best Life Now: 7 Steps to Living at Your Full Potential*. New York: Hachette, 2004.

Pannenberg, Wolfhart. *Systematic Theology, Volume. 1*. Translated by Geoffrey W. Bromiley. Grand Rapids: Eerdmans, 1991.

Papanikolaou, Aristotle. "Person, *Kenosis* and Abuse: Hans Urs von Balthasar and Feminist Theologies in Conversation." *Modern Theology* 19 (2003) 41–65.

Perriman, Andrew, ed. *Faith, Healing and Prosperity: A Report on the 'Word of Faith' and 'Positive Confession' Theologies*. Carlisle: ACUTE Paternoster, 2003.

Pinnock, Clark. *Flame of Love: A Theology of the Holy Spirit*. Downers Grove, IL: IVP Academic, 1996.

Plantinga Jr., Cornelius. *Not the Way It's Supposed to Be: A Breviary of Sin*. Grand Rapids: Eerdmans, 1995.

Plüss, Jean Daniel. "Pentecostalism in Europe and the Former Soviet Union." In *The Cambridge Companion to Pentecostalism*, edited by Cecil M. Robeck Jr. and Amos Yong, 93–111. Cambridge: Cambridge University Press, 2014.

Poloma, Margaret. *Main Street Mystics: The Toronto Blessing and Reviving Pentecostalism*. New York: Altamira, 2003.

Pope, Stephen. "Jesus Christ and Human Flourishing." Paper presented at the Yale Center for Faith and Culture Consultation on Christ and Human Flourishing, New Haven, CT, December 2014.

Ramirez, Daniel. "Pentecostalism in Latin America." In *The Cambridge Companion to Pentecostalism*, edited by Cecil M. Robeck Jr. and Amos Yong, 112–31. Cambridge: Cambridge University Press, 2014.

Reno, R. R. "The Empire of Desire." Paper presented at the Yale Center for Faith and Culture Consultation on Desire and Human Flourishing, New Haven, CT, December 10–11, 2010.

Richard, Lucien. *Living the Hospitality of God*. New York: Paulist, 2000.

Robeck, Cecil M., Jr. "The Origins of Modern Pentecostalism." In *The Cambridge Companion to Pentecostalism*, edited by Cecil M. Robeck Jr. and Amos Yong, 13–30. Cambridge: Cambridge University Press, 2014.

Roberts, Oral. *God is a Good God: Believe It and Come Alive! Your Key to an Abundant Life*. Indianapolis: Bobbs-Merrill, 1960.

———. *The Miracle of Seed Faith*. Tulsa, OK: Oral Roberts Ministries, 1982.

Bibliography

Robinson, James. *Divine Healing: The Formative Years: 1830–1880: Theological Roots in the Transatlantic World.* Eugene, OR: Pickwick, 2011.

———. *Divine Healing: The Holiness-Pentecostal Transition Years, 1890–1906: Theological Transpositions in the Transatlantic World.* Eugene, OR: Pickwick, 2013.

———. *Divine Healing: The Years of Expansion 1906–1930: Theological Variation in the Transatlantic World.* Eugene, OR: Pickwick, 2014.

Russell, Letty M. *Just Hospitality: God's Welcome in a World of Difference.* Louisville: Westminster John Knox, 2009.

Sacks, Daniel W., et al. "The New Stylized Facts About Income and Subjective Well-Being." *Emotion* 12 (2012) 1181–87.

Second General Conference of Latin American Bishops. "Poverty of the Church." In *The Church in the Present-Day Transformation of Latin America in the Light of the Council: Second General Conference of Latin American Bishops, Bogotá, 24 August, Medellín, 26 August–6 September, Colombia 1968. Vol. 2. Conclusions*, edited by Louis Michael Colonnese. Bogota: General Secretariat of CELAM, 1970.

Self, Charlie. *Flourishing Churches and Communities: A Pentecostal Primer on Faith, Work and Economics for Spirit-Empowered Discipleship.* Grand Rapids: The Christian Library, 2012.

Seligman, Martin E. P. *Authentic Happiness: Using the New Positive Psychology to Realize Your Potential for Lasting Fulfillment.* New York: Atria, 2002.

———. *Flourish: A Visionary New Understanding of Happiness and Well-being.* New York: Atria, 2012.

Sen, Amartya. *Commodities and Capabilities.* Oxford: Oxford University Press, 1999.

———. *Development as Freedom.* Oxford: Oxford University Press, 2000.

Shweder, Richard A., et al. "The Big Three of Morality (Autonomoy, Community, and Divinity), and the Big Three Explanations of Suffering." In *Morality and Health*, edited by Allan Brandt and Paul Rozin, 119–72. New York: Routledge, 1997.

Silk, Danny. *Culture of Honor: Sustaining a Supernatural Environment.* Shippenberg, PA: Destiny Image, 2009.

Smith, Calvin L. "The Politics and Economics of Pentecostalism: A Global Survey." In *The Cambridge Companion to Pentecostalism*, edited by Cecil M. Robeck Jr. and Amos Yong, 175–94. Cambridge: Cambridge University Press, 2014.

Smith, James K. A. *Thinking in Tongues: Pentecostal Contributions to Christian Philosophy.* Grand Rapids: Eerdmans, 2010.

Soskice, Janet M. *Metaphor and Religious Language.* Oxford: Clarendon, 1985.

Steptoe, Andrew, et al. "Positive Affect and Health-Related Neuroendocrine, Cardiovascular, and Inflammatory Processes." *Proceedings of the National Academy of Sciences of the United States of America* 102 (2005) 6508–12.

Stoebe, H. J. "Raḥum." In *Theological Lexicon of the Old Testament, vol. 3*, edited by Ernst Jenni and Claus Westermann, 1230. Translated by Mark E. Biddle. Peabody, MA: Hendrickson, 1971.

Stone, Bryan. *Compassionate Ministry.* New York: Orbis, 2002.

Storkey, Alan. "Post-Modernism Is Consumption." In *Christ and Consumerism: A Critical Analysis of the Spirit of the Age*, edited by Craig Bartholomew and Thorsten Moritz, 100–17. Carlisle: Paternoster, 2000.

Studebaker, Steven M. *From Pentecost to the Triune God: A Pentecostal Trinitarian Theology.* Grand Rapids: Eerdmans, 2012.

Bibliography

Swinton, John. *From Bedlam to Shalom: Towards a Practical Theology of Human Nature, Interpersonal Relationships, and Mental Health Care*. New York: Peter Lang, 2000.

Tanner, Kathryn. "Power of Love." Paper presented at the Yale Center for Faith and Culture Consultation on Good Power—Divine and Human, New Haven, CT, October 5–6, 2007.

Taylor, Charles. *A Secular Age*. Cambridge, MA: The Belknap Press of Harvard University Press, 2007.

Thomas, John Christopher. "Pentecostal Theology in the Twenty-First Century." *Pneuma* 20 (1998) 3–19.

Thompson, Marianne Meye. "Alpha and Omega—And Everything in Between: Jesus Christ and Human Flourishing." Paper presented at the Yale Center for Faith and Culture Consultation on Christ and Human Flourishing, New Haven, CT, December 2014.

———. "The Trees Clap Their Hands." In *Joy and Human Flourishing: Essays on Theology, Culture, and the Good Life*, edited by Miroslav Volf and Justin E. Crisp, 17–38. Minneapolis: Fortress, 2015.

Torrance, Thomas F. *The Ground and Grammar of Theology*. Charlottesville, VA: University Press of Virginia, 1980.

Vaillant, George E. *Adaptation to Life*. Cambridge: Harvard University Press, 1977.

———. *Aging Well: Surprising Guideposts to a Happier Life*. Cambridge: Harvard University Press, 2002.

———. *Triumphs of Experience: The Men of the Harvard Grant Study*. Cambridge: Harvard University Press, 2012.

Volf, Miroslav. *After Our Likeness: The Church as the Image of the Trinity*. Grand Rapids: Eerdmans, 1998.

———. "The Crown of the Good Life: A Hypothesis." In *Joy and Human Flourishing: Essays on Theology, Culture, and the Good Life*, edited by Miroslav Volf and Justin E. Crisp, 127–35. Minneapolis: Fortress, 2015.

———. *The End of Memory: Remembering Rightly in a Violent World*. Grand Rapids: Eerdmans, 2006.

———. *Exclusion and Embrace: A Theological Exploration of Identity, Otherness, and Reconciliation*. Nashville: Abingdon, 1996.

———. *Flourishing: Why We Need Religion in a Globalized World*. New Haven: Yale University Press, 2015.

———. "Materiality of Salvation: An Investigation in the Soteriologies of Liberation and Pentecostal Theologies." *Journal of Ecumenical Studies* 26 (1989) 447–67.

———. "Original Crime, Primal Care." In *God and the Victim*, edited by Lisa B. Lampman and Michelle D. Shattuck, 17–35. Grand Rapids: Eerdmans, 1999.

———. *A Public Faith: How Followers of Christ Should Serve the Common Good*. Grand Rapids: Brazos, 2011.

Vondey, Wolfgang. *Beyond Pentecostalism: The Crisis of Global Christianity and the Renewal of the Theological Agenda*. Grand Rapids: Eerdmans, 2010.

Walton, Jonathan L. "Empowered: The Entrepreneurial Ministry of T. D. Jakes." *Christian Century* (July 2007) 25–28.

Wariboko, Nimi. *The Pentecostal Principle: Ethical Methodology in New Spirit*. Grand Rapids: Eerdmans, 2012.

Bibliography

Wawrykow, Joseph. "Aquinas and Bonaventure on Christ and Human Flourishing." Paper presented at the Yale Center for Faith and Culture Consultation on Christ and Human Flourishing, New Haven, CT, December 2014.

Warrington, Keith. *Pentecostal Theology: A Theology of Encounter*. Edinburgh: T. & T. Clark, 2008.

Whybray, Norman R. *The Good Life in the Old Testament*. London: T. & T. Clark, 2002.

Wilkinson, Michael. "Sociological Narratives and the Sociology of Pentecostalism." In *The Cambridge Companion to Pentecostalism*, edited by Cecil M. Robeck Jr. and Amos Yong, 215–34. Cambridge: Cambridge University Press, 2014.

Williams, Daryl E. "Can't the Goodness of God be more Empirically Grounded?" *Journal of Bible and Religion* 25 (1957) 311–16.

Williams, David T. "The Heresy of Prosperity Teaching: A Message for the Church in its Approach to Need." *Journal of South African Theology* (1987) 33–44.

Wolterstorff, Nicholas. "The Contours of Justice: An Ancient Call for Shalom." In *God and the Victim*, edited by Lisa B. Lampman and Michelle D. Shattuck, 107–30. Grand Rapids: Eerdmans, 1999.

———. "God's Power and Human Flourishing." Paper presented at the Yale Center for Faith and Culture Consultation on Desire and Human Flourishing, New Haven, CT, December 10–11, 2010.

———. *Lament for a Son*. Grand Rapids: Eerdmans, 1987.

———. *Until Justice and Peace Embrace*. Grand Rapids: Eerdmans, 1983.

Wright, Christopher J. H. *Old Testament Ethics for the People of God*. Downers Grove, IL: IVP Academic, 2004.

———. *The God I Don't Understand: Reflections on Tough Questions of Faith*. Grand Rapids: Zondervan, 2008.

Wright, N. T. "Joy: Some New Testament Perspectives and Questions." In *Joy and Human Flourishing: Essays on Theology, Culture, and the Good Life*, edited by Miroslav Volf and Justin E. Crisp, 39–61. Minneapolis: Fortress, 2015.

Yoder, John Howard. *The Jewish-Christian Schism Revisited*, edited by Michael G. Cartwright and Peter Ochs. Grand Rapids: Eerdmans, 2003.

———. *The Politics of Jesus*. Grand Rapids: Eerdmans, 1972.

Yong, Amos. *The Bible, Disability, and the Church: A New Vision of the People of God*. Grand Rapids: Eerdmans, 2011.

———. "Instead of a Conclusion: A Theologian's Interdisciplinary Musings on the Future of Global Pentecostalism and Its Scholarship." In *The Cambridge Companion to Pentecostalism*, edited by Cecil M. Robeck Jr. and Amos Yong, 313–20. Cambridge: Cambridge University Press, 2014.

———. *Spirit of Love: A Trinitarian Theology of Grace*. Waco, TX: Baylor University Press, 2012.

———. *The Spirit Poured Out On All Flesh: Pentecostalism and the Possibility of Global Theology*. Grand Rapids: Baker Academic, 2005.

———. *Spirit-Word-Community: Theological Hermeneutics in Trinitarian Perspective*. Eugene, OR: Wipf & Stock, 2002.

———. *Theology and Down Syndrome: Re-Imagining Disability in Late Modernity*. Waco: Baylor University Press, 2007.

Yong, Amos, and Attanasi, Katherine. *Pentecostalism and Prosperity: The Socio-Economics of the Global Charismatic Movement*. New York: Palgrave Macmillan, 2012.

Bibliography

Zehr, Howard. "Restoring Justice." In *God and the Victim*, edited by Lisa B. Lampman and Michelle D. Shattuck, 131–59. Grand Rapids: Eerdmans, 1999.

Author Index

Adeboye, O., 99
Albrecht, D., 14
Althouse, P., 21, 140
Archer, K., 14, 15, 21
Arendt, H., 44, 47, 48, 165
Attanasi, K., 2, 114

Balthasar, H., 147–49, 162
Bauckham, R., 7, 25, 34, 41, 46–50, 55, 68, 144, 161–65
Berger, P., 1–2, 88
Berry, M., 37
Bianchi, M., 142
Bloom, P., 53–54
Bondi, R., 94
Bowler, K., 6, 16, 18
Brother Lawrence, 119
Brown, B., 61–63, 69, 96, 99
Brueggeman, W., 91, 142, 144, 147, 162, 175
Buxton, G., 143

Callen, B., 145
Carter, R. K., 13
Cartledge, M., 20
Charry, E., 46, 101
Childs, B., 38
Clark, M., 13–14
Clifton, S., 113
Cloninger, R., 57–62, 69, 95, 174
Cohen, A., 66–67, 113
Cohen, M. M., 36, 38

Cone, J. H., 7, 72, 76–80, 83, 95, 102, 123
Coppes, L. J., 150

Dayton, D., 12–13, 17
Diener, E., 66
Donovan, M. A., 108
Dreze, J., 65

Ehrenreich, B., 57
Eisland, N. L., 109–10, 130
Elshtain, J. B., 94

Fayard, C., 174
Fortune, M., 93, 129
Fuhrman, J., 174

Green, J. B., 26–27, 38, 40, 108
Gutierrez, G., 7, 72–76, 102, 134

Heschel, A., 146
Hollenweger, W. J., 14
Homer-Dixon, T. F., 175
Howard, E., 14
Huntzinger, J. D., 146
Husbands, M., 158

Johnson, B., 19–20, 28, 39, 127, 140
Johnson, E. A., 7, 72, 80–83, 100, 102, 135
Johnson, K. A., 66–67, 113
Jones, L. G., 92

Author Index

Kärkkäinen, V. M., iii, x–xii, 12, 17, 38, 107–9, 112, 119–20, 135–36, 138, 152
Kelsey, D. H., 8, 33, 35, 117–23, 129–30
Kifer, Y., 64–65, 69, 97
Kross, E., 62

Ladd, G. E., 24, 26, 39, 89, 131, 140
Lampman, L. B., 90
Land, S. J., 14, 17, 20
Lederle, H. L., 13–14
Lee, S., 2
Luther, M., 85, 87, 108, 136

Macchia, F. D., 42
Mannoia, K., 145
McClymond, M. J., 12
McConnell, D. R., 21
McFague, S., 82, 134–37
Middleton, J. R., 107
Migliore, D., 145
Moltmann, J., xii, 7, 9, 21, 25–26, 35, 41–50, 55, 68, 71–73, 120, 134, 136–38, 161, 165, 173
Murphy, N., 38
Myers, C., 92
Myland, D. W., 21

Neff, K., 50
Newlands, G., 152–53
Nussbaum, M., 66–67, 70, 97

Ornstein, R. E., 174
Osteen, J., 169

Pannenberg, W., 138
Papanikolaou, A., 162
Pinnock, C., 142
Plantinga Jr., C., 37, 164
Pope, S., 56, 63

Reno, R. R., 33

Richard, L., 153
Roberts, O., 27, 139
Russell, L. M., 152–53, 155

Sacks, D. W., 64, 69
Self, C., 20
Seligman, M. E. P., 56–57, 69
Sen, A., 64–66, 70, 112
Shattuck, M. D., 90
Shweder, R. A., 67
Silk, D., 28, 88, 98
Smith, A., 152–53
Smith, C. L., 22, 178
Smith, J. K. A., 15
Sobel, D. S., 174
Soskice, J. M., 136
Steptoe, A., 174
Stoebe, H. J., 150
Stone, B., 91–93, 95
Storkey, A., 47
Swinton, J., 37

Taylor, C., 6, 15, 31–34, 50, 103
Thorsen, D., 145
Torrance, T. F., 141

Vaillant, G. E., 61
Volf, M., 7–8, 25, 32, 35, 41, 47, 51–55, 68–69, 84–86, 91, 154, 159, 161, 164, 166

Warrington, K., 14
Williams, D. T., 23
Wolterstorff, N., 37, 52, 91, 93, 116
Wright, N. T., 25, 35

Yoder, J. H., 39, 178–79
Yong, A., xi–xii, 2, 12, 19, 29, 39–40, 107–8, 110–11, 113–14, 130, 140

Zehr, H., 90–91

Subject Index

Abundance
  as Abundance-thinking, 9–11, 37, 39–40, 70, 126, 159–60, 169, 171–80
  as Scarcity-thinking, 9, 173–79
Already-not yet, 24, 27, 39–40, 89, 131
Anger. *See* Character of God.
Anthropological perspectives. *See* Human Flourishing.
Ascetic Life. *See* Holiness.
Autonomous self. *See* Self.

Blindness to legitimate victimization. *See* Prosperity Gospel.

Character of God
  as Compassion and favor, 143, 146, 149–50, 152, 155, 162, 167, 173
  as Covenant and Loving-kindness, 108, 109, 143, 147–50, 167
  as Goodness and Justice, 40, 90–93, 143, 146–48, 152, 154–57, 159, 167, 173–74, 179
  as Holiness as wholeness, 29, 37–38, 79, 83, 87, 91–94, 102, 106, 125, 140, 145–46, 157, 159–60, 165–66, 171–73
  as Justice and covenant, 108–9, 143, 147–48, 167
  as Justice and shalom. *See* Shalom.
  as Kenotic relationality of God, 8–10, 68, 101, 108, 141, 151, 154, 157–62, 164, 166, 168–69, 173
  as Loving-kindness and Truth, 143–44, 147, 149, 167
  Questioning the goodness of God, 90
  as Restorative anger, 91, 146–47
  as Righteousness and kenosis, 143, 146–48, 157, 167
Christian Freedom. *See* Freedom.
Civilized self. *See* Modern Worldview.
Compassion. *See* Character of God.
Consecration. *See* Holiness.
Cooperativeness. *See* Temperament and Character Inventory.
Covenant. *See* Character of God.
Cycles of poverty, 2, 4, 21, 54, 86–87, 102, 113, 124, 125

Death. *See* Human Flourishing.
Deficiencies of the Prosperity gospel. *See* Prosperity Gospel.
Dehumanization. *See* Sin.
Disability, Imago Dei. *See* Imago Dei.
Disability or chronic illness. *See also* Human Flourishing.
Discipleship. *See* Kenotic paradigm of God's relationality.
Dominion theology, 22, 26, 28, 178

Subject Index

Economic perspectives. *See* Human Flourishing.
Egalitarianism, 68, 73, 76, 81, 83, 137–38, 151–52, 154, 157–59, 161, 167
   of autonomous selves, 158
   of kenotic selves, 158–61
Empowerment, 2–5, 7–9, 11, 13, 15, 20, 32, 55, 69, 72, 77, 80, 83–84, 86, 88–89, 94–99, 101–2, 106, 111–17, 123–25, 129–31, 133–34, 139–41, 151, 154–57, 159–61, 164–76, 180
   Affirmation of, 169–71
   in Liberation theology. *See* Liberation theology.
   as Empowering Believers, 5, 7, 13, 88–89
   as Empowerment as intrapersonal peace. *See* Shalom.
Enchanted view of the world. *See* Modern Worldview.
Epicureans. *See* Modern Worldview.
Eschatology of Hope, 25–26, 43, 71–73
Ethic of contentment. *See* Human Flourishing.
Ethic of hunger. *See* Human Flourishing.
Evangelically sound theology of prosperity. *See* Prosperity Gospel.
Extravagant lifestyles of the Prosperity gospel. *See* Prosperity Gospel.

Favor. *See* Character of God.
Feasting. *See* Shalom.
Five-fold full gospel. *See* Pentecostalism.
Flourishing. *See* Human Flourishing.
Freedom
   as Self-determination, 46–47
   as Self-limitation in love, 48–49
   as Self-discipline for excellence, 54
   as the ability to begin something new, 44, 47
   Martin Luther's Freedom of a Christian, 85

Glamorization of poverty. *See* Poverty.

Grieving. *See* Human Flourishing.
Good Power. *See* Health.
Goodness of God, 90, 139–48, 150, 160, 166–67, 173
   in Good as a supra-adjective attribute, 151
   in "Is God Good?," 90, 101
   as The God who takes sides, 91, 101
   as The Good God. *See* Naming God.

Health
   as Good Power, 7, 64, 66, 94–99, 101–3, 114, 163–65, 171
   as Other-regard, 61, 63, 163
   as Self-love, 63, 67, 99, 159, 172
   as Social connection/cooperativeness, 57–61, 69
Holiness
   as Asceticism, 1, 4, 14, 16, 18–20, 22, 25–26, 34, 37, 86–87, 125–26
   as Consecration, 19–20, 22, 26, 87, 140
Hospitable God Theology. *See* Naming God.
Human Flourishing, 5–11, 17, 19, 24, 27–28, 30–41, 43–45, 47–53, 55–57, 59–63, 65–70, 86, 97, 103, 105–9, 111–12, 114, 117–18, 120–21, 123, 126, 128–31, 133–39, 141, 144–45, 150–51, 154–55, 157, 160, 163–64, 166–68, 170, 172, 174, 180
   as Affirmation of life, 41–46
   Anthropological perspectives of, 66–70
   Ascetic views of, 34
   Bridging Theistic and Humanistic views of, 36
   in Disability or chronic illness, 8, 106–7, 109–14, 117, 122–24, 128, 130–31
   Economic and Political perspectives of, 63–66, 68–70
   as Ethic of contentment, 122–123, 126
   as Ethic of empowerment, 129–130
   as Ethic of hunger, 123–126

Subject Index

as Flourishing of communities, 3, 5, 19, 45, 88, 103, 166, 179
Humanistic views of, 33, 35–36, 41, 63, 69, 70, 166, 174
in sickness and in dying, 119–120
in Mourning and grieving, 114, 116–17
NT perspectives on flourishing as Kingdom of God, 38–40, 68–70
as Ordinary flourishing, 6–9, 11, 17, 24, 28, 30–31, 33–35, 38, 40–41, 45, 48, 50, 56, 68, 70, 103, 105, 117, 128–31, 139, 160, 163–64, 167, 168, 172, 174
OT perspectives on flourishing as shalom, 36–38, 68–70
Psychological perspectives of, 56–61, 68–70, 87
as Quotidian, x, 117–23, 127–31
Redefined views of, 36
Sociological perspectives of, 2–3, 21, 61–63, 68–70, 88
Tri-partite vision of, 52, 54
as Well-being vs. flourishing, 37, 52, 57, 59–61, 63–67, 69, 85, 87, 97, 113, 119–21, 126, 129, 142, 146, 174
Humanistic perspectives. *See* Human Flourishing.

Imago Dei, 92–93, 106–14, 117, 121–23, 127–28, 130
as faculty of rationality, 106–7, 112, 147, 175
as functional stewardship of creation, 107–8, 112, 122, 168, 173
as relational, 108–9, 112, 114, 117, 121–22, 127–28, 130,
in disability, 106–7, 109–14, 117, 122–24, 128, 130–31
in marginalization, 83, 110, 112–13, 128
Immanent frame. *See* Modern Worldview.
Inner man. *See* Salvation.
Institutionalized poverty. *See* Poverty.

Justice, 4–5, 9, 15, 19, 37, 39–40, 63, 68, 74, 76–78, 83–84, 90–93, 100–101, 112–16, 135, 140, 143, 146–48, 152, 154–57, 159, 167, 173–74, 179

Kenotic model of God. *See* Naming God.
Kenotic paradigm of God's relationality, 8–10, 68, 101, 108, 141, 151, 154, 157–62, 164, 166, 168–69, 173
in Discipleship as rehabilitation, 160, 162–63, 168, 170, 172, 174
in Forgiveness as overcoming narratives of victimization, 163
in Repentance as a re-sensitization of the conscience, 163

Latter Rain eschatology, 13–15, 21–22, 25–26, 140
Legal right. *See* Prosperity Gospel.
Legitimate victimizations. *See* Victim.
Liberation Theology
as Challenging the status quo, 54, 73, 76–80, 101–2, 123, 125, 135, 155
Conversion in, 13, 83–84, 87
as Empowerment, vii, x, 4–5, 7–9, 11, 13, 32, 69, 70, 77, 83–84, 86, 88, 94–95, 97–98, 102, 106, 113–17, 123, 129–31, 133–34, 139–41, 151, 154–57, 160–61, 165, 167, 169, 170–73, 175, 180
as Liberation from patriarchalism, 80–84, 137, 186
in Loss of Personal power, 68, 83, 88, 94–95, 97–98,
of the sinned-against. *See* Theology of the Sinned-against.
as Preferential option for the poor, 1, 75–76, 80, 102
as Socio-political liberation, 72, 73–76, 87
Lordship, 7, 9, 30–31, 40–41, 46, 48, 50–51, 55, 63, 67–68, 158, 160–62, 164, 166
Loss of depth and meaning. *See* Modern Worldview.

197

Subject Index

Loving-Kindness. *See* Character of God.

Marginalization. *See* Imago Dei.
Materiality of Salvation, 4, 6, 15, 17, 22, 26, 28, 55, 84–86, 139–40, 152, 160, 172
Metaphors of God. *See* Naming God.
Models of God. *See* Naming God.
Modern Worldview
  in Christian vision of flourishing undermining ordinary flourishing, 33–34
  as Civilized self, 32
  as against an enchanted view of the world, 6, 15, 32–33, 50
  vs. Epicureans, 31
  as Immanent Frame, 6–7, 31, 33–35, 44, 50–51, 61, 68, 70, 103, 105, 117–18, 126–27, 129, 132–33, 138, 157, 160, 162, 172, 180
  as Invention of privacy, 32
  as Loss of depth and meaning, 32
  as Rival cross pressures, 33
  vs. Stoics, 32
Mourning. *See* Human Flourishing.

Naming God
  in the Kenotic model of God, 8–10, 68, 101, 133, 139, 141, 143–47, 149–50, 154, 157–73, 176, 178, 179, 180
  in Models of God, 133, 135, 137–38, 150–52, 154, 157, 167
  in Plethora of metaphors, 80–82, 135–39, 151, 167
  in Root Metaphors, 101, 136–37, 151
  as The Good God, 8, 27, 101, 133–34, 138–40, 143–47, 150–51, 154, 157–59, 166–68
  as The Good, Hospitable, and Liberating God, 160
  as The Hospitable God, 8–9, 101, 151–60, 166–68, 170, 172–73
  as The Liberating God, 9, 81, 93, 152–54, 157, 159–60, 166–68
Narcissism
  as fear of being ordinary, 62
  of Pride, 9, 144, 162, 170, 172
  of Shame, 62–63, 67, 96, 99, 144, 170
  Narratives of Victimization, 4, 7–8, 44, 69, 88–89, 94, 101, 114, 116, 125, 129, 141, 154–57, 160–61, 164–65, 167–70

Oppression, definition of, 93
Ordinary Flourishing. *See* Human Flourishing.
Other-worldly salvation. *See* Salvation.

Patriarchalism. *See* Liberation theology.
Pentecostal identity. *See* Pentecostalism.
Pentecostal Spirituality. *See* Pentecostalism.
Pentecostalism
  as Classical, 6, 11, 17–21
  as Five-fold full gospel, 6, 11–12, 15–17
  in Maturing of Themes, 6, 10–11, 13, 16–23
  as Ordinary Human Flourishing. *See* Human Flourishing.
  as Pentecostal identity, 6, 11–17, 19, 21
  Prosperity theology, definition of, 16–17
  as Spirituality, 13–16
Personal agency, 2, 4–5, 7, 101, 114, 124, 164–65
Political perspectives. *See* Human Flourishing.
Positive confession. *See* Prosperity Gospel.
Poverty, 17, 25, 40
  Cycles of, 2, 4, 21, 54, 86–88, 102, 113, 124–25, 129
  Glamorization of, ix, 1, 126
  in Institutionalized poverty, 73
  in Power poverty, 64
Power poverty. *See* Poverty.
Powerlessness. *See* Victim.
Preferential option for the poor. *See* Liberation Theology.
Pride, 9, 144, 162, 170, 172
Privacy. *See* Modern Worldview.

Subject Index

Prosperity gospel, ix–x, 1–3, 6, 11, 13, 15–16, 18, 24, 29, 75, 111
   in Blindness to legitimate victimization, 7, 8, 114–17, 166
   Deficiencies of, 3–4, 23
   in Disability or chronic illness, 8, 106–7, 109–14, 117, 122–24, 128, 130–31
   Evangelically sound Theology of, 5–6
   Extravagant lifestyle of, 2
   as Generosity, 27–28, 97–99, 126
   as Good power. *See* Health.
   as Legal right (name it and claim it), 24–25, 27
   as Offshoot of Pentecostalism, 16–17
   as Positive Confession, 27
   as Seed Faith, 27
   Sociological benefits of, 2–3
   Theology of, 1
Prosperity theology, definition of. *See* Pentecostalism.
Psychological perspectives. *See* Human Flourishing.

Quotidian, definition of, 118

Radical Affirmation of Materiality, 4, 6, 15, 17, 22, 26, 28, 55, 84–86, 139–40, 152, 160, 172
Rationality. *See* Imago Dei.
Relational self. *See* Self.
Relational, Imago Dei. *See* Imago Dei.
Repentance. *See* Kenotic paradigm of God's relationality.
Responsible agents of change, 2, 96, 170
Righteousness. *See* Character of God.
Root Metaphors. *See* Naming God.

Salvation, 4, 7, 13, 18, 28, 30, 37, 45, 55, 74–76, 84–87, 102, 133, 136–37, 139–40, 145, 152, 172
   in Martin Luther's inner vs. outer transformation, 85, 87
   Other-worldly dimensions of, 4, 74
   This-worldly dimensions of, 4, 30, 74, 79, 85, 87

Seed faith. *See* Prosperity Gospel.
Self
   as Autonomous, 46, 48–50, 158–59, 167
   as Relational, 50, 69, 141
Self-care, 9, 155, 165–66, 174
Self-determination. *See* Freedom.
Self-directedness. *See* Temperament and Character Inventory.
Self-discipline for excellence. *See* Freedom.
Self-Limitation in love. *See* Freedom.
Self-love. *See* Health.
Self-transcendence. *See* Temperament and Character Inventory.
Shalom, 5–6, 9, 19–21, 24–27, 36–41, 48, 52, 68, 70, 90, 92–93, 96, 126, 139, 140, 145–47, 154–55, 157, 160, 162, 164, 166, 168, 171–74, 176, 179, 180
   in Empowerment as intrapersonal peace, 157, 161, 167
   as Feasting, 19, 45, 173
   in Hospitality as interpersonal peace/righteousness, 152–60, 166, 168, 172
   in Liberation as intracommunal peace/justice, 5, 9, 68, 74, 76–78, 84, 90–91, 93, 100–101, 114, 140, 152, 154, 156–57, 159, 167
Shame, 62–63, 67, 96, 99, 144, 170
Sickness. *See* Human Flourishing.
Sin, 7–8, 13, 17, 19, 24, 37, 48–50, 55, 69, 71, 75–76, 79–81, 83–84, 88–93, 102, 110, 129, 143, 147, 152, 156, 161–65, 168, 170
   as Obstruction of wholeness, 83, 92–93, 102
   as dehumanization, 92
   as Systemic sin, 3, 5, 8, 55, 75, 84, 90, 92, 114–16, 152, 154–57, 161, 167–68, 170, 173
Sinned-against. *See* Liberation Theology.
Social connection. *See* Health.
Social justice, 5, 9, 68, 100–101, 114
Social mobility, 1, 2, 69

Subject Index

Socio-political liberation. *See* Liberation Theology.
Sociological benefits of the prosperity gospel. *See* Prosperity Gospel.
Sociological perspectives. *See* Human Flourishing.
Spirituality of overflow, 9, 126, 142, 146, 165, 169, 171–72, 179
Stewardship. *See* Imago Dei.
Stoics. *See* Modern Worldview.
Systemic sin. *See* Sin.

Temperament and Character inventory
   in Cooperativeness, 57–60
   in Self-directedness, 57–58, 60–61
   in Self-transcendence, 57, 59–60
Theology of the Prosperity gospel. *See* Prosperity Gospel.
Theology of the Sinned-against, 7, 84, 89–94, 102, 116, 129, 147
   in Questioning the goodness of God, 90
   as The Restorative anger of God, 91, 146–47
   as Trialogue of God, sinner, and sinned-against, 91

Trialogue of Scripture. *See* Theology of the Sinned-against.
Tri-partite vision of flourishing. *See* Human Flourishing.
This-worldly salvation. *See* Salvation.
Truth. *See* Character of God.

Victim
   as Legitimate Victimizations, 7–8, 114, 127
   as Narratives of victimization, 4, 7–8, 44, 69, 88–89, 94, 101, 114, 116, 125, 129, 141, 154–57, 160–61, 164–65, 167–70
   as Powerlessness of Victimhood, 4, 94, 96, 98, 101
   as Victimization caused by sin, 4, 7–8, 69, 88–89, 156, 161–62, 164–65
Victimization caused by sin. *See* Victim.
Vulnerability, 63, 97, 99

Well-being. *See* Human Flourishing.
Wholeness, 29, 37–38, 79, 83, 87, 91–94, 102, 106, 125, 140, 145–46, 157, 159–60, 165–66, 171–73

www.ingramcontent.com/pod-product-compliance
Lightning Source LLC
Chambersburg PA
CBHW070326230426
43663CB00011B/2235